Praise for *H. P. Lovecraft and the Black Magickal Tradition*

"I am enthralled by this outstanding study. As one who has practiced as a solitary witch, and who now practices as a weaver of Lovecraftian fiction, I can appreciate this book on many levels. In its approach to biographical matters, it paints an honest portrait of H. P. Lovecraft. A magnificent work!"

—W. H. Pugmire, author of *Some Unknown Gulf of Night*

"At the time of his death in 1937 H. P. Lovecraft was little more than a minor pulp author. He regarded himself as a failure. Three-quarters of a century later he is accepted as a serious figure in literature, one whose standing and influence grow almost daily.

But was he 'merely' a writer of horror stories, or was there something more to his works? Were his many weird beings and alien gods purely the products of his imagination, or did Lovecraft tap into some greater and more esoteric truth than the average reader of *Weird Tales* or *Astounding Stories* realized?

In *H. P. Lovecraft and the Black Magickal Tradition*, John L. Steadman addresses this question head-on. Whether Lovecraft was himself a practicing, if covert, occultist, as some devotees believe, or solely a practitioner of the tale-spinner's art, his works fall clearly within the occult traditions of cultural and even supernatural beliefs stretching back to classical Greece, Egypt, and Mesopotamia.

Steadman's scholarship is impressive and the revelations in his book may well be as shocking to skeptics (including me!) as they are reassuring to believers. I recommend this book unreservedly to any admirer of Lovecraft, whichever camp the reader may belong to."

—Richard A. Lupoff, author of *Marblehead: A Novel of H. P. Lovecraft* and *Lovecraft's Book*

"John L. Steadman's fascinating look at the intersection of Lovecraft and the occult is both comprehensive and comprehensible—even to the non-occultist—and provides a wealth of information and inspiration for the aficionado or the practitioner of the weird tale."

—Orrin Grey, author of *Never Bet the Devil and Painted Monsters*

"John L. Steadman has opened the door to the study of neo-mythology in *H. P. Lovecraft and the Black Magickal Tradition*. Funny and dark, cynical and powerful, Steadman takes on the many-faced monster that is rising out of the R'lyeh of the collective unconscious."

—Don Webb, author and occultist

"John L. Steadman's treatise *H. P. Lovecraft & the Black Magickal Tradition* provides a fresh angle of context for the man, the myth, and the legend. A fine addition to the library of any Lovecraft enthusiast, whether or not you believe in magic."

—Cherie Priest, author of *Boneshaker* and *Bad Sushi*

"H. P. Lovecraft's influence on modern horror fiction is indisputable. John L. Steadman explores a more obscure aspect of his legacy, dissecting and analyzing the research into the occult that underpins the Cthulhu mythos, and describing how the rites and metaphysics in Lovecraft's fiction have influenced the practice of contemporary magic. A fascinating and valuable contribution to Lovecraftian scholarship."

—Paul McAuley, author of *Four Hundred Billion Stars*
(Philip K. Dick Award winner, 1988) and *Fairyland*
(Arthur C. Clarke Award winner, 1996)

"Author John L. Steadman's intriguing book is a fascinating and well-researched treatise on the influence of magickal thought with respect to the output of one of the recent giants of Weird Literature. With concision and insight into the historical underpinnings of Black Magick and its adherents, Steadman's volume is indispensable reading for neophyte Lovecraft readers, longtime fans, or simply individuals with a casual interest in the Old Gentleman from Providence, as well as those curious about the history of magick in literature and in popular culture. A stimulating and informative reading experience."

—Jason V. Brock, author of *Disorders of Magnitude*

"Not just for students of the occult! Lovecraftian horror fans and writers will find this well-researched volume a brisk and fascinating read."

—Lon Prater, author of *Head Music* and over a dozen Lovecraftian horror stories

"In *H. P. Lovecraft and the Black Magickal Tradition*, John Steadman has written a compelling and unusual study of the Chthulu Mythos. By locating Lovecraft's work in the narrative of black magic systems and interrogating the various intersections between the Mythos and real magickal practices, this fantastic book casts new light onto both. A must read for anybody interested in either Lovecraft or black magic, and fascinating for newcomers and scholars alike."

—Tom Fletcher

H. P. LOVECRAFT

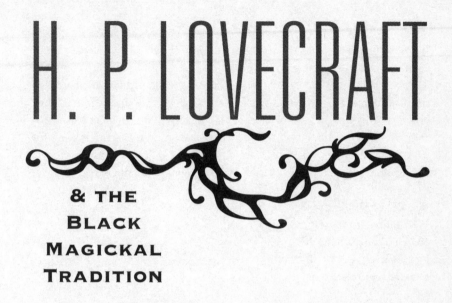

& THE BLACK MAGICKAL TRADITION

THE MASTER OF HORROR'S INFLUENCE ON MODERN OCCULTISM

JOHN L. STEADMAN

WEISER BOOKS
San Francisco, CA / Newburyport, MA

This edition first published in 2015 by Weiser Books, an imprint of

Red Wheel/Weiser, LLC
With offices at:
665 Third Street, Suite 400
San Francisco, CA 94107
www.redwheelweiser.com

Copyright © 2015 by John L. Steadman

ISBN: 978-1-57863-587-0

Library of Congress Cataloging-in-Publication Data available upon request.

Cover design by Jim Warner
Cover photographs © Valery Sideinykov, © lynea
Interior by Deborah Dutton
Typeset in Adobe Calson text, with Copperplate Gothic and Univers display

Printed in Canada.
MAR

10 9 8 7 6 5 4 3 2 1

To my beautiful wife, Pamela,
and my beautiful daughter, Ligeia.

CONTENTS

ACKNOWLEDGMENTS

I want to express my gratitude to S. T. Joshi, the foremost Lovecraft scholar in the world, for his endorsement and for taking time away from his own creative labors to read the manuscript of a relatively unknown writer such as myself and then provide substantial feedback that ended up enriching the book as a whole. In my day, we had a phrase: a gentleman and a scholar. If any person deserves to be described in such a fashion, that person is S.T. Joshi.

I also want to acknowledge and thank my two editors at Red Wheel/Weiser, Kim Ehart and Amber Guetebier, along with Rachel Leach, Eryn Carter, and Sylvia Hopkins, among others. Although I am the author of this book, there wouldn't really be a "book" at all if it weren't for these individuals and for the work of all of the other fine professionals at Red Wheel/Weiser.

INTRODUCTION

Since his death in 1937, H. P. Lovecraft has become a major figure in popular culture and critical circles. From the popular standpoint, Lovecraft's Cthulhu Mythos has inspired a variety of theatrical films, television shows, and even children's cartoons, along with a wealth of interactive and role-playing games—all of which have made Lovecraft and his imaginative constructs familiar to a broad range of individuals, young and old alike, many of whom have never read a single word of his writing. As for the critical response, Lovecraft is now indisputably accepted by scholars as one of the leading writers of horror and science fiction in the United States and Europe, due in large part to the labors of S. T. Joshi, who wrote the standard biography *H. P. Lovecraft: A Life* (1996) and such influential studies as *H. P. Lovecraft: The Decline of the West* (1990).

The fact that Lovecraft has finally "arrived" is further confirmed by the 2005 Library of America publication of Lovecraft's stories, *H. P. Lovecraft: Tales* and the single volume publication of

Lovecraft's fiction, *H. P Lovecraft: The Fiction* (2008) in the Barnes and Noble Library of Essential Writers series. Both publishers have issued authoritative editions of the writings of Washington Irving, Nathaniel Hawthorne, Herman Melville, and Edgar Allan Poe. By including Lovecraft among these illustrious authors, they position Lovecraft as more than merely another writer who is simply trying to scare us or find original ways to say "boo", but rather as an authentic literary figure with serious purposes to his work. Lovecraft elaborates on his reasons for writing in numerous letters to friends and business acquaintances. Like Poe, Lovecraft is concerned with exploring the psychological and often physiological effects of fear, which he defines as the "oldest and strongest emotion of mankind."[1] Also, Lovecraft is interested in providing an accurate yet terrifying vision of man's insignificance in the cosmos, a vision that is, according to Peter Straub, "fearsome in its pessimistic view of human destiny."[2]

Lovecraft's influence, however, is not confined to the field of imaginative literature. Contemporary occultists, particularly those who are drawn to the darker aspects of Western magick and mysticism, have likewise been influenced by Lovecraft's work, and this provides another important dimension to Lovecraft's overall impact on Western culture. In fact, a diverse group of prominent magickal practitioners have made extensive use of Lovecraft's Cthulhu Mythos in their own magickal organizations. These occultists include the late Kenneth Grant, former head of the Typhonian O.T.O.; Peter Carroll, author of *Liber Kaos* (1992) and *Liber Null & Psychonaut* (1987); the late Anton Szandor LaVey, founder of the Church of Satan in San Francisco; and Donald Tyson, who has published two volumes of magickal rites that utilize Lovecraft's mythological entities in actual ritual settings, *Grimoire of the Necronomicon* (2008) and *The 13 Gates of the Necronomicon* (2010). All of these occultists argue that Lovecraft's works are not merely fictional artifacts, but rather that

Lovecraft had, either consciously or unconsciously, been "initiated" into the mysteries and thus been in contact with real extraterrestrial entities. In *The Magical Revival* (1972), Grant claims that Lovecraft was a practicing magickian, but was too terrified to complete his initiation into the higher Qabalistic realms.

> But Lovecraft seems not to have passed the final pylons of Initiation, as evidenced by his stories, and particularly his poems, in which, at the last dreadful encounter, he invariably recoiled, resolved not to know what horror lay concealed behind the mask of his most critical incarnation. He was haunted by his "dweller on the threshold," failed to resolve the enigma of his own particular sphinx, and, because of this, no doubt, feared to use drugs in case his nightmare-vision swept him beyond the point of no recall. Understandably terrified of crossing the Abyss, he forever recoiled on the brink, and spent his life in a vain attempt to deny the potent Entities that moved him. Little wonder the tales he wrote are among the most hideous and powerful ever penned.[3]

Grant, of course, cannot establish that Lovecraft was actually performing magick, but he claims that Lovecraft did manage, via dream control, to channel or "port" the same types of elements utilized by magickians in the Western hermetic tradition, particularly those found in the works of such master occultists as Aleister Crowley. As Peter Levenda notes in *The Dark Lord: H. P. Lovecraft, Kenneth Grant and the Typhonian Tradition in Magic* (2013), Grant was convinced that Lovecraft and Crowley were in contact with the same extraterrestrial influences:

> While these associations [between the twin gods Horus and Set and between Wilbur Whateley and his twin brother] may seem fanciful, we need only remember how definite were Lovecraft's stories when matched against corresponding dates

and events in Thelema . . . In order to understand the Necro-nomicon gnosis, it is necessary to grasp some of the essential elements as transcribed by Lovecraft (and those of his circle) and then to "port" them over to Thelemic elements and note their correspondence. If Lovecraft received many of his ideas through his dreams, as he often admitted in writing to friends, then his process was consistent with Grant's dream control the-ory and practice. What is startling is that the dreams of Love-craft would so neatly correspond to the inspirations received by Crowley. They were both dreaming the same dream.[4]

In *The Satanic Rituals* (1972), Anton LaVey shares a similar view of Lovecraft's knowledge of Western magick. As LaVey describes it: "There is no doubt that Lovecraft was aware of rites not quite "nameless," as the allusions in his stories are often identical to actual ceremonial procedures and nomenclature, especially to those prac-ticed and advanced around the turn of the last century."[5]

Both Grant and LaVey are making two rather remarkable as-sumptions here: Lovecraft's knowledge of Western occultism and magick was extensive enough to qualify him as a bona fide initiate; and Lovecraft's actual magickal experiments were, in fact, successful, since he was able to achieve some level of contact with extraterrestrial entities. However, it is important to observe that neither occultist of-fers any evidence to support his views. Even more troubling, neither Grant nor LaVey (or any other magickal practitioner or scholar, for that matter) can demonstrate any viable connection between Love-craft and occult theory or practice. Indeed, with the exception of a few isolated articles and online squabbles, and Levenda's book, Love-craft's connection with contemporary occultism—and particularly with the black magickal tradition—has not been adequately studied.

My book is meant to remedy this situation. I start out with a description of the theory and practice of black magick, including a full analysis of the black magickal methodologies as they developed in Africa, Egypt, Greece, and Rome. Next, I focus specifically on the life and works of H. P. Lovecraft. I explain in detail exactly what Lovecraft knew and how much he knew about the Western magickal tradition. In so doing, I determine conclusively if the two assumptions raised by Grant, LaVey, and other magickal practitioners are valid. Following this, I examine the various versions of the Necronomicon, Lovecraft's fictional book of spells used for summoning the Great Old Ones, and determine which of these may, in fact, serve as an efficacious magickal grimoire. I also compare Lovecraft's pantheon of extraterrestrial entities with the archetypes of the other magickal traditions in order to determine their ontological status, and whether or not these so-called "fictional" entities can be used in bona fide magickal workings. Finally, I provide a detailed look into Lovecraft's specific connection with the great black magickal systems of the contemporary world, focusing not only on the more traditional systems, such as the Vodou and Wicca religions, but also on such relatively recent esoteric groups as LaVey's Church of Satan, Grant's Typhonian O.T.O., Carroll's deconstructionist chaos magick rites, and Simon's Necronomicon Gnosis, which is based on Sumerian mythology.

This book will, I hope, find favor with New Age readers as well as academics, historians, and countless fans of Lovecraft and his weird tales who may find themselves drawn to the field of magick and occultism. Being an academic and scholar myself, I am aware that when students approach these genres, they are immediately confronted with a vast amount of literature. This scholarship is invariably lumped under the category "New Age," though there are two separate and seemingly diverse groups of writers who produce this type of material. On the one hand, there are the New Age writers themselves, who believe in magick and magickal theories of the universe. At the other end of the spectrum are the academics who are, for the most part, non-practitioners, and who are drawn from a multiplicity of intellectual disciplines. Invariably, these latter writers do not acknowledge the reality of magick; thus, they tend to treat the subject solely in terms of its psychological, social, or cultural dimensions. Consequently, there is little common ground between the New Age writers, who believe in magick, and the academics, who do not. The existence of this divide prompted me to wonder if there might be a way to bridge the gap.

Accordingly, in this book, I approach the subject of magick in an objective, scholarly manner. I remain faithful to the empirical facts, keeping speculation and credulity minimal, as I identify what I take to be genuine manifestations of magick in Western culture. My goal throughout is not to convince the reader to become a believer in magick, but rather to keep an open mind, and to simply approach the subject of magick much in the same way as Lovecraft himself approached the subject. Intellectually, Lovecraft was a materialist; he denied the existence of any non-tangible, subtle form of life such as the spirit or soul—and thus, by implication, the existence of God, gods, demons, or otherworldly entities. He also rejected the notion that there was any purpose to human life; his cosmic view of the universe invariably placed human life in a secondary, even inessential role, when compared to the universe as a whole. However, in spite of his intellectual beliefs, Lovecraft also acknowledged the deep power and efficacy of the unconsciousness, and he was always willing and ready to adopt a "what if" attitude to the cosmos and to accept the possibility, if not quite the probability, that there could be something more to the universe than what he himself was willing to acknowledge intellectually.

1

THE PURPOSES AND METHODOLOGIES OF BLACK MAGICK

In his magnum opus, *Magick* (1974), the great twentieth-century occultist Aleister Crowley offers a succinct definition of magick: "Magick is the Science and Art of causing Change to occur in conformity with Will."[6] Crowley defines the principle of "change," that the magickian is expected to effect over the course of his magickal career. According to Crowley, the magickian must seek to attain union with his higher self, or Holy Guardian Angel—an experience that is virtually equivalent to the mystical union of man with his God. In fact, as far as Crowley is concerned, all magickal workings are merely particular instances of this ultimate goal. As Crowley states it:

> There is a single main definition of the object of all magical
> Ritual. It is the uniting of the Microcosm with the Macrocosm.
> The Supreme and Complete Ritual is therefore the Invocation
> of the Holy Guardian Angel; or, in the language of Mysticism,
> Union with God. All other magical Rituals are particular cases
> of this general principle, and the only excuse for doing them

is that it sometimes occurs that one particular portion of the microcosm is so weak that its imperfection or impurity would vitiate the Macrocosm of which it is the image, Eidolon, or Reflexion.[7]

Later occultists who have attempted to define magick generally acknowledge Crowley's definition and invariably offer similar definitions. However, there are serious problems with the Crowleyan view of magick. First, Crowley's definition is too broad to be useful in clarifying the difference between an act of magick and any other kind of human action. The application of the proper kind and degree of force can effect any change. Thus, the simple act of getting in the car and driving to the store to purchase a gallon of milk could be interpreted as an act of magick. So could a trip to the movie theater. Essentially, Crowley's definition does nothing more than transform the word "magick" into a synonym for "action" or "acting." The second problem with Crowley's definition is that it applies strictly to the practice of white magick. Historically, white magick focuses predominantly on the goal of spiritual attainment, as opposed to the less rarified goals common among practitioners of black magick. Examples of white magickal organizations include the Hermetic Order of the Golden Dawn, where Crowley received his initial training; Crowley's own magickal organization, the A∴A∴ (commonly termed the Argenteum Astrum, or Silver Star); and the Thelemic O.T.O. By associating all magickal rites with the ultimate goal of the white magickal systems, Crowley collapses the practice of magick into one particular magickal rite. In doing so, he willfully ignores the complexity and the sheer vitality of the Western magickal tradition in its entirety.

The only way to arrive at a satisfactory definition of magick is to examine the characteristics common to all magickal practices, irrespective of "denomination." When one does this, it is clear that magick can be defined basically as *the use of language, gestures, symbolic objects, and stylized settings for the purpose of establishing contact with extraterrestrial entities.* The first part of this definition stipulates the elements present in most types of magickal rites. The second part accurately identifies the goal of magickal practice as the linking of human intelligence to intelligences of an order of being much more sophisticated than mankind. At first glance, the phrase "extraterrestrial" may seem inappropriate. This phraseology is typically used in conjunction with the UFO abduction phenomenon that permeated Western popular culture in the 1950s and 60s and dwindled in importance in the new millennium. A more appropriate term might be simply gods, or deities. In the earliest forms of magick, extraterrestrial entities were interpreted as Apollonian deities like the Christian God and the divine beings that acted as his servitors (archangels, angels, and spirits) or as Dionysian deities like Pan or Bacchus. The reason I use the term "extraterrestrial" will become clearer when we examine the nature of the Dionysian gods and goddesses, particularly the amorphous, thoroughly non-human entities envisioned by Lovecraft. All of these entities have little in common with the glamorous deities of the Western tradition. Indeed, an entity like Cthulhu, which Lovecraft describes as a gigantic, gelatinous being with an octopus-like head, sharp claws, and flabby wings, could only be labeled as extraterrestrial; to describe him as "divine" would be a misnomer at the very least. Also, many of the beings contacted via magickal workings aren't really gods or deities at all. For instance, Crowley's Holy Guardian Angel is decidedly not a god—it is more like a glorified human being. Similarly, the Qliphothic entities, important in Kenneth Grant's system, are even further removed from the status of Godliness. These are potent energy sources that guard the Tunnels of Set, closer in nature to elementals than deities.

DIFFERENCES BETWEEN BLACK AND WHITE MAGICK

The theory and practice of black magick is deeply rooted in the Dionysian principle. The Dionysian personifies the mysterious, irrational, and chaotic aspects of the universe. The term is taken from the Greek god Dionysus, son of Zeus and Semele. In Greek mythology, Dionysus was the god of vegetation and was associated with wine and good fellowship. Over time, Dionysus was perceived as a deity who inspired ecstatic, orgiastic worship, and the frenetic celebrations in his honor became occasions for licentiousness and intoxication. "Dionysian" is a perfect label for the principle that runs counter to order, decorum, and the daytime world. In its highest metaphysical development, the Dionysian can be equated with the concept of the Void, or Emptiness, as exemplified in the Buddhist concept of Sunyata. In Qabalistic doctrine, the Dionysian was associated with the Ain Soph Aur, the realm of nothingness that exists outside the known universe. Subjectively, the Dionysian signifies the primal, unconscious elements of the human psyche. The Dionysian is female, and passive, as opposed to the aggressive, masculine elements of the cosmos. In her monumental study of Western culture, art, and literature, *Sexual Personae* (1991), Camille Paglia describes the Dionysian in a series of eloquent and memorable passages that capture the full range of meanings associated with this principle.

> Dionysus is energy, hysteria, promiscuity, emotionalism. The quarrel between Apollo and Dionysus is the quarrel between the higher cortex and the older limbic and reptilian brains ... Dionysus is our body's automatic reflexes and involuntary functions, the serpentine peristalsis of the archaic. Apollo freezes, Dionysus dissolves. Apollo says, "Stop!" Dionysus says, "Move!"[8]

The earliest manifestation of the Dionysian in the Western world appeared in Africa around 10,000 BC, well before the advent of the Egyptian empire. The primitive beliefs and traditions of the ancient African tribes ultimately crystallized into the religious rites and practices known today as Vodou. From Africa, the Dionysian principle was carried into Egypt, where the Dionysian reached its first great apotheosis. During a period of roughly 1,500 years, from 3100 to 1570 BC, the Dionysian deities were worshipped by the Star cults, which rivaled the great Apollonian solar cults that were centered on the sun god Ra. But after this period, the solar cults began to supplant the Star cults in importance, a process that was facilitated by the replacement of stellar time keeping with solar time keeping. The solar cults dominated the religious practices of the Egyptians in the later dynasties. In Greek and Roman culture, the Dionysian tradition was kept alive by the Bacchanali rites, which presented alternatives to the staid, orderly rites of Zeus, Apollo, Artemis, and the other anthropomorphic entities. However, the frenetic orgies of the bacchantes drew criticism from the authorities, and by the second century the Bacchanali rites were banned in Roman Italy. With the advent of Christianity in the fourth century and the implementation of laws and ordinances forbidding the worship of pagan deities, the Dionysian tradition was forced to go underground in order to survive. Yet the original beliefs and practices were kept alive by witchcults in Western Europe. Ultimately, in the nineteenth century, the laws forbidding magickal practices were abolished. At this point, the Dionysian tradition began to regain its former status in the world.

The black or Dionysian magickian establishes contact with extraterrestrial entities primarily to gain knowledge of different beings and alternate levels of existence. In effect, the black magickian attempts to subordinate the self to the noumenal realms and by so doing, align himself or herself more completely with the entities that inhabit these realms. This type of alignment is particularly evident in the current practices of the Vodou cults, and among the Wiccan covens. The Vodou houn'gans and mam'bos subordinate the self to such an extent that the loa, i.e. Vodou god-forms, are able to possess their bodies and minds. Once this occurs, then and only then is knowledge possible. In a similar fashion, the members of the Wiccan covens are expected to subordinate themselves to Nature, as personified by the Great Goddess, an archetype that is virtually equivalent to the Mother Goddess of the Seven Stars in Egypt, and the moon goddess Mawu in the Vodou religion. In effect, the magical power of the coven stems from the Great Goddess, since this power is utilized by the psychic and intuitive faculties of individual witches. In *A Witches' Bible* (1996), Janet and Stewart Farrar describe this power as a "gift" from the Goddess.

> Wicca, by its very nature, is concerned especially with the development and use of "the gift of the Goddess"—the psychic and intuitive faculties—and to a rather lesser degree with "the gift of the God"—the linear, logical, conscious faculties. Neither can function without the other, and the gift of the Goddess must be developed and exercised in both male and female witches.[9]

Contemporary black magickal systems also instruct their practitioners to subordinate the self to their dark gods and goddesses in order to achieve knowledge. Anton LaVey, the charismatic founder of the Church of Satan, does not speak of psychic and intuitive powers as a "gift," but his magical system is also allied with the spirit of Nature, particularly human nature. LaVey frankly disavowed the possibility of human perfectibility. In his estimation, the self was not meant to be elevated, but it was not meant to be debased either. Quite simply, the self was to be indulged. By such indulging, the Satanist was yielding to Nature and gaining knowledge of himself, and thus becoming more whole and complete. As LaVey states it:

Satanism encourages its followers to indulge in their natural desires. Only by so doing can you be a completely satisfied person with no frustrations . . . It is the frustration of our natural instincts which leads to the premature deterioration of our minds and bodies.[10]

Like LaVey, Kenneth Grant felt that a new magickal dispensation was needed to more accurately reflect the realities of the magickal universe. Grant, who started out as a disciple of Aleister Crowley during the last years of Crowley's life, and who, after Crowley's death, became arguably the most original interpreter of Crowley's Thelemic system, set up his own Typhonian New Isis O.T.O. lodge in the 1950s. On the surface, Grant's O.T.O. resembled the traditional Apollonian O.T.O., but Grant truly believed that the O.T.O. system of spiritual attainment, which he dismissed as "unwieldy" and "masonic," was no longer in accordance with New Aeonic consciousness.[11] Moreover, in Grant's estimation, New Aeonic consciousness involved the use of magick for selfless knowledge, and for exploring the shadow-matter dimensions ruled by the Qliphoth. As Grant perceived it, there was no longer any room for the Apollonian merging of the lower self with the higher self; in fact, the self would interrupt the smooth, fluidic link between the god-forms and the magickian.

The sex-magical formulae used in the O.T.O. in connection with the VIIIth, IXth and XIth degrees comport forms of control . . . [b]y means of [which] direct contact may be established with the transplutonic radiations of Nu-Isis . . . It was the work of the New Isis Lodge to prepare the ground and . . . to establish terrestrial outposts for these alien creatures.[12]

Another important difference between the black magickian and the white magickian is the black magickian's emphasis on gaining magickal power. Magickal power can be generated for the purposes of promoting health, well being, and longevity, but it can also be used for more mundane reasons, like attracting a lover, finding a job, or ridding oneself of an enemy. These types of concerns are viewed as instances of "low" magick by the more high-minded white magickians; often, low magick is denigrated as being "evil." However, the concept of light and dark, or white and black, has nothing to do with good or evil, and determining whether or not an action is evil depends solely on impartial judgment of the action itself and its effects. Certainly, a black magickian can be considered good if he acts ethically, while a white magickian can be considered evil if his actions are harmful to others. In *Real Magic* (1993), Isaac Bonewits, founder of neopagan Druid fellowship Ar nDraiocht Fein, argues that the association of white with good and black with evil is the result of cultural bigotries, and that this type of labeling is beside the point because moral judgments have no place in magickal practice.

> There is nothing that we as scientists (and all magicians are scientists) can label "Black Magic" or "White Magic" just as we cannot as scientists label anything "Good" or "Evil." That is the job of ethics, not science . . . Magic is a science and an art, and as such has nothing to do with morals or ethics. Morals and ethics come in only when we decide to apply the results of our research and training. Magic is about as moral as electricity. You can use electricity to run an iron lung or to kill a man in the electric chair. The fact that the first is preferable does not change the laws of physics. It would be nice if the words "destructive" and "creative" could be interchanged with "Black" and "White" when describing acts of magic, but the facts of history will not allow it.[13]

THE ELEMENTS OF BLACK MAGICKAL PRACTICE

The necessary elements for successful magickal working, as identified previously, include language, gestures, symbolic objects, and stylized settings. Of these four, language is the most important. The text of the ritual can be written in any spoken language. However, the actual words that bring about the summoning of an extraterrestrial entity are invariably written in one of the so-called magickal scripts. In the earliest Western magickal rituals, the Hebrew alphabet served as the principal magickal script. Transliterations of Hebrew god-names proliferate in magickal librettos. The most common of these were usually inscribed around the perimeter of the magickal circle as well as spoken during the performance of the ritual. In later magickal systems like the Golden Dawn rituals, and in the black magickal tradition, the words of power—or, as black magickians refer to them, the barbarous names—are combinations of sounds that are unintelligible to the mind in its normal state, yet are nevertheless peculiarly adapted to the unsealing of the unconscious power of the magickian. Frequently used magickal scripts are the Runic or Futhorc alphabet, the Malachim alphabet, the Masonic or Rosicrucian alphabet, the Sumerian alphabet, and the Ogham script, which some occultists believe to have been part of the written language of Atlantis. One of the most influential of these scripts is the Enochian or Angelic alphabet, which originated with the magickal skrying of Dr. John Dee and Sir Edward Kelley in the sixteenth century and was later incorporated into the Golden Dawn knowledge lectures. Dee and Kelley's system was fairly straightforward. They obtained five large, square tablets filled with letters, all of which corresponded to the elements of the ancient world. These were known as the Enochian tablets. Dee would customarily sit at a table with one or more of these tablets in front of him, while Kelley sat in front of a large crystal, or shewstone. Gazing into the crystal, Kelley would see an angel holding its own tablet, and the angel would point with a wand to various letters on this tablet. Kelley would indicate where the angel pointed, and Dee would write it down. Through this process, Dee created a series of magickal invocations called the Forty-Eight Angelic Keys or Calls.

The potency of the barbarous names lies not in their meaning. The words are more than an arrangement of syllables or a means of communication. They are an intrinsic part of what they reference; thus, there is an intimate connection between the words and the phenomena of the ritual. Kenneth Grant explains the elemental nature of this affinity.

> Much of the potency of an evocation, as in the case of mantra yoga, lies in its vibratory affinity with elemental phenomena; the violence and thunder of the storm, for the element Air; the seductive and insidious plashing of fountains, for Water; the lambency of flickering flame, summer lightning, for Fire; and the booming echoes of chthonian reverberations, for earth. The strings of words rise and fall, fitfully or with majesty according to the nature of the operation. The plasticity of the human mind exalted to a pitch of evocative suggestibility is molded into words and names containing intrinsic magickal energies. The result is a compelling incantation capable of tapping and unsealing the caverns of Hell—the Subconsciousness.[14]

As Grant's description makes clear, the words are not spoken—the magickian must actually vibrate the words of power. The technique of vibration is described in the Golden Dawn knowledge lectures and by Crowley in *Liber O vel Manus Et Sagittae*.[15] The magickian begins by breathing the word in through the mouth and nostrils. He lets the word descend slowly from the lungs to the heart, the navel, the penis, and down to the feet. When the word reaches the feet, the magickian should be at a midpoint in his vibration and will find that the word will quickly rush back up through the body and out through the mouth. This latter movement is a reaction to the momentum of the inhalation. Generally, the word should be sucked into the body with as much force as the magickian can muster; the exhalation will then occur naturally, like a well-coiled spring, which then uncoils with a violence that is directly proportional to the strength of the coiling. To someone outside the Place of Working who listens to the magickian as he vibrates one of the barbarous names, the vibration initially has a chant-like quality, then slowly crescendos into an animalistic, inhuman cry. In *The Magical Revival* (1973), Kenneth Grant devotes a whole chapter to this subject. As the following description makes clear, the barbarous words are often so inhuman that they could be considered alien, and not of the earth at all.

> [The barbarous names] are not unintelligible in the absolute
> sense, for their meaningless is their meaning, in much the
> same way as are the barbarous names of Goetic sorcery. [Goety
> means "howling."] Similarly, Crowley notes in *The Confessions*
> that Goety is "the technical word employed to cover all the
> operations of that magick which deals with gross, malignant,
> or unenlightened forces." The spells do in fact suggest very
> strongly the howling of wolves, the baying of jackals and the
> shrill tittering ululations of the hyaena, animals traditionally
> associated with sorcery and the hidden world . . . The expression
> "barbarous names" evidently refers to "monstrous speech," or
> the speech of monsters, and this is the key to the meaning of
> the word "goety," howling (like a beast).[16]

A sign that the vibration is being done correctly is a slight erosion of the magickian's normal energy level at the completion of the practice. With regard to the vibration of sentences and phrases, a sign that these are being vibrated correctly is a feeling of momentary exhaustion. The magickian should hear the words ringing in his ears as they issue forth; they might even sound as though they are being vibrated by a multitude of voices rather than a single voice.

The second essential element in the performance of magickal workings is the set of gestures utilized by the magickal practitioner over the course of the rites. There are two basic types: the magickal signs that are drawn in the air or on the ground, and the bodily positions that are assumed during the working itself. Gestures can be used at any time during a ritual, but they are generally employed in the banishing and consecration portions. Banishing represents a purification of the Place of Working; this is needed to dispel all undesirable or superfluous influences. In his description of the proper technique of banishing, Crowley rightly stresses the psychological effects of banishing on the mind and temperament of the magickian; this part of the ritual is more important for the mind than the body.

> The first task of the Magician in every ceremony is therefore to
> render his circle absolutely impregnable. If one littlest thought
> intrude upon the mind of the Mystic, his concentration is
> absolutely destroyed . . . In more elaborate ceremonies it is usual
> to banish everything by name. Each element, each planet, and
> each sign . . . But this process, being long and wearisome, is not
> altogether advisable in actual working. It is usually sufficient to
> perform a general banishing . . . Let the banishing, therefore,
> be short, but in no wise slurred—for it is useful as it tends to
> produce the proper attitude of mind for the invocations.[17]

The consecration portion of a rite follows the banishing, which is only logical, since the Place of Working and the tools used by the magickian must be pure before they can be actively employed for magickal ends. By consecrating, the magickal practitioner is dedicating a symbolic object or a magickal weapon to the single purpose of the rite. As Crowley defines it:

> The method of consecration is very simple. Take the wand, or the holy oil, and draw upon the object to be consecrated the supreme symbol of the force to which you dedicate it. Confirm this dedication in words, invoking the appropriate God to indwell that pure temple which you have prepared for Him.[18]

Generally, both white and the black magickians include some type of banishing or consecration ceremony in their rituals. The magickal gestures and the signs are traced with one of the magickal weapons, usually an "active" weapon such as the wand or a sword. As the magickian traces, she visualizes the sign outlined in glowing colors. She then "charges" the sign, i.e. renders it magickally efficacious, by stabbing at it with the weapon and vibrating an appropriate god-name or word of power. If the ritual includes bodily gestures, they normally follow the charging of the sign. A good example of a preliminary magickal ritual that involves the use of magickal gestures is the Lesser Ritual of the Pentagram. Versions of this ritual have been published in various places, but the original version was part of the Golden Dawn knowledge lectures; it is this version that Crowley later revised and published in *Magick* (1974). Contemporary black magickians, particularly chaos magickians and Satanists, find the Christian symbolism of the pentagram rite distasteful and thus prefer to use banishing and consecration rituals drawn from the darker side of the magickal universe. For example, in his *Nocturnicon* (2006), Konstantinos advises the black magickian to perform a general banishing ritual before any other ritual in order to orient herself and the Place of Working to the purposes of the working. The magickian must begin with a technique known as Drawing in the Darkness. In this ritual, when the magickian feels the darkness pressing around her, she inhales and then exhales it, evoking a f "cosmic aloneness" accompanied by the sounds of s "swishing" in the darkness.[19] Following this, the black performs the technique known as a Sphere in the Cosmos the magickian uses gestures to create a dark sphere both within and outside herself. This sphere, like the glowing pentacles in the Lesser Ritual of the Pentagram, not only protects the magickian from entities that might be harmful, but also effectively prepares the body and mind for further occult explorations.

Symbolic objects, including all the tools, weapons, and devices the magickian employs in his rites, represent the third essential element in the successful performance of magickal workings. On occasion, the magickian's arsenal can be fairly extensive. The *Key of Solomon* grimoire, for example, requires three swords, two knives, a scimitar, a sickle, a poniard, a dagger, a lance, a staff, a wand, a censer, forty or so pentacles, and various lesser devices such as incense burners, perfumes, candles, and lamps. In contrast, the Abramelin system mentions only two weapons: the wand and the censer. There is, thus, a certain degree of latitude regarding the number of symbolic objects necessary for a working and the relative importance of these objects in the schemata of the ritual. However, most Western magickal systems, both white and black, agree that four weapons are essential. These are the wand, the cup, the sword, and the sigils.

The wand, attributed to the element of fire, is the principal magickal weapon. The wand is an active, creative weapon, a symbol of the magickian's will. It is linear and unyielding. In *Sexual Personae*, Camille Paglia describes the outstretched arm of the Apollo Belvedere as the straight line of the aggressive Western nature; the wand is the objectification of this straight line. In the practice of sex magick, the wand is the male penis; erect, it represents magickal power coursing through the body of the magickian, energizing the power zones. In the black magickal tradition, the wand is not so much a symbol of human perfectibility as a symbol of the will's control over the other elements of consciousness. For the black magickian, the wand is the Dionysian Will-to-Power, similar to the Apollonian Will-to-Power that Crowley identifies; the only difference is that the black magickian uses the will solely for knowledge and power, not perfection.

The cup, attributed to the element of water, is the exact opposite of the wand. The cup is a passive, receptive weapon, a symbol of the structuralization of the Will-to-Power. It is round and curvaceous, unlike the wand, which is hard and pointed. In terms of sex magick, the cup is the vagina; it receives the combined sexual fluids of the magickian and his partner, magickally charged during the course of the working. From the standpoint of the black magickal tradition, the magickal practitioner characteristically ignores the lower self/higher self dichotomy in his magickal workings. The cup symbolizes the aspect of the human psyche in which knowledge and power take root and reach fruition. Thus, in the cup, there is a hidden or occult mechanism that makes it possible for the magickian to understand and interpret the phenomena that result from a successful outcome.

The sword, attributed to the element of air, is less vital as a weapon than the wand or cup. Nevertheless, the sword serves a very useful purpose in magickal workings. It represents the analytic faculty of the magickian; it is intellectual rather than creative. The magickian must have a sharp intellect in order to cleanse the mind and free his perceptions from the tangled web of the emotions. The magickian who is armed with the sword possesses a disciplined mind, balanced and in control, dissipating illusions. This "dissipating" aspect, indeed, is one of the key functions of the sword, and it differentiates the sword from the wand. The sword doesn't generate magickal energy but rather destroys it, particularly superfluous energy that may create problems for the magickian. In effect, the black magickian uses the sword to clarify the purposes of the working—to categorize, to mold, to shape, and at times, to protect.

The sigils, attributed to the earth, likewise serve as protection for the magickal practitioner. They are employed not merely to summon extraterrestrial entities, but also to control them. In *Nocturnicon*, Konstantinos clarifies the role of the sigils.

> A sigil is a symbol used to represent something . . . If you're not new to the occult, you may have come across or even used sigil magick of some type. In basic candle magick, sometimes symbols of desire are carved into candles before they're burned. In the advanced art of evocation, sigils are used as signatures of sorts, representing the entity being called forth.[20]

The standard magickal sigil is the Pentacle. Generally, however, the black magickian uses particular sigils for particular rites. Sigils have traditionally been constructed through a method known as Aiq Bekr, or the "Qabalah of Nine Chambers," a technique that is described in the introduction to S. L. MacGregor Mathers' *Kabbalah Unveiled* and in Israel Regardie's *Golden Dawn* volumes. The best description of this method, however, is given by Francis King in his introduction to *The Grimoire of Armadel,* an ancient magickal manuscript that Mathers discovered in the Bibliotheque d'Arsenal in Paris and translated into English in 1897. In his introduction to the 1980 publication of *Armadel,* King offers an example of how to construct the sigil of Bartzabal, a spirit of Mars, using the magick square of Mars as the basis on which to draw the image.

> The "cabbalah of nine chambers" is neither more or less than a Hebrew form of "Theosophical Addition," a numerological technique which still has many devotees, and it simply involves "knocking the noughts off the end" of the numerical values of the Hebrew alphabet. The letter Shin, for example, which has

a numerical value of 300, is taken as 3. The names of the planetary spirits are first written out in Hebrew, then transposed into their simplest numerical form; finally, lines are drawn on the "magic square" of the particular planet, connecting up the appropriate numbers, thus giving the required seal.[21]

There are less formal methods for constructing sigils. Konstantinos provides a rather effective approach, which he calls the mechanical method. The magickian sits at a table with two blank pieces of paper and a pen. She closes her eyes and formulates in her mind an image of the entity she wants to summon, or else, an image of what she wants to accomplish with a particular ritual. Then, she writes a phrase that expresses this desire on one sheet of paper. Next, she rewrites the phrase, eliminating any letters that appear more than once. The magickian must then randomly select one of the letters of this new phrase and draw a somewhat larger version of that letter. After this, she adds the other letters to the larger letter, creatively blending them to form a symbol. Once a single shape has been fashioned, the magickian can add any additional artistic embellishments that will make the symbol "look more arcane."[22]

The fourth and final element necessary to the performance of magickal workings is the stylized setting—the Place of Working or magickal temple. This place can be indoors or outdoors, depending on the magickian's personal preferences, and it commonly contains one or more magickal circles. The main circle is designed to accommodate the magickian and his assistants. According to Aleister Crowley's *Magick, Part II,* the magickian chooses a circle rather than another geometrical shape to affirm his identity with the Infinite ("as above, so below," as the alchemical maxim goes), and to uphold the equal balance of his working, since all points on the circumference of the circle are equidistant from the center.[23] The black magickian uses the circle to concentrate the energies of the magickal working; after all, a circle contains space and whatever else is inside this space. In effect, the magickal energies are generated inside the circle, enhanced in part by the movement of the black magickian and his coworkers. Indeed, many black magickal rituals involve the use of circumambulation, or dance. In the Vodou and Wiccan systems, for example, the movement of the participants around the perimeters of the circle is integral to the success of the working. William Gray describes this movement as "circling." He explains how circling can assist the black magickian in achieving the desired results.

> The so-called "Magic Circle" is really the ground-plan of whatever Cosmos or consciousness the ritualist intends to manifest through. In olden times, the idea was to run round and round the circle until sheer giddiness resulted in disorientation and disassociation from physical surroundings ... bodily movement around a circle is a genuine help in all ritual practice. Apart from anything else, it co-ordinates effort and brings people together. The mere fact of circular movement through the earth's magnetic field, induces minimal electric changes in the human body of a beneficial kind. Moreover, if a number of people are involved, they are moving through each other's electric fields and auric influences so as to pick up each other's energies and tune these for the common purpose.[24]

It is important to note that black magickians rarely use the magick circle for protective purposes; after all, they are seeking contact with extraterrestrial entities and it would be counterproductive to bar them from entry. Occasionally, unwelcome entities are drawn to the vicinity of a magickal working, but the black magickian is more than capable of dealing with these entities if they become a problem. Janet and Stewart Farrar clarify the differing attitudes of black and white magickians with regard to the magick circle in *A Witches' Bible*.

There is a difference of emphasis from the medieval magician's Circle; the power he hoped to tap was that of spirits summoned into the Triangle outside the Circle, and his Circle was cast partly to protect himself in such a dangerous encounter. Any weakness in it could blast him as surely as a puncture in an astronaut's space-suit. Witches do not summon the kind of nastiness which medieval magicians hoped to control like lion-tamers ... So containment, rather than exclusion, is the main function of their Circle.[25]

In addition to the circle, the Place of Working customarily includes an altar, which is placed in the exact center of the magick circle, and a triangle, which is usually inscribed outside the circle in the quarter where the entity being summoned will appear. Basically, the altar serves a utilitarian purpose; it holds all the weapons, the text of the ritual, the lamp, the braziers, the sigils, and any other devices or objects that are needed for the rite. The altar is similar to the architect's drawing board or the surgeon's operating table; it contains neither more nor less than what the magickal practitioner requires at any given point in time. The triangle, on the other hand, plays a much more important role in the magickal working. In effect, the triangle serves as the focal point for the magickian's visualization—it contains the entity that the magickian is working with. Entities associated with the air will appear in a triangle located outside the circle in the eastern quarter; entities associated with the earth materialize in a triangle situated in the northern quarter; entities associated with the element of fire appear in a triangle inscribed in the southern quarter; and entities associated with water materialize in a triangle situated in the western quarter.

Often, the magickian places a censer or brazier in the triangle. These can be constructed from a metal bowl that is filled halfway with sand or shingle and then covered with charcoal blocks. The charcoal is treated with fuel and then lit. After it burns for a few minutes, it settles down into a smoldering bed of red-hot coals. Before his invocation or evocation, the magickian scatters incense on the coals, creating a billowing cloud of smoke. The entity that the magickian is attempting to summon can then use the smoke to shape a visible body—if, of course, the entity feels it necessary to concoct a physical body at all. Indeed, as Lovecraft rightly suggests in "The Dunwich Horror" (1929), an entity such as Yog-Sothoth is not a denizen of our space-time continuum; it is rather egocentric, or perhaps more accurately human-centric, to assume that Yog-Sothoth would manifest in a form that is compatible with our expectations, or to the material and spiritual laws of our cosmos.

BLACK MAGICKAL METHODOLOGIES

The most time-honored method for contacting extraterrestrial beings is through actual physical and/or psychic possession in which the body and mind of the magickal practitioner is temporarily "taken over" by an alien entity. This method dates back to the beginnings of the Dionysian tradition itself. The first historical instance of the use of possession as part of religious or magickal workings occurred in ancient Africa. The central deities of the original African black magickal cults were Mawu, Lissa, and Danbhalah. These deities were prototypes of the contemporary Vodou "trinity" of Erzulie, Legba, and Danbhalah Wedo in Haiti. In the practice of religious rites, the African priests and priestesses "awakened" the deep, Dionysian energies of Danbhalah, the serpent god, by assuming the god-forms of Mawu and Lissa. The rites that accomplished this goal were pure Dionysian, involving wild dancing, chanting, singing, alcohol and drug use, and sexual intercourse between the priestesses and priests.

After these rites spread to ancient Egypt, the crisis of possession became an integral part of Egyptian magickal and religious practices. The secret Dionysian rites of ancient Egypt were attended only by the priestesses, priests, and initiated members of the cults. The rites celebrated the relationship between the female principal, deified as one of the goddess archetypes (Maat, Nuit, Hathor, or Isis), and the male principal, deified as one of the son-brother-lover archetypes. Basically, this involved the acting out of the "sacred" marriage between the god and goddess and included sexual intercourse between the priestess and the priest, which led, in turn, to the crisis of possession on the part of both participants.

In ancient Greece and Rome, the basic god/goddess pattern of the Egyptian mythos was retained in the Mystery cults. The rites themselves were known as the *Rites of Eleusis*, held in the city of Eleusis in east central Greece. These rites were structurally similar to the ancient African rites and the rites of the stellar and lunar cults in Egypt, and featured the preponderant biune deity, in this case Dionysus, who was invoked or "charged" by the participants. The purpose of these rites mirrored that of the African priests and priestesses—the bodies of the participants were possessed by Dionysus in a violent "sparagmos" (a convulsion or divine seizure that was virtually equivalent to the possession of the African priestess or priest by the loa). This same sort of sparagmos is evident later in the early Judeo-Christian period. The principal black magickal rite was the Sabbat, practiced in Europe during the fourteenth and fifteenth centuries and in the New World in the seventeenth century. Accounts of the Sabbat, as derived from the confessions of witches and warlocks who gave statements to investigators and judges connected with the Medieval Inquisition in Europe, bear a remarkable resemblance to black magickal rites in ancient Africa, Egypt, and Greece. The Sabbat reached its culmination when the bodies of the practitioners were literally possessed by the presiding entities. In recent years, both black and white magickians have made use of a refined, rather controlled form of possession for the purpose of attaining knowledge of alternate realms. This technique is known as the Assumption of the God-Form. The magickian visualizes a particular god-form and then "assumes" this god-form—in other words, the magickian "puts on" the god-form, much like a person donning an item of clothing. When the identification between the magickian and the god-form is complete, the actual entity represented by the god-form takes possession of the mind and body of the magickian.

A second method for contacting extraterrestrial entities involves the use of dream control. The ancient Africans discovered that dreams were a very important element in the practice of magick. In fact, specialized groups of priestesses, known as "Oracles," devoted themselves to the worship of a particular god or goddess and used dreams and visions in the practice of their art. The ancient Egyptians, Greeks, and Romans also made use of dream control in their magickal practices. Like the ancient Africans, the Greeks and Romans had special temples that housed the oracles of various gods and goddesses. These functioned in a fashion similar to the Igbo oracles in Africa. The most well known of these was the oracle at Delphi, which flourished during the middle and late 500s BC, until it suffered a decline when Christianity started to take hold in the Roman provinces. The modern use of dream control stems from the writings of Austin Osman Spare (1886–1956), a contemporary of Aleister Crowley and one of the few modern magickal practitioners who developed a truly self-created, self-contained magickal system. In 1913, Spare published his magnum opus, *The Book of Pleasure*. According to Spare, the magickian performs his workings entirely on the astral plane and then uses the magickal energy generated from these workings to accomplish his purposes on the material plane.

The purpose of the dream control ritual is transubstantiation. The magickian first creates a sigil, which is very much like a Vodou veve or nkisi in that it is meant to store magickal energies. The actual design of the sigil represents the object or goal of the ritual. Specifically, when the sigil is charged, the object of the rite is realized. The magickian can charge the sigil through two techniques: a heterosexual magick operation with a priestess on the physical plane, or a masturbatory magick operation with a dream woman on the astral plane. If the magickian favors a heterosexual operation, the sigil will be prepared previously. The priest must be able to visualize this sigil in full, complete detail, for he will create it in the astral realm. During the performance of the rite with the priestess, the priest visualizes the sigil while the priestess falls into a magickal sleep akin to a state of self-induced hypnosis. Ultimately, the magickal energies generated by the body of the priestess are embodied in the astral sigil—these energies issue forth from her vagina in the form of secretions (or the combined fluids from the priest and priestess). The priest then places the physical form of the sigil below the vagina of the priestess, where it absorbs the magickal energies of the working. Through the "grace" or "agency" of the priestess, who is possessed by the goddess, the sigil thus passes from the magickian's subconsciousness through the astral realm and back again to the material plane.

If, on the other hand, the magickian favors the masturbatory operation, before he retires for the night, the sigil must be placed within reach. The priest then practices the technique known as "karezza"— he must masturbate while visualizing the sigil until sleep occurs; this will make it possible for him to visualize the sigil properly when he reaches the dream state.[26] During this initial stage of masturbation, the priest must not ejaculate; the semen must be retained so that the priest will be able to successfully ejaculate in the subsequent part of the ritual. Eventually, the priest falls asleep and he gradually progresses into the dream state. In this state, the priest encounters a sexual partner who serves as surrogate for the priestess on the physical plane. This surrogate, or Shadow-Woman, personifies the Kundalini—as does the priestess in real-time rituals—and the sigil is magickally transferred from the waking state in karezza to the dream state. The sex rite culminates when the priest reaches orgasm in the dream state, and, by implication, on the astral plane; the energies thus generated are used to "charge" the mental image of the sigil. When the priest awakes, the sigil on the material plane, linked metaphysically with the same sigil on the astral plane, is likewise charged, and the dream has effectively become reality.

The third method for contacting extraterrestrial entities is ritual magick. There are three different categories of magical rites: ceremonies, evocations, and invocations. The first of these, the ceremony, can be defined as a formal or symbolic series of actions or observances in which the magickal energies of the magickian are only minimally engaged. The typical modern black magickal ceremony consists of the dramatization of legends or the actions of gods or extraterrestrial entities on the physical plane. These rituals are important to contemporary Wiccan covens and to most of the larger black magickal groups, including Satanist groups associated with LaVey's Church of Satan and even the chaos magick pacts. However, because the ceremony doesn't usually involve any direct contact with entities, deities, or "forces," it doesn't differ too much from secular ceremonies, like high school graduations. As a result, many contemporary black magickians tend to view the ceremony in a disparaging fashion, and small covens and individual practitioners often refrain from engaging in ceremonial work except for initiation purposes.

The evocation rite, on the other hand, is common to all black magickal groups. Evocation is specifically designed to summon an extraterrestrial entity to visible appearance. It represents a "calling forth" of the entity into the Place of Working, and requires the full engagement of the practitioner's magickal energies. The target entity is usually summoned to manifest inside the triangle, while the magickian is careful to remain safely inside his or her circle. Aleister Crowley describes evocation as the bringing of a live spirit from dead matter, emphasizing the entity rather than the magickian. But perhaps it is more useful to focus on the inner aspect or connection that makes possible the external conjuring. This aspect, in fact, determines whether or not the evocation will be a success. It differs in degree (rather than in kind) from the psycho-magickal mechanics necessary to the performance of effective invocations. In his highly original study of Western magick, *Magical Ritual Methods* (1969), William Gray defines the importance and the limitations of magickal evocation.

> "Evocation" means *calling out of.* It signifies that we are calling upon our Inner Contacts to approach more closely toward our Outer terms of consciousness. If we evoke, we ask the Inner Ones to come out of us so that we may meet them nearly as possible at material level . . . We cannot expect to be met by Divine Ones in human guise, using human language, without allowing for the distortions and errors of which we are capable. If we insist They confine Their consciousness to human phraseology, then we must accept the shortcomings of our language and the degree to which we understand it. This is not likely to help communication. Provided we are prepared to make such allowances, evocation may be of some value when seen in its proper light.[27]

The invocation, unlike the evocation, is designed to summon an extraterrestrial entity within the magickian himself. Thus it represents a "calling-in" rather than a "calling-forth." Crowley describes the practice of invocation in terms that stress the importance of "letting go" of the self on the part of the magickian; he sums up the secret trick to a successful invocation in four words: "Enflame thyself in praying."[28] In effect, the mind of the magickian must be uplifted until it is no longer conscious of itself. Once this occurs, the magickian is able to connect fully with the entity he or she wishes to invoke, and, by so doing, partake fully in the metaphysical experience identified by the god-name. Crowley describes very vividly what transpires during a successful invocation.

> The mind must be exalted until it loses consciousness of self. The Magician must be carried forward blindly by a force which, though in him and of him, is by no means that which he in his normal state of consciousness calls I. Just as the poet, the lover, the artist, is carried out of himself in a creative frenzy, so must it be for the Magician.[29]

The black magickal invocation rite normally involves leaving the physical body at some point during the ritual. This is known by the acronym "OBE," or "out-of-body experience." Equivalent terms are astral traveling and rising on the planes. The magickian creates a body of light, which is composed of the same substance as the astral plane, and then transfers his consciousness to this body. Once the magickian has done this, he can explore alternate dimensions. Or, if he is so inclined, the magickian can explore the astral plane itself, where the thought-forms of all living creatures reside. He can also travel to different places on the material plane and imbibe some of their underlying spiritual qualities and characteristics.

2
H. P. LOVECRAFT: PROPHET OF THE AEON OF THE GREAT OLD ONES

Howard Philips Lovecraft has become a prominent figure in the occult world over the last fifty or sixty years, particularly among black magickal practitioners. In fact, a number of contemporary occultists view Lovecraft as a virtual progenitor of a new aeon of black magick—an aeon ruled by an ancient pantheon of entities that predate the pagan deities of Africa, Greece, and Rome and which are known only as the Ancient Ones or the Great Old Ones. These occultists argue that Lovecraft was a knowledgeable, conscious progenitor, versed in arcane lore and magickal practices. More conservative black magickians, like Konstantinos, see Lovecraft's role as more passive, even largely unconscious—they believe that Lovecraft inspired black magickians by his imaginative literary constructions and clever manipulation of psychological and psychic realities. A good example of this latter approach to Lovecraft's work is described in Erik Davis's essay, "Calling Cthulhu: H. P. Lovecraft's Magick Realism."

Lovecraftian magick is an imaginative and coherent reading set in motion by the dynamics of Lovecraft's own texts, whose thematic, stylistic, and intertextual strategies constitute what I call Lovecraft's Magick Realism . . . Lovecraft constructs and then collapses a number of intense polarities—between realism and fantasy, book and dream, reason and its chaotic Other. By playing out these tensions in his writing, Lovecraft also reflects the transformations that modern occultism has undergone as it confronts the new perspectives of psychology, quantum physics, and existentialism. And by embedding all this in an intertextual Mythos of profound depth, he draws the reader into the chaos that lies "between the worlds" of magick and reality.[30]

Lovecraft might have been amused by this interest from occultists; nevertheless, the interest is very real. It is important to determine the validity of some occultists' claims that Lovecraft's pantheon of ancient entities are not merely literary constructs that are efficacious in "drawing the reader" into alternative dimensions, but rather actual extraterrestrial entities that are directly accessible to the magickal practitioner.

LOVECRAFT'S LIFE AND WORKS

H. P. Lovecraft was born on August 20, 1890 in Providence, Rhode Island. His father, Winfred Scott Lovecraft, and his mother, Sarah Susan Phillips, were members of the New England upper middle class. But when Lovecraft turned two, his father began to suffer from hallucinations and was placed in a mental institution. As a result, Lovecraft was brought up by his mother, who took him to live in her father's house. Here, under the influence of his mother and his grandfather, Whipple Phillips, both of whom were avid bookworms, Lovecraft became a voracious reader, developing a taste for scientific treatises (particularly on astronomy), mythology, gothic fiction, and, somewhat later, the works of Edgar Allan Poe and Lord Dunsany. Lovecraft also was subject to psychosomatic illnesses, and his mother, who was suffering with mild depression, had a tendency to coddle her son, allowing him to attend school on a less than regular basis during his psychosomatic interludes. In 1898, Lovecraft's father died from general paresis due to tertiary syphilis. The same year, Lovecraft had his first nervous breakdown. Lovecraft had another nervous breakdown in spring of 1899, causing him to leave school. In 1904, his grandfather died, so Mrs. Lovecraft and her son moved again. Lovecraft attended a classical high school for a few years, but his formal education ended in 1908 when, at the age of seventeen, he suffered another nervous breakdown.

Lovecraft continued his studies on his own. He had started writing poetry and stories at the age of fourteen, and managed to publish many of his earlier pieces in local magazines and newspapers. In 1914, Lovecraft discovered amateur journalism. He was invited to join the United Amateur Press Association (UAPA) by one of its members, Edward F. Daas. Lovecraft began contributing essays and reviews to various UAPA publications, including their official organ, *The United Amateur*. Lovecraft also served as chairman of the UAPA's department of literary criticism and, in 1915, as the first vice president of the organization. At this time, Lovecraft commenced his correspondence with a large number of acquaintances whom he had met through his association with amateur journalism. His correspondents eventually included many of the rising stars of the horror and fantasy genres, notably Clark Ashton Smith, Robert E. Howard, and August Derleth. In 1919, Lovecraft's mother suffered a mental breakdown and was admitted to Butler Hospital, the same institution where her husband had died twenty-one years earlier. She died soon after, and Lovecraft went to live with his aunts, Annie Gamwell and Lillian Clark.

Later that year, Lovecraft attended the annual convention of the National Amateur Press Association (NAPA), where he met Sonia Haft Greene, a successful businesswoman and aspiring writer who worked as a manager at a Manhattan women's clothing store. Lovecraft began to visit Greene in her Brooklyn apartment whenever he could. During this period, Lovecraft started writing the stories that would eventually make him famous. One of these, "Hebert West—Reanimator" (1922), was published in *Home Brew*; this was Lovecraft's first professional publication. In 1923, Lovecraft began to submit his stories to a new magazine, *Weird Tales*.

Lovecraft and Sonia Greene were married on March 3, 1924, and they took up residence in New York. They were an odd couple—Sonia was glamorous and extroverted, while Lovecraft was reclusive and introverted. At first, Lovecraft came out of his shell a little; he worked for a brief period as a salesman for a collection agency, but was unable to find editorial or publishing work. Sonia supported them both with her millinery shop until the end of the year, when the shop failed. She was forced to move to Cincinnati, where she worked in a department store. Lovecraft moved to a one-room apartment in Brooklyn Heights. Sonia left her Cincinnati job and returned to Brooklyn for a brief visit in the winter of 1925, but she left again soon after. Clearly, the marriage was in trouble.

In 1926, Lovecraft finally admitted that he was unwilling to sever his ties with his beloved New England and decided to leave New York. This turned out to be a good decision for his literary career, for 1926 marks the beginning of Lovecraft's mature phase as a writer. He returned to Providence and took an apartment in the same building as his Aunt Lillian. Almost immediately, Lovecraft began to write his best fiction. He sold his favorite story, "The Colour Out of Space" (1927), to *Amazing Stories*, and his critical essay "Supernatural Horror in Literature" (1927) appeared in *The Recluse*. In 1928, Lovecraft visited Sonia in Brooklyn and they apparently attempted to mend their damaged relationship, but this didn't work and Sonia filed for divorce.

Lovecraft's Aunt Lillian Clark died in 1932, so Lovecraft moved to a new apartment with his aunt Annie Gamwell. Lovecraft did a lot of traveling at this time; he visited his young friend Robert Barlow in Florida in 1934 and again in 1935; and he traveled extensively in New York, Charleston, Washington, and Philadelphia. In late 1936, Lovecraft's health began to break down; he had digestive and eye problems. By the winter of 1937, he had lost a great deal of weight and was having difficulty eating. According to his biographer, L. Sprague de Camp, Lovecraft likely had a suspicion that these symptoms were manifestations of a more serious illness; in a letter to his friend and *Weird Tales* colleague August Derleth, he described himself as being near the "end of [his] life."[31] Lovecraft was diagnosed with cancer of the small intestine on March 2nd, and he died on the morning of March 15th. He was buried with his parents in Swan Point cemetery.

H. P. Lovecraft's most important tales are referred to as the Cthulhu Mythos stories. These stories focus on the Great Old Ones, Lovecraft's pantheon of extraterrestrial entities. The term "Cthulhu Mythos" was not used by Lovecraft himself—it was invented by his friends and admirers. There are different opinions regarding which of Lovecraft's stories should be included in the Mythos. Most readers, however, agree that the following stories represent the core documents of the series: "Nyarthathotep" (1920), "The Nameless City" (1921), "The Hound" (1922), "The Festival" (1922), "The Horror at Red Hook" (1925), "The Call of Cthulhu" (1926), "The Strange High House in the Mist" (1926), "The Dream-Quest of Unknown Kadath" (1927), "The Case of Charles Dexter Ward" (1927), "The Colour Out of Space" (1927), "The Dunwich Horror" (1929), "The Whisperer in Darkness" (1930), "The Shadow Over Innsmouth" (1931), "At the Mountains of Madness" (1931), "The Dreams in the Witch House"

(1932), "The Thing on the Doorstep" (1933), "The Shadow Out of Time" (1934), and "The Haunter of the Dark" (1935).

LOVECRAFT'S PHILOSOPHICAL VIEWS

Lovecraft states his philosophical views fairly clearly in a letter to Zealia Brown Reed, one of his ghostwriting clients, in 1927, and later, in a letter to his colleague Frank Belknap Long, in 1929. Lovecraft identifies himself as a materialist, or, as he phrases it, "mechanistic materialist," by which he means he is a believer in the doctrine that nothing exists apart from matter, and that all the facts of existence and experience can be explained in reference to the laws of material substances. Furthermore, Lovecraft embraces the view of matter and energy as articulated by modern quantum physics. The quantum physicists, following the speculations of Niels Bohr and Werner Heisenberg, argue that reality is multi-dimensional. From the standpoint of the individual human being, the body is composed of quantas of energy and is usually localized in time and space, and yet, due to the existence of a wave function, that same body is also disaggregated and therefore can appear simultaneously in different places and times. Because of this, the universe can be seen as a fluidic field of energy in which different levels of alternate realities are possible, each level superimposed on one another. As the following two excerpts from Lovecraft's letters make clear, Lovecraft does indeed accept the conclusions of Bohr and Heisenberg and their successors, but he is careful to observe that the "energy-aspect" of matter does not change the essential fact that matter remains material and must ultimately perish.

I have a parallel nature or phase devoted to science and logic, and do not believe in the supernatural at all—my philosophical position being that of a mechanistic materialist of the line of

Leucippus, Democritus, Epicurus, and Lucretius—and in modern times, Nietzsche and Haeckel.[32]

The truth is, that the discovery of matter's identity with energy—and its consequent lack of vital intrinsic difference from empty space—is *an absolute coup de grace to the primitive and irresponsible myth of "spirit." For matter, it appears, really is exactly what "spirit" was always supposed to be.* Thus it is proved *that wandering energy always has a detectable form*—that if it doesn't take the form of waves or electron-streams, *it becomes matter itself;* and that the absence of matter or any other detectable energy-form indicates *not the presence of spirit, but the absence of anything whatsoever.*[33]

With regard to the belief in the continued existence of human beings after death, Lovecraft is equally clear: there is no such thing as personal immortality, and there is no such thing as the survival of the life force—or, by implication, of the mind or soul—upon the death of the body.

We have found that the body of a human being is composed of certain energy-streams which gradually undergo transformations (though retaining the form of matter in various decomposition products) after the withdrawal of the chemical and physical process called life, are we any more justified in believing that these demonstrable streams are during life accompanied by another set which gives no evidence of its presence, and which at the cessation of the life reactions retains its specialized grouping, contrary to all laws of energy, and at a time when even the solid streams of matter—energy—whose existence is really capable of proof—are unable to retain a similar grouping?[34]

This rather bleak view of human existence had its origins in Lovecraft's early readings in his grandfather's library at the

Phillips family home. Among the volumes in this library was a copy of Lucretius's *De Rerum Natura*, which articulated an atomistic view of the cosmos. Lovecraft also read widely among the early Greek materialists such as Leucippus, Democritus, and Epicurus, and this reinforced his inclinations toward the empirical. Lovecraft refined his mechanistic materialism after 1918, when he read Ernst Haeckel's *The Riddle of the Universe* (1899) and Hugh Elliot's *Modern Science and Materialism* (1919). In particular, Lovecraft was influenced by Elliot's three principles of mechanistic materialism: the uniformity of law; the denial of teleology; and the denial of any form of existence other than those envisaged by physics and chemistry. Lovecraft accepted these three tenets for his whole life, and even went so far as to assert later that quantum theories of the universe did not upset, but rather only confirmed the validity of Elliot's principles.

Interestingly, there is another possible source for Lovecraft's materialism that the critics have largely overlooked. This can be found in the works of Edgar Allan Poe, who was one of Lovecraft's major literary influences. I am referring to Poe's cosmological treatise *Eureka: A Prose Poem* (1848). Although there is no direct evidence that Lovecraft actually read or studied *Eureka*, I am conjecturing that he likely did so, since Poe's ideas in this treatise are so congenial to Lovecraft's own ideas. In *Eureka*, Poe equates the material universe with God. However, Poe's concept of God bears no resemblance to the standard, anthropomorphic images that one usually associates with the term. Basically, Poe identifies three principles at work in the cosmos; these principles are responsible for the origin, existence, and eventual destruction of the universe. The first principle is Oneness, or Unity, which, Poe speculates, was the result of the first action of creation by the godhead. The second principle, Expansion, represents a cosmic movement away from Oneness. Poe identifies Expansion as the secondary cause of existence, since the result of expansion is the actual creation of the universe. The third principle is Contraction, which represents a movement back to Oneness. Poe argues that Contraction will be the eventual cause of the destruction of the universe, because the movement back to Oneness will result in the annihilation of the expanded universe. In Poe's view, it is inevitable that the diffusing, radiating, repulsing energy, the Expansion, grows progressively weaker as it moves away from the Oneness, and when the radiated particles can no longer withstand the principle of Contraction, then these particles return to the Oneness and their material existence is terminated.

On a superficial level, Poe's view of the Oneness seems less Lovecraftian and more similar to the standard view of the Oneness articulated by many Eastern religions and philosophical systems, and by the Concord Transcendentalists, particularly Ralph Waldo Emerson, who felt that the human mind and the external world were part of one spiritual reality—the Oversoul, or God. However, when we examine Poe's conception of the Oneness, it is clear that he isn't really referring to a Oneness at all. He offers an abstract of the thesis of *Eureka* in an 1848 letter to his friend George W. Eveleth. Poe lays out the thesis in seven points; the 5th, 6th, and 7th points are of particular interest.

> 5: Mind is cognizant of Matter only through its two Properties, attraction and repulsion. Therefore, Matter is only attraction and repulsion: a fully consolidated globe of globes, being but one particle, would be without attraction, i.e., gravitation: the existence of such a globe presupposed the expulsion of separative ether which we know to exist between the particles as of present diffused: thus the final globe would be matter without matter, i.e., no matter at all: it must disappear: thus unity is nothingness.
>
> 6: Matter, springing from unity, springs from Nothingness, i.e., was created.
>
> 7: All will return to Nothingness, in returning to Unity.[35]

Poe here identifies his three principles and defines the relationship between them. Nothingness is clearly described in 5 and 6; Poe qualifies his depiction of Oneness by a deft, logical argument that reveals the Oneness as actually nothingness, or Death. The argument can be stated in a syllogistic manner as follows.

Matter consists of only the two principles of attraction and repulsion.
Oneness, or Unified Matter, has no attraction or repulsion.
Therefore: Oneness is Not-Matter, or Nothingness.

Clearly, Poe's cosmology is a cosmology of nothingness. Poe is essentially arguing that the universe arises out of No-Matter. But No-Matter is merely another term for nothingness; therefore, the universe must necessarily and ultimately return to nothingness. This view of the cosmos is very similar to Lovecraft's own view with regard to the ultimate disposition of matter in general.

THE CTHULHU MYTHOS AS A MAGICKAL SYSTEM

Since Lovecraft was a materialist, and clearly did not believe in either the reality or the efficacy of magickal practices, it is necessary to offer some explanation as to why many magickal practitioners, myself included, have seen fit to make use of the Mythos as the foundation for a bona fide magickal system. Indeed, in his letters to acquaintances and business associates, Lovecraft himself clearly indicates that his works are only fiction, written to entertain and hopefully inspire his reader with fear of the unknown. However, there are two reasons why the Mythos *can* be used as the basis of a magickal system, irrespective of Lovecraft's strongly professed materialistic inclinations.

First, in an important passage from a letter to his fellow writer Clark Ashton Smith, dated October 17, 1930, Lovecraft himself admits that, on an unconscious level, there does seem to be a reality of sorts associated with the basic, archetypal sources of his own dreams and visions. In the following excerpt from that letter, Lovecraft refers to the dreams and waking visions he has had in the past and suggests that his conscious experiences (and, by implication, his imaginative work) can be interpreted as an attempt to "recapture" the "fleeting & tantalizing mnemonic fragments" derived from those dreams and visions.

> In fact I *know* that my most poignant emotional experiences are those which concern the lure of umplumbed space, the terror of the encroaching outer void, & the struggle of the ego to transcend the known & established order of time, (time, indeed, above all else, & nearly always in a backward direction) space, matter, force, geometry, & natural law in general. My most vivid experiences are efforts to recapture fleeting & tantalizing mnemonic fragments expressed in unknown or half-known architectural or landscape vistas . . . Some instantaneous fragment of a picture will well up suddenly through some chain of subconscious association—the immediate excitant being usually half-irrelevant on the surface—& fill me with a sense of wistful memory and bafflement; with the impression that the scene in question represents something that I have seen & visited before under circumstances of superhuman liberation & adventurous expectancy, yet which I have almost completely forgotten, & which is so bewilderingly uncorrelated & unoriented as to be forever inaccessible in the future . . . The more recent an experience is—be it objective, pictorial, or verbal—the more sharply vivid it has to be in order to gain a place in this subconscious reservoir of vision-material.[36]

Lovecraft goes a bit further than this in a subsequent letter to his friend Frank Belknap Long from February 27, 1931, in which he clearly indicates that his "fleeting, mnemonic" dream-visions are not only useful for artistic purposes, but also that these visions may represent a valid, and thoroughly real, supplementary source of knowledge to humanity.

> The only permanently artistic use of Yog-Sothothery, I think, is in symbolic or associative phantasy of the frankly poetical type; in which fixed dream-patterns of the natural organism are given an embodiment & crystallization. The reasonable permanence of this phase of poetical phantasy as a possible art form . . . seems to me a highly strong probability . . . But there is another phase of cosmic phantasy (which may or may not include frank Yog-Sothothery) whose foundations appear to me as better grounded than those of ordinary oneiroscopy; personal limitation regarding the *sense of outsideness* . . . The time has come when the normal revolt against time, space & matter must assume a form not overtly incompatible with what is known of reality—when it must be gratified by images forming supplements rather than contradictions of the visible & measurable universe.[37]

Despite the jocularity of his reference to the Great Old Ones as "Yog-Sothothery," Lovecraft, in his discussion of the second phase of "cosmic phantasy," is making two claims here: that humans have incomplete and limited knowledge of reality, i.e. of "what is or is not possible in the universe"; and that there may be entities or life-forms in the vast universe that "supplement" rather than "contradict" our current, limited perceptions of what is or is not possible. Although Lovecraft is definitely not arguing that it is probable, or even possible, that his own Great Old Ones exist in some ontological sense, he is still entertaining the possibility that entities that have previously been misinterpreted as being gods or goddesses could nevertheless really and truly exist—not as gods or goddesses but as extraterrestrial entities. S. T. Joshi, in fact, in *The Rise and Fall of the Cthulhu Mythos* (2008),[38] argues that Lovecraft, particularly in his later work, "demythologized" his gods and goddesses, making them more "amenable" to his materialistic view of the cosmos.[39]

A second reason why the Cthulhu Mythos can serve as the basis for magickal practice is the simple fact that this system, unlike strictly fictional mythologies, does seem to reference actual archetypes that are equivalent in scope and power to the traditional archetypes that black magickal systems utilize in their workings. This fact is supported by the experiments and the writings of many notable magickians. Kenneth Grant, for example, asserts that Lovecraft's work was based on the older magickal systems; in his three *Typhonian Trilogies*, Grant argues that Lovecraft, through the agency of the dream state, established a connection with real, Dionysian deities, and that these deities bear an affinity with the Sumerian magickal tradition and with the more Dionysian aspects of Crowley's Thelemic Cult. Grant even provides a table in *The Magical Revival* (1972) contrasting elements of the Cthulhu Mythos with corresponding elements in Crowley's system. A number of these associations are intriguing. For example, Grant observes the similarity between the title of Lovecraft's principal grimoire, *Al Azif*, and the title of Crowley's *Book of the Law, Al vel Legis*. Similarly, Grant associates Yog-Sothoth with Sut-Thoth or Sut-Typhon, names which Crowley gave to his own Holy Guardian Angel. Grant, likewise, equates Azathoth, the blind idiot god at the center of infinity, with Hadit, the Chaos at the center of Infinity; Hadit is one of the three important deities spoken of in *The Book of the Law* (1904).[40] To justify these associations, Grant is careful to point out that Lovecraft was unacquainted with Crowley's work. Thus, Grant's view represents a type of psychic absorption.

Fiction, as a vehicle, has often been used by occultists. Writers such as Arthur Machen, Brodie Innes, Algernon Blackwood and H. P. Lovecraft are in this category. Their novels and stories contain some remarkable affinities with those aspects of Crowley's Cult dealt with in the present chapter, i.e. themes of resurgent atavisms that lure people to destruction. Whether it be the Vision of Pan, as in the case of Machen and Dunsany, or the even more sinister traffic with denizens of forbidden dimensions, as in the tales of Lovecraft, the reader is plunged into a world of barbarous names and incomprehensible signs. Lovecraft was unacquainted with the name and work of Crowley, yet some of his fantasies reflect, however, distortedly, the salient themes of Crowley's Cult.[41]

More recently, Donald Tyson argues that the Great Old Ones are just as potent and "real" as any of the "archetypal realities that lie on the edges of human consciousness," and which have found expression in various veiled forms in our religious myths. In his *Grimoire of the Necronomicon,* Tyson picks up on many of the themes in Lovecraft and makes these the foundation of a projected magickal order devoted to the Great Old Ones. Rather fancifully, Tyson has named this group the Order of the Old Ones—even though, as yet, it has no priests or priestesses, and no initiates. According to Tyson, the individual magickal practitioner who embraces and creatively makes use of Lovecraft's archetypes can attain to a higher level of consciousness that is nothing short of a genuine, personal apocalypse, equivalent in scope to the apocalypse referred to in Christian mythology.

The great work of the Old Ones may be identical to the apocalyptic vision foretold in the biblical book Revelation. It will be marked by a transformation that necessitates widespread destruction of the present existing state of the world, followed by the emergence of a more spiritual condition. In Lovecraft's fiction, those who survive the great work of the Old Ones will be those chosen by the Old Ones, who have put off their lower earthly natures and been transformed into something less tangible that approaches pure mind.[42]

The goal of Tyson's current magickal endeavors is further clarified by the author; Tyson argues that mankind should not "fear" the Old Ones, or dread contact with these extraterrestrial beings, as Lovecraft's narrators invariably do, but rather that mankind (or at least that portion of mankind devoted to magickal practices) should bond together into a community dedicated to actively achieving contact with the Great Old Ones.

Given Lovecraft's own admissions regarding the possible unconscious validity of his imaginative constructs, and taking into account the aforementioned testimony of prominent magickal practitioners, I would further argue that Lovecraft's view of the cosmos is, in actuality, not at odds with the postmodernistic magickal view of the cosmos in general. The principal black magickal systems posit a view of the cosmos that is remarkably akin to the views of the leading quantum physicists of today, and these views are virtually equivalent to Lovecraft's concept of the universe. I have already noted that early quantum physicists and Lovecraft shared similar views of the human being as an energy stream. In fact, Lovecraft had done some study of quantum physics, for he alludes to the works of Planck, Einstein, and Heisenberg in "The Dreams in the Witch House." In the 1960s, over twenty years after Lovecraft's death, the modern quantum physicists, extending the work of Bohr and Heisenberg, developed string theories; in 1984, Schwarz and Green of Queen Mary's College in London combined string theory with the concept of supersymmetry, leading to the superstring theory. Building on this, contemporary quantum physicists developed the theory that there are hidden or shadow-matter dimensions.

The concept of hidden dimensions first originated in the work of the Swiss American Fritz Zwicky, who in 1930 calculated that galaxies in large clusters moved so fast that the gravity provided by their visible stars was insufficient to hold the galaxies together. Thus, Zwicky concluded, hidden or shadow-matter must exist. Lovecraft, of course, died long before the string and superstring theorists, and before Zwicky's work was used as a rationale for the existence of hidden dimensions; thus, Lovecraft could not have given us his impression of the latter-day quantum physicists. Nevertheless, there are many definitions of alternate dimensions scattered throughout Lovecraft's fiction and poetry.

The best definition of Lovecraft's view of alternate dimensions is provided in "The Dunwich Horror." The black magickian Wilbur Whateley visits the library at the fictional Miskatonic University to consult the Necronomicon. He is deep in his reading when the librarian, Dr. Henry Armitage, glances over his shoulder at a passage: "The Old Ones were, the Old Ones are, and the Old Ones shall be. Not in the spaces we know, but between them, They walk serene and primal, undimensioned and to us, unseen."[43] According to this definition, the dimensions of the Great Old Ones are located "between" the regular spatial/temporal boundaries characteristic of phenomenal existence. These dimensions are, thus, identical to the types of shadow-matter dimensions postulated by contemporary quantum physicists. In Lovecraft's estimation, human beings are essentially confined to their own dimensions, physically as well as metaphysically. In some of the stories I will be examining in the final section of this chapter, the humans who do manage to find their way into alternate dimensions in their natural state can only exist in those dimensions for a brief time. For Lovecraft, though humans are composed of energy-streams, these streams break down at the moment of death, i.e. "after the withdrawal of the chemical and physical processes called life."[44] As such, Lovecraft retains his materialistic view of mankind and his place in the cosmos; mankind, in his view, is merely a transient, rather insignificant incident when reckoned against the background of the universe.

LOVECRAFT'S KNOWLEDGE OF WESTERN MAGICK AND OCCULTISM

Lovecraft had a general, academic acquaintance with a number of the central documents of the Western magickal tradition, but his knowledge of Western magick could not be described as profound in any sense. Thus, the claims of some modern occultists that Lovecraft was an initiate and an accomplished practitioner of magickal rites are patently false. Likewise, the readers and critics who argue that Lovecraft was totally ignorant of occultism are equally mistaken.

Lovecraft's acquaintance with magick and occultism developed slowly but steadily from 1910 to the late 1920s and can be studied in terms of three distinct periods. The first phase, from 1910–1919, is centered on Lovecraft's readings on the New England witchcraft crisis in the late seventeenth century. The earliest influence on Lovecraft was the Boston minister Cotton Mather (1663–1728), who played an instrumental role as chief apologist for the witchcraft trails in Salem, Massachusetts in 1692. In February of that same year, the daughter of Reverend Samuel Parris and another girl were seized by fits and convulsions, and the cause was attributed to a presumed coven of witches operating in Salem Village, headed by George Burroughs, a former pastor of the village who had relocated to Maine. The ranks of the afflicted girls grew steadily over the next few months, and soon the jails were filled with accused witches. On August 5, a special court called the Oyer and Terminer ("Hear and Determine") was set up to try the accused witches. After the first two group executions, public opinion was turning against the witchcraft trials and many people were questioning the validity of the proceedings. In support of the court, Mather attended the third execution on August 19 and gave a speech to the observers that quieted any potential dissent and allowed the executions to proceed. Mather also wrote *The Wonders of the Invisible World* (1692), which was published in mid-October; this book used actual court documents and documented five of the trials. Somewhat later, Mather returned to the witchcraft trials in his monumental history of New England, *Magnalia Christi Americana* (1702). Lovecraft was familiar with both volumes. According to his biographer, L. Sprague de Camp, Lovecraft considered the latter volume to be the most valuable item in his library; de Camp cites Rheinhart Kleiner's account of a visit to Lovecraft in 1702.

> Although Lovecraft said he had no interest in rare books as such, he had inherited an impressive ancestral collection of old volumes. Besides his bound files of eighteenth-century periodicals, he had about one hundred books published before 1800, including several seventeenth-century books and one from 1567. His most valuable single item, he said, was a copy of Cotton Mather's *Magnalia Christi Americana* of 1702.[45]

Mather, in his analysis of the witchcraft trails, had come to the conclusion that the practice of black magick was not merely an isolated phenomenon in New England—rather, it was an underlying, widespread cancer that was eating away at the very foundation of American society. In fact, Mather equated witchcraft with Satanism, and considered them both as a kind of conspiracy against the church and state on the deepest levels. As Mather describes it:

> Now, by these Confessions 'tis Agreed, That the Devil has made a dreadful Knot of Witches in the Country, and by the help of Witches has dreadfully increased that Knot ... That at prodigious Witch-Meetings, the Wretches have proceeded so far, as to Concert and Consult the Methods of Rooting out the

Christian Religion from this Country, and setting up instead of it, perhaps a more gross Diabolism, than ever the World saw before.[46]

This same view of black magick cultism was adapted by Lovecraft and applied to his own version of "diabolism," as is evident in one of the earliest Cthulhu Mythos stories, "The Festival." The unnamed narrator of this story returns to the city of Kingsport to celebrate Yuletide with his kin. It is winter, and the narrator is aware of the fact that the celebration will likely not be a traditional Christmas festival. As he observes: "It was the Yuletide, that men call Christmas though they know in their hearts it is older than Bethlehem, and Babylon, older than Memphis and mankind."[47] Yet, the narrator is still drawn to return to the place of his ancestors. An old man and his wife welcome him, but the old man's face seems to be a mask and the narrator finds himself slowly becoming frightened. As he waits for the hour of the festival, he examines the library of the old house, which contains a collection of rare black magickal works, including the Necronomicon. Presently, the old man, the old woman, and their visitor don black robes and leave the house, joining the other inhabitants of the village in a procession that winds through the silent streets of the town, moving into the church and then down into a vast, subterranean world beneath Kingsport. There is a large, sunless lake, lit by a column of leprous green fire. In a distant grotto, an amorphous flute player plies its instrument, as the celebrants perform their nameless rites. Eventually, a horde of winged, flying creatures descends on the celebrants and all of them ride off on these beings, except for the narrator, who plunges into the river and is later found half-frozen in Kingsport Harbour. At the hospital, the narrator learns that his adventure must have taken place in ancient Kingsport, since the Kingsport where he is now hospitalized is a modern, New England city. What is interesting about this story is the fact that the black magickal practices witnessed by Lovecraft's narrator are widespread; the inhabitants of the town are all "in" on the festival, and though they are not paying homage to the Devil in the strictest sense, they are united and clearly involved in a conspiracy of sorts against mankind. This view of black magick parallels Mather's view, and undoubtedly, Lovecraft embraced this view for his own literary purposes. Indeed, in subsequent Cthulhu Mythos stories, such as "The Shadow Over Innsmouth," Lovecraft posits similar scenarios, pitting a lone narrator against a large, hidden network of evil.

The second phase of Lovecraft's studies in Western occultism ran from the early- to mid-1920s. The book Lovecraft read during this period was *The Witch-Cult in Western Europe* (1921). The author, Dr. Margaret Murray, was a noted anthropologist and Egyptologist; her thesis in the book is centered on the theory that black magick and witchcraft were part of an organized, pre-Christian religion that spanned the entire continent of Europe as well as the New World. Lovecraft indicated that he had, indeed, studied this book in a letter to his colleague, Clark Ashton Smith, written on October 9, 1925.

> The idea that black magic exists in secret today, or that hellish antique rites still survive in obscurity, is one that I have used & shall use again ... Meanwhile, let me urge you, as I did over a year ago, to read *The Witch-Cult in Western Europe*, by Margaret A. Murray. It ought to be full of inspiration for you.[48]

Before Murray's book, scholars and historians tended to view witchcraft as an isolated phenomenon. There were actual witches here and there, of course, but they weren't seen as being organized in any larger sense. Basically, the academic view of the witch involved four criteria: the witch was usually an older woman, or man, who lived apart from others in a town or village, and was generally unpopular due to ill temper and/or an unattractive appearance; the witch was the repository of the superstition and folk beliefs that had flourished in the old country, and he or she had a working knowledge of natural magick, herbs, healing, charms, and such; the witch suffered from delusions and believed that he or she had supernatural powers; and, finally, the witch believed that he or she derived magickal power from the Devil, or Satan. Dr. Murray, however, challenged these assumptions by approaching the subject of witchcraft as an anthropologist. She examined the documents associated with European witchcraft, which included legal records associated with the trials; pamphlets detailing the lives of individual witches; and the writings of inquisitors, witch-hunters, theologians, judges, court officials, witnesses, and other interested parties. Murray also read the numerous statements given to the court by the accused or convicted witches themselves. In the course of her studies, Murray found it necessary to distinguish between the minor practices of charms and spells, which she labeled operative witchcraft, and ritual witchcraft, which included the practice of organized, group rites. Her conclusion was that ritual witchcraft was, in fact, practiced by a large, extensive organization of witches in both Europe and America in pre-Christian times. She refers to this organization as the "Dianic Cult" in reference to the Moon goddess Diana, who is one of the three deities in the Triple Goddess pantheon.

> Ritual Witchcraft—or, as I propose to call it, the Dianic cult—
> embraces the religious beliefs and ritual of the people known
> in late mediaeval times as "Witches." The evidence proves that
> underlying the Christian religion was a cult practiced by many
> classes of the community, chiefly, however, by the more igno-
> rant or those in the less thickly inhabited parts of the country
> . . . The organization of the hierarchy was the same throughout
> Western Europe, with the slight local differences which always
> occur in any organization.[49]

Clearly, the above theory closely parallels Lovecraft's fictional premise of the Cthulhu Cult as a widespread, occult organization operating beneath the veneer of Christianity; the fact that Murray's theory tended to lend a degree of corroboration to Mather's earlier supposition was likely not lost on Lovecraft as well.

The Witch-Cult in Western Europe served as a source of practical information to Lovecraft, and he made use of it as a kind of source-book to flesh out some of the concrete details in a number of his most important tales. In particular, Lovecraft derived his knowledge of Sabbats (Murray uses the term "Sabbaths") and Esbats from the fourth chapter of Murray's book, where she treats of the assemblies of the witch covens. Lovecraft demonstrates his knowledge of these assemblies in "The Dunwich Horror." When the story opens, Lavinia Whateley gives birth to her son Wilbur Whateley at 5 a.m. on Sunday, February 2, 1913. Lovecraft informs us that this is Candlemas, which "people in Dunwich curiously observe under another name"—here, Lovecraft is referring to the first of the Greater Witches' Sabbats, which is also known as Imbolg, Oimelc, and Imbolc.[50] This Sabbat celebrates the first stirring of spring; it is a time of cleansing and ritual purification, and a preparation for the coming year. Thus, the fact that Wilbur Whateley is born on this day is significant, for he represents the ultimate Necronomicon magickian who will open the Gates between the phenomenal and noumenal realms, and cleanse the earth for the advent of the Great Old Ones. Later, Lovecraft alludes to two other Greater Sabbats, Bealtaine on April 30th, or May-Eve, which is known more famously as Walpurgis Night, and Samhain, or All Hallows Eve, on the 31st of October: "For a decade the annals of the Whateleys sink indistinguishably into the general life of a morbid community used to their queer ways and hardened to their May-Eve and All Hallows orgies."[51] In "The Shadow Over Innsmouth," Captain Obed Marsh, in a visit to the South Sea Islands, encounters a tribe of natives who are in communion with a race of amphibious fish-frog creatures that dwell under the sea; these creatures supply the natives with abundant fish in return for human sacrifices, and Marsh learns how to communicate with these creatures when he returns to Innsmouth. Although the Islanders are not related ethnically or culturally to European civilization, or to the witch-cults or pagan cults examined by Murray, nevertheless, they, too observe the same two Greater Sabbats that the Whateleys observe. As Zadok Allen, the old rummy who lives in Innsmouth, states it: "Them things liked human sacrifices. Had had 'em ages afore, but lost track o' the upper world arter a time . . . They give a sarten number o' young folks to the sea-things twict every year—May-Eve an' Hallowe'en- reg'lar as cud be."[52] May-Eve is also important in "The Dreams in the Witch House"; Walter Gilman is spirited away to Walpurgis Night revels by the witch Keziah and her familiar, Brown Jenkin, at the climax of the story.

There is some indication that Lovecraft was familiar with the works of another prominent writer on occult subjects, Montague Summers (1880–1948), the famous British scholar. Summers wrote a number of erudite books on witchcraft, demonology, and related subjects: *The History of Witchcraft and Demonology* (1926), *The Geography of Witchcraft* (1927), *The Vampire: His Kith and Kin (*1928), *The Vampire in Europe* (1929), *A Popular History of Witchcraft* (1937), and *Witchcraft and Black Magic* (1938). Summers disputed Murray's theory about the existence of a Dianic cult in pre-Christian Europe; he considered this to be a fanciful speculation. In fact, his critique of Murray, based on his reading of an article written by her in the *Encyclopedia Britannica*, is rather vitriolic—he describes her scholarship as a collection of "ignoble fatuities" and "monstrous extravagances."[53] In spite of this, however, Summers' own view on witchcraft isn't too dissimilar to Murray's, and it is virtually equivalent to Cotton Mather's view. Summers believed that there was a universal satanic cult in operation in the nineteenth century, and that this cult represented a threat to Western civilization.

Up and down England there is hardly a village without a witch. In our great cities, our large towns, our seats of learning, Satanists abound and are organized (as of old) into covens of wickedness. Black Masses are celebrated in Mayfair and Chelsea; in Wapping and Shoreditch; in Brighton; in Birmingham; in Liverpool; in Edinburg. Under conditions of peculiar horror a Black Mass was celebrated in the ruins of Godstow Nunnery near Oxford. A band of Satanists have their rendezvous not far from the city of Cambridge. . . . there are (I fear) few persons who realize how far-spread and how cunningly organized are these Societies of Evil. To the ordinary man Satanism often seems incredible, or at any rate a myth of the remote Dark Ages. He does not realize, and he is happy in his ignorance, the devil's fires that burn just a very little way beneath the thin and crumbled crust of our boasted modern civilization.[54]

Lovecraft doesn't refer directly to any of Summers' works in his letters or other writings, other than to mention in a 1933 letter to August Derleth that he, Lovecraft, read *The Geography of Witchcraft* (1927). But it is certainly telling that in a 1925 letter to his *Weird Tales* colleague, Clark Ashton Smith, Lovecraft asked Smith to provide recommendations for background reading that he, Lovecraft, might do to bolster his knowledge of occultism and black magick. There is no record of Smith's reply, but Smith had received a similar request from Virgil Finley, an illustrator, and Smith's reply was preserved: "Aside from fiction, I recommend the books of Montague Summers, such as *The Geography of Witchcraft, The History of Witchcraft and Demonology*."[55] Thus, it is entirely probable that Smith provided the same information to Lovecraft and if so, then Lovecraft would have had additional confirmation of the possible existence of black magickal cults in both medieval and modern times.

During the third period of Lovecraft's magickal studies, from the mid to late 1920s, Lovecraft began writing the central documents of his Cthulhu Mythos. These works illustrate just how deeply he had delved into Western occultism. In a letter to Willis Conover, dated July 29, 1936, Lovecraft identifies two occultists that he had read at this period in his literary life.

> The first really scholarly material of the sort was the work of the eccentric Frenchman Alphonse-Louis Constant (middle of nineteenth century), who wrote under the pseudonym of "Eliphas Levi." More compilation of the same kind has been done by Arthur Edward Waite (still living, I believe)—who has also translated "Eliphas Levi's" books into English. If you want to see what the actual "magical" rites and incantations of antiquity and the Middle Ages were like, get the works of Waite—especially his Black Magic and History of Magic. . . . Other stuff can be found in Waite's translations of "Eliphas Levi."[56]

The first of these occult writers, Arthur Edward Waite (1857–1942), had been a member of the Isis-Urania Temple of the Hermetic Order of the Golden Dawn, but didn't take an active role in the order until after 1903, when he played a major administrative role in the governing of the Stella Matutina, one of the branches of the order. Although Waite was, by all accounts, a mediocre magickian, he was an accomplished scholar and he wrote a number of important books that are still essential reading for serious students of Western occultism. His most popular work, *The Book of Black Magic and of Pacts* (1898), was the book that Lovecraft was referring to above; an expanded, more accurate version of this same book was published in the late 1960s under the title *The Book of Ceremonial Magic* (1961). The other writer that Lovecraft refers to is Eliphas Levi Zahad, the pseudonym of Alphonse Louis Constant (1810–1875), who was one of the most famous magickians of the nineteenth century. As a young man, Levi became a clerical novitiate at St. Suspice, in France, and rose to be a deacon in the Roman Catholic Church. He was subsequently appointed professor of the Petit Seminaire of Paris, but was soon expelled for holding beliefs and opinions on magick that were not sanctioned by the Church. After his expulsion, Levi studied deeply in the occult arts and began to produce important works in this field. These included *Dogme de la Haute Magie* (1855), *Rituel de la Haute Magie* (1856), *Historie de la Magie* (1860), and *La Clef des Grands Mysteres* (1861). Lovecraft's knowledge of Levi's writings was derived from a collection of Levi's writings published by Waite in *The Mysteries of Magic*, first in 1896 and later in 1897.

Lovecraft's use of Waite is clearly evident in "The Horror at Red Hook." When the story opens, Thomas F. Malone, a detective of the New York City Police Department, has been assigned to investigate a cult of black magickians who are operating in the Red Hook district of Brooklyn. Malone identifies the members of the cult as Eastern or "Mongoloid stock" Kurdish and Yezidic devil worshippers (this, of course, demonstrates Lovecraft's ignorance of the Kurds and the Yezidis, both of whom are relatively benign ethnic groups centered in the Middle East). The leading figure in the cult is Robert Suydam, a former scholar, who is mysteriously slain along with his new bride while on his honeymoon. On a raid of Suydam's house in Parker Place, Malone discovers circles and pentacles inscribed on the floors, and, on one of the walls, the following words of power, which Lovecraft describes as "the most terrible daemon-evocations of the Alexandrian decadence."[57]

HEL · HELOYM · SOTHER · EMMANVEL · SABAOTH · AGLA · TETRAGRAMMATON · AGYROS · OTHEOS · ISCHYROS · ATHANATOS · IEHOVA · VA · ADONAI · SADAY · HOMOVSION · MESSIAS · ESCHEREHEYE.[58]

In *Lovecraft: Tales* (2005), Peter Straub notes that this incantation was copied by Lovecraft word for word from an article named "Magic" in the ninth edition of the *Encyclopedia Britannica*; Straub's observation here was taken from S. T. Joshi's note in his edition of H. P. Lovecraft's *The Dreams in the Witch House and Other Weird Stories*. However, Lovecraft could have found nearly all of these words in a perusal of Waite's *Book of Black Magick*. Indeed, these so-called "daemon" evocations are, in reality, various divine names representing the Hebrew God and his angels, which were drawn from ancient Hebrew and Jewish documents. In *The Book of Black Magic*, part 2, chapter 6, Waite provides the text of the Grand Conjuration of Spirits whom the ceremonial magickian desires to make a pact with. The conjuration is addressed to Lucifuge Rofocale, or as this demon is more commonly known, Lucifer, the "light giver," a demon who has been equated with Satan by various Church fathers, including St. Jerome. The magickian threatens Lucifer with a series of words of power, exhorting the demon to appear visibly in the Place of Working. Among the words of power are SOTER, EMANUEL, MESSIAS, SABAOTH, and ADONAI.[59] Soter, or Sother, is referred to in *The Hebrew Book of Enoch* (1928) as a prosecuting angel-prince who serves the throne of divine judgment—the name means he "who stirs up the fire of God." Emmanuel means "God with us"; this is used commonly in hymns and prayers to God in both the Hebrew and Christian tradition. Messias is, of course, Messiah, another name for Christ, Savior, or God; Sabaoth is one of the seven angels in the Gnostic and Qabalistic lore who was closest to God and assisted in the creation of the universe; and Adonai can be translated as "God" and is used as another word for Jehovah in the Old Testament.[60] In *The Book of Black Magic*, part 2, chapter 7, Waite presents a Universal Conjuration from the *Grimoire of Honorius*, a conjuration that can, in turn, be used to evoke any evil spirit or demon. During the course of the exhortation to the spirit, the magickian uses the following words of power: TETRAGRAMMATON, JEHOVA, OTHEOS, ATHANATOS, ISCHYROS, AGLA, and SADAY.[61] In a later conjuration in the same chapter, the name HOMOSION is used by the magickian.[62] Tetragrammaton is the secret name of God, IHVH, i.e. Yod, He, Vau, He, used by ceremonial magickians since the Middle Ages up to the present time; Jehovah is another name for God used in Hebrew and Christian texts, hymns, and rituals; Otheos is a spirit of earth used by Qabalistic magickians for conjuring; Athanatos is a name for God used for discovering hidden treasure; Ischyros is another name for God; Agla is the name of God which Joseph invoked when he was delivered from his brothers in the Old Testament—the name means "Thou art forever mighty, O Lord"; Saday is a diminutive for El-Shaddai, another name of God; and Homosion is a corruption of the title "Son of Man," which is an alternate name for Christ.[63] The remainder of the words in Lovecraft's evocation do not appear in Waite directly, but these are all further examples of divine names in Hebrew and Christian mythology. "Hel" is a name for God, mentioned in Scot's *Discoverie of Witchcraft*; "Heloym" is an obvious corruption of "Elohim," which is a name of God that conceives of God as androgynous, i.e. "eloh," a female singular, and "im," a masculine plural.[64] "Va" is likely "Via," which in Latin means "way," and thus refers to Christ as "the way, the truth and the light." Finally, "Eschereheye" refers to "Eserchie/Oriston," which is the name of God invoked by Moses when he brought the plague of frogs on the Egyptians in the Old Testament.

Lovecraft's use of Waite is also readily apparent in "The Case of Charles Dexter Ward." In this story, Charles Dexter Ward, a young antiquarian living in his parents' spacious mansion in Providence, becomes fascinated with his great-great-great grandfather Joseph Curwen, who settled in Providence in 1692. Curwen was secretly a black magickian who never seemed to age; he specialized in necromantic rites that allowed him to revive dead persons, using the "essential saltes" of the corpse as the material basis. Over the course of the story, Ward uses necromantic arts to raise up his great-great-great grandfather and question him; later, he becomes a fairly proficient black magickian himself. There are two specific references to magick circles used by Curwen/Ward and his associates. The first reference is a brief allusion to the remnants of a circle etched on the floor of Ward's bedroom. Dr. Willett, a friend of the family, is asked to visit Charles by Charles' father. He happens to glimpse the circle when he pays an unexpected visit to the Ward residence.

> Frequently, he [Willett] noted peculiar things about; little wax images of grotesque design on the shelves or tables, and the half-erased remnants of circles, triangles, and pentagrams in chalk or charcoal on the cleared central space of the large room. And always in the night those rhythms and incantations thundered, till it became very difficult to keep servants or suppress furtive talk.[65]

Later in the story, Dr. Willett explores Curwen's subterranean laboratory, which is located underneath the Pawtuxet farm, and discovers a similar magickal chamber, though this latter chamber is much more elaborate.

> The room beyond the door was of medium size . . . the two vacant walls . . . were thickly covered with mystic symbols and formulae roughly chiseled in the smooth dressed stone. The damp floor also bore marks of carving; and with little difficulty Willett deciphered a huge pentagram in the centre, with a plain circle about three feet wide half way between this and each corner. In one of these four circles, near where a yellowish robe had been flung carelessly down, there stood a shallow kylix of the sort found on the shelves above the whip-rack; and just outside the periphery was one of the Phaleron jugs from the shelves in the other room.[66]

In this room, Curwen and his associates use the "essential saltes" of dead bodies to raise them up again and to question them in an effort to learn about the secrets of life and death. On the walls of the room, Willett deciphers the words of a chant taken from the work of Eliphas Levi, previously alluded to in the story (I shall be discussing this chant shortly). Lovecraft's description of the pentagram and the four circles at the corners of the chamber shows the influence of Waite's *Book of Black Magic,* since there are a number of illustrations of magickal circles and pentacles in that book that could have served as the basis for the magickal chambers described by Lovecraft. In *The Book of Black Magick*, part 2, chapter 4, Waite provides a diagram of a magickal circle with four pentagrams at the four corners of the chamber, which is very similar to Lovecraft's chamber, except for the fact that there are four circles instead of pentacles at the corners, and the circle is replaced by a great pentagram. Lovecraft, no doubt, transposed the types of symbols used for his own fictional chamber. In chapter 6 of his book, Waite provides three more magickal circles that might have inspired Lovecraft: the Grand Kabbalistic Circle; the Circle of White Magic; and a particularly noxious-looking Goetic Circle of Pacts (this last circle showing a dead bat, the head of a cat, the horns of a bull, and a skull & crossbones at each of the corners of the room). Finally, in chapter 6, Waite offers the reader an illustration of the Magic Circle of Honorius; there is a place at the perimeter of the circle referred to as the "Spiritus Locus," i.e. the Place of the Spirit, which is clearly meant to accommodate the body of the spirit that arises in response to the evocation of the magickal practitioner. It seems likely that this particular illustration served as the inspiration for Lovecraft's placement of the Phaleron jug outside the perimeter of Curwen's circle in the Pawtuxet temple. Indeed, Willet himself, as he stands in the temple, attempts to collate the text of one of the evocations to a similar text that he encountered in Ward's room and, chanting the words of the text to himself, unwittingly causes a shadowy shape to form from the pile of yellowish dust that had been left behind in the kylix on the floor of the chamber.

Lovecraft's debt to Levi is much more direct and tangible than his debt to Waite. In "The Case of Charles Dexter Ward," Charles Dexter Ward, while living with his family and still free from the obsessive influence of Joseph Curwen, performs one of his first evocations, using the saltes taken from a body interred in the North Burial Ground in Providence. On a Good Friday afternoon, Ward enkindles a pungent, unidentified incense and then begins his ritual, repeating a particular magickal formula over and over again for two hours.

Per Adonai Eloim, Adonai Jehova,
Adonai Sabaoth, Metraton On Agla Mathon,
Verbum pythonicum, mysterium salamandrae,
Conventus sylvorum, antra gnomorum,
Daemonia Coeli Gad, Almousin, Gibor, Jehosua,
Evam, Zariatnatmik, veni, veni, veni.[67]

At first, Ward's evocation causes all the dogs in the quiet Providence neighborhood to howl and bark, and Mrs. Ward, Charles' mother, takes her stand outside her son's door to listen. Presently, she detects a "hideous, all-pervasive odour," and there is a flash of light. Then it appears that the evocation has succeeded, for Mrs. Ward hears a thunderous voice responding to her son's call—a voice that is not Charles' voice, but the voice of the entity he is evoking. Mrs. Ward can only catch one phrase spoken by the voice: "DIES MIES JESCHET BOENE DOESEF DOUVEMA ENITEMAUS."[68] After this, the skies darken, and Charles Dexter Ward is chanting again. In a few minutes, Mrs. Ward hears her son shriek once, followed by another shriek, which occurs concurrently with the shriek of the other voice. At this point, Mrs. Ward succumbs to the terror of the situation and faints outside her son's door, where she is discovered by her husband later when he returns home from work. As he carries his wife downstairs, Mr. Ward can hear his son conversing with some other being in the room, cautioning the being to not speak, but to simply write. It is apparent that Charles Dexter Ward's evocation has been successful and Charles is communicating with the reanimated body of the person whose saltes had been procured from the cemetery.

Ward's evocation is taken verbatim from *The Mysteries of Magic*, ed. A. E. Waite (1886), as S. T. Joshi observes in his notes on the story in *The Thing on the Doorstep and Other Weird Stories* (2001). But this evocation appears also in chapter 15 of Eliphas Levi's *The Ritual of Transcendental Magic* (1971). In this chapter, Levi delineates the techniques for performing infernal evocations. He explains that the black magickian must use a magick fork as his principal weapon, which should be cut from a hazel or almond and "armoured" with iron or steel. The evocation is best performed at night between a Monday and Tuesday or a Friday and Saturday; in a solitary place— ideally, a place that is haunted by evil spirits, or where a murder has been committed. The black magickian must wear a black robe, and outside the perimeter of his circle, he must have placed the head of a black cat, the body of a dead bat, the horns of a goat, and the skull of a man who has killed a child. The actual evocation, Levi informs us, can be found in a grimoire known as the *Magical Elements of Peter of Apono*, and in the Grand Grimoire known as the *Red Dragon*. The text of the evocation is written in Latin; this is the same as the text Lovecraft used. Levi offers his readers the following translation.

> By Adonai Eloim, Adonai Jehova, Adonai Sabaoth, Metraton
>   On Agla Adonai
> Mathon, the Pythonic word, the Mystery of the Salamander,
>   the Assembly of
> Sylphs, the Grotto of Gnomes, the demons of the heaven of
>   Gad, Almousin, Gibor
> Jehosua, Evam, Zariatnatmik: Come, Come, Come![69]

Obviously, Lovecraft didn't understand the purpose of Ward's evocation at all, for this text certainly has no connection with the professed necromantic goal of Ward's ritual, and certainly, the text would not be efficacious in evoking the spirit of a dead person, or in reanimating a dead body. Indeed, the evocation is merely a general address to three of the legendary order of creatures that Paracelsus associated with the four elements of the ancient world: the Sylphs, spirits without a soul who live in the air; the Gnomes, earth beings who live underground; and Salamanders, elemental fire spirits who dwell in fire (the fourth order, the Undines, not mentioned in the evocation for some inexplicable reason, are water nymphs who live under the sea). It is difficult to understand how this particular evocation would help Ward at all; the excessive use of the various names of God common to medieval grimoires (Adonai, Eloim, Jehova, etc.), would likely subvert the daemonic purposes of black magickians like Ward and Curwen.

The subsequent fragment of speech overheard by Mrs. Ward after the evocation likewise appears in the same chapter of Levi's book. In fact, it can be found immediately following the Grand Grimoire evocation in chapter 15. Levi tells us that this passage is derived from the fourth book of Agrippa's *Philosophia Occulta*.

> The Grand Appellation of Agrippa consists only in these words:
> DIES MIES JESCHET BOENEDOESEF DOUVEMA
> ENITEMAUS. We have no pretense of understanding their
> meaning; possibly they possess none, assuredly none which is
> reasonable, since they avail in evoking the devil, who is the sov-
> ereign unreason. Picus de Mirandola, no doubt from the same
> motive, affirms that in Black Magic the most barbarous and
> unintelligible words are the most efficacious and the best.[70]

In using this fragment, Lovecraft is surely on firmer ground, since this passage is, indeed, unintelligible; it looks as though the passage combines garbled words and sounds derived from a variety of different languages, including French, Latin, and German. Levi also informs us that the passage was used to evoke the Devil, and this goal is, admittedly, closer to the nefarious goals of Ward, Curwen, and their magickal associates. But Levi is being rather disingenuous when he claims that the passage is wholly incomprehensible. Surely, the first three words can be roughly translated as "Days of my Jesus," or perhaps, "Days of the Lord." These words indicate the likelihood that this passage was taken from yet another medieval grimoire written in one or more European languages, since the authors of these grimoires were so fond of stringing together the names of God and Jesus in their evocations of devils and demons.

LOVECRAFT'S VIEW OF THE BLACK MAGICKIAN

Lovecraft presents his readers with three good examples of black magickians in his fictional works, and all of them correspond rather closely to the traditional image of the black magickian, as defined in chapter 1. Likewise, Lovecraft's black magickians are perceived as "evil," even though these magickal practitioners rarely engage in malefic actions directed toward specific individuals. The evil arises out of the fact that they have goals that are alien to the majority of people around them. The most fully developed black magickian in Lovecraft's fiction is Wilbur Whateley, the protagonist of "The Dunwich Horror." This tale focuses on a decadent family living in Dunwich, a decaying town located in central Massachusetts. The patriarch of the family, Old "Wizard" Whateley, and his daughter, an albino woman named Lavina, have a reputation for performing black magick. They hold rites twice a year on Halloween and Walpurgisnacht. The rites are performed on the site of an outdoor temple that crowns Sentinel Hill. This temple was presumably constructed by the Indians for the worship of their ancestral gods, which bear a close resemblance to the Ancient Ones. Although Lavina is unmarried and has no lover, she nevertheless gives birth to a child whom she names Wilbur. This child is goat-like in appearance, and develops very quickly, reaching the size of a full-grown man by the age of ten. Wilbur is trained in the black arts by his grandfather, and the two men begin a process of remodeling the farmhouse, converting the upper part of the house into living quarters for some unseen creature, or person. Eventually, Old Whateley dies and Lavina disappears, and Wilbur continues his magickal studies. He also continues expanding the farmhouse to accommodate the rapidly growing creature that inhabits it. Wilbur Whateley visits the library of nearby Miskatonic University to consult the Necronomicon; he possesses an imperfect copy of this book, translated by Dr. John Dee, but he wishes to examine the Olaus Worminus Latin version, which is kept under lock and key at the library. As Wilbur consults the volume, he attracts the attention of Dr. Henry Armitage, the librarian. Armitage suspects that Wilbur is going to use one of the Necronomicon rituals to open the Gates between our world and the dimensions of the Great Old Ones. This suspicion is confirmed when Armitage later reads an excerpt from Wilbur Whateley's diary.

> Grandfather kept me saying the Dho formula last night, and I think I saw the inner city at the 2 magnetic poles. I shall go to those poles when the earth is cleared off, if I can't break through with the Dho-Hna formula when I commit it. . . . I wonder how I shall look when the earth is cleared. . . . He that came with the Aklo Sabbath said I may be transfigured, there being much of outside to work on.[71]

Certainly, Wilbur Whateley's goal here is knowledge and power; the diary mentions that the earth will be "cleared off" when Wilbur succeeds in opening the gates, but this is likely metaphorical. After the rite, Wilbur Whateley will end up dwelling in another dimension, experiencing a different type of life altogether, while the real world will presumably continue as usual. Thus, Wilbur is not really doing anything evil at all; certainly, he is not directing any malefic magick toward his fellow men. About the only questionable thing that Wilbur does is to attempt to steal the copy of the Necronomicon from the library. However, he is attacked and killed by the watchdog that guards the library. Shortly after, Armitage arrives and discovers, while examining the body, that Whateley was only half human. Below the waist, his body is covered with thick black fur, and from the abdomen twenty or so long greenish-gray tentacles with red sucking mouths are visible. There are rudimentary eyes on each hip as well, and his posterior terminates in a purple trunk or feeler, which seems to be an undeveloped mouth. The body decomposes swiftly; soon, all traces of it have vanished, except for a fetid stench. Following this incident, the gigantic, invisible creature imprisoned in the Whateley farmhouse back at Dunwich breaks out and ravages the countryside, leveling houses and devouring cattle and people. When Armitage hears about this, he and two fellow professors go to Dunwich and perform a ritual on the top of Sentinel Hill that effectively banishes the monster back to the dimensions of the Great Old Ones. At the end of the story, it is revealed that this creature was Wilbur's twin brother, and that the father of both Wilbur and this creature was Yog-Sothoth, one of the principal Great Old Ones in the Lovecraftian pantheon.

The other two important black magickians in Lovecraft's work are very similar to Wilbur Whateley in their single-minded devotion to knowledge and power. The first of these characters, Joseph Curwen in "The Case of Charles Dexter Ward," has committed his life to his necromantic experiments with the corpses of illustrious dead persons; he reanimates the dead to gain knowledge from the past, which, in turn, increases his own power over life and death. Unlike Wilbur Whateley, however, Curwen is an evil black magickian; he has no compunction about sacrificing a certain number of his own sailors as fodder for the half-human creatures that remain as the failed by-products of his experiments at the Pawtuxet farm. The second Lovecraftian magickian, Ephraim Waite in "The Thing on the Doorstep," practices black magick in order to raise up the Great Old Ones; upon death, he takes possession of his daughter Asenath's body (she willingly allows him to do this) and continues his magickal practices. Lovecraft makes it clear that Waite's goal involves the acquisition of knowledge and power.

> He talked about terrible meetings in lonely places, of Cyclopean ruins in the heart of the Maine woods beneath which vast staircases lead down to abysses of nighted secrets, of complex angles that lead through invisible walls to other regions of space and time, and of hideous exchanges of personality that permitted explorations in remote and forbidden places, on other worlds, and in different space-time continua.[72]

Lovecraft, in describing the activities of his black magickians and the non-human entities and alien beings that align themselves with the Ancient Ones, takes particular delight in the use of "purple-passages" and extravagant adjectives that underscore just how evil these characters are. But quite frankly, most of Lovecraft's wicked protagonists are not very evil at all; rather, they are committed to expanding their minds, bodies, and souls into alternative levels of knowledge and existence.

LOVECRAFTIAN MAGICK:
THE CRISIS OF POSSESSION

In his fiction, Lovecraft makes use of the same black magickal methodologies that I have identified in chapter 1. The first method is centered on the crisis of possession, and is important thematically in three of the key stories in Lovecraft's Cthulhu Mythos, "The Case of Charles Dexter Ward," "The Thing on the Doorstep," and "The Shadow Out of Time." In the first story, as we have seen, Charles Dexter Ward, a young antiquarian, learns about his ancestor, Joseph Curwen, who came to Providence in 1692 and conducted strange, alchemical experiments at an isolated farmhouse. Charles Dexter Ward digs up Curwen's "essential saltes" and reanimates him using his fledgling necromantic skills. After this, Curwen possesses Ward to a greater or lesser degree, dominating his mind and his will. He eventually murders Ward, then assumes his identity since there is a strong resemblance between the two of them. However, the deception is unsuccessful. Eventually, Ward's father and a physician, Dr. Willett, have Ward confined to a mental hospital. Dr. Willett discovers Curwen's subterranean laboratories and the horrifying, reanimated corpses.

In "The Thing on the Doorstep," the possession is more direct and complicated; it is, in fact, multi-layered. Edward Pickman Derby, a young student of the occult, falls in with a dissolute set at Miskatonic University. He dabbles in black magick. He meets a co-ed named Asenath Waite with similar tastes. Her father, Ephraim Waite, was a notorious sorcerer, and Asenath, like him, is an intense, strong-willed person who is able to exchange personalities with others through the use of hypnosis. Asenath and Derby get married and Asenath uses her magickal powers to take possession of her husband's body. Gradually, it becomes clear that Asenath's personality is not really her own, but that of her father, Ephraim. Thus, Derby is possessed by Asenath, who, in turn, has been possessed by Ephraim. The story ends when Derby, imprisoned in the decomposing, liquescent body of Asenath, drags himself out of the grave in the cellar of his house and shows up on the doorstep of his best friend, Daniel Upton.

In "The Shadow Out of Time," there is a simultaneous type of possession that spans centuries. Nathaniel Wingate Peaslee, a professor of economics at Miskatonic University, experiences a form of amnesia beginning in 1908 and lasting six years; he has no memory of his former self and his whole personality changes, causing him to lose his wife and his career. After Peaslee returns to his normal consciousness in 1913, he begins to have recurrent dreams of his life as a member of an alien race, the "Great Race" that ruled the earth in Triassic times. The Great Race resemble immense, rugose cones that are ten feet or so in height, with their heads and other organs attached to foot-thick distensible limbs that spread out from their apexes. The Great Race move by expanding and contracting a viscous layer of membrane attached to their bases; they communicate by telepathy and by the clicking or scraping of claws attached to the ends of their limbs. These beings live in great cities, and they have developed the ability to travel through time and space mentally, exchanging their personalities with the personalities of other beings in other ages and on other planets. The visiting personalities are invited by the Great Race to provide records of their own civilizations, which they transcribe into books that are housed in metal cases and then filed away in city libraries and archives. Peaslee realizes that his dreams are actually memories of what he experienced during his bout of amnesia, and he suspects that he has, indeed, been forced to exchange personalities with one of the members of the Great Race. Peaslee puts together an archaeological dig in a place near Pilbarra, West Australia, where some blocks of stone were discovered that are reminiscent of the stones used for the buildings in the cities of the Great Race. One night, Peaslee wanders away from the rest of the crew and discovers an entrance to the buried remains of one of the cities. At these remains, he discovers one of the metal cases and the writings that he has, in his own hand, transcribed for the Great Race. Thus, Peaslee has empirical evidence that he had, in fact, exchanged personalities with one of the members of the Great Race, but unfortunately, he loses this evidence as he escapes from the buried city.

LOVECRAFTIAN MAGICK: DREAM CONTROL

The second type of black magickal methodology, dream control, is engineered by Lovecraft's extraterrestrial entities rather than by the individuals who experience these dreams; the dreams, in turn, lead to the creation of a "waking" dream state, or OBE. The OBE is effectively described in one of Lovecraft's best stories, "The Dreams in the Witch House." In this story, Lovecraft makes use of the dream state as well as the OBE, but the dream state quickly merges into an alternate state of reality. The main character, Walter Gilman, is an undergraduate at Miskatonic University, like Edward Derby. He is studying fourth-dimensional calculus and quantum physics. He rooms in a house in Arkham which had once harbored Keziah Mason, a witch, and her familiar, an odd creature named Brown Jenkin, which resembled a large rat with a human head and feet like human hands. Keziah had lived in Salem during the late seventeenth century and fled during the witch trials. Gilman soon begins to experience dreams in which he encounters Keziah and Brown Jenkin. Both these beings now exist in alternate dimensions and are able to take Gilman into these realms. Interestingly, Keziah and Brown Jenkin take on different forms in the alternate dimensions. Keziah appears as "a rather large congeries of iridescent, prolately spheroidal bubbles," while Brown Jenkin manifests as "a much smaller polyhedron of unknown colors and rapidly shifting surface angles."[73] At first, Gilman thinks that his encounters with the witch and her familiar are confined to the dream state. But it becomes clear that these are out-of-body experiences. While Gilman is moving about the alternate dimensions in one of his dream sequences, he steps outside and finds himself back in his own dimension, but not back in his room.

During the night of April 19–20 the new development occurred. Gilman was half involuntarily moving about in the twilight abysses with the bubble-mass and the small polyhedron
floating ahead, when he noticed the peculiarly regular angles
formed by the edges of some gigantic neighboring prism-
clusters. In another second he was out of the abyss and standing
tremulously on a rocky hillside bathed in intense, diffused green
light. He was barefooted and in his nightclothes, and when he
tried to walk discovered that he could scarcely lift his feet. A
swirling vapor hid everything but the immediate sloping terrain
from sight, and he shrank from the thought of the sounds that
might surge out of that vapor. Then he saw the two shapes
laboriously crawling toward him—the old woman and the little
furry thing . . . Spurred by an impulse he did not originate,
Gilman dragged himself forward along a course determined
by the angle of the old woman's arms and the direction of the
small monstrosity's paw, and before he had shuffled three steps
he was back in the twilight abysses. Geometrical shapes seethed
around him, and he fell dizzily and interminably. At last he
woke in his bed in the crazily angled garret of the eldritch
old house.[74]

Gilman begins to experience longer OBEs. On one occasion, he
enters a cyclopean city that exists in a prehistoric time period reminiscent of the Triassic world of the Great Race in "The Shadow Out
of Time." Upon awakening, Gilman finds that he has inadvertently
brought back a tangible souvenir of his journey: a statuette of an extraterrestrial that he had broken off from a balustrade. This is certainly tangible proof that his experiences are, indeed, real, but Gilman
still refuses to accept this. Later on, he enters the cramped, boarded-
up enclosure attached to his room where the earthly remains of Keziah Mason and Brown Jenkin reside. The story ends with the death

of Walter Gilman, who thwarts the nefarious purposes of the witch and her familiar and pays for it with his life.

LOVECRAFTIAN MAGICK: RITUAL MAGICK

The last type of black magickal methodology involves the performance of magickal rituals, and this method is important in five of Lovecraft's Mythos stories. In these tales, Lovecraft doesn't provide any actual rituals; he relies on half-glimpsed hints of mysterious assemblies, and half-heard fragments of chanting and intonation. Since Lovecraft's knowledge of Western magick was rather superficial, as we have seen, the fact that the rites are cloaked in mystery is not hard to understand. In "The Festival," discussed previously, the mysterious congregation engages in magickal Yuletide rites in a deep vast grotto. There are no specific incantations or gestures associated with these rites, and Lovecraft offers no descriptions of any symbolic objects or ritualistic trappings; he merely tells us that the celebrants stand in a semi-circle and perform "stiff, ceremonial motions" and "groveling obeisance."[75] In "The Horror at Red Hook," Robert Suydam, a reclusive scholar living in the Red Hook district of Brooklyn, presides over a cult of Asian devil worshippers. The main character, Thomas F. Malone, a New York City detective, observes the devil worshippers performing their rites in a subterranean place similar to the grotto in "The Festival." Again, Lovecraft offers no specific descriptions of these ceremonies, but he does give the reader the text of a chant, which is presumably directed toward Hecate, the Crone aspect of the Wiccan Triple Goddess.

> O friend and companion of night, thou who rejoicest in the baying of dogs and spilt blood, who wanderest in the midst of shades among the tombs, who longest for blood and bringest

terror to mortals, Gorgo, Mormo, thousand-faced moon, look favourably on our sacrifices![76]

In "The Case of Charles Dexter Ward," both Charles' mother and Dr. Willett get a glimpse of the magick circles drawn on the floor in the attic of the Ward mansion in Providence, and in Joseph Curwen's hidden, underground chamber below the Pawtuxet farmhouse. Unlike the previous stories, this tale does provide two small ritual texts. The first text, written in Latin, has already been examined previously; the second text consists of two "mystic" formulas, one associated with the astrological symbol known as the Dragon's Head, or Caput Draconis, which designates the point of intersection between the path of the moon and the path of the sun when the moon is ascending, and the other associated with the Dragon's Tail, or Cauda Draconis, which signifies the crossing of the path of the moon downward through the path of the sun. Lovecraft was most certainly unaware of these astrological attributions; in his story, the Dragon's Head incantation is used to conjure a given extraterrestrial entity to visible appearance, while the Dragon's Tale incantation is used to dismiss the entity. The word Yog-Sothoth refers to this extraterrestrial entity, but Lovecraft offers no translation of the other words in these two incantations and it seems likely that they are made up of nonsense words that Lovecraft devised himself.

Y'AI NG'NGAHOGTHROD AI'F
YOG-SOTHOTHGEB'L-EE'H
H'EE-L'GEBYOG-SOTHOTH
F'AI THRODOG 'NGAH'NG AI'Y
UAAAH ZHRO[77]

In "The Dunwich Horror" and "The Haunter of the Dark," Lovecraft is equally vague in his portrayal of actual magickal rites. In the former story, Wilbur Whateley and his father, "Wizard" Whateley, as we have seen, are in the habit of performing magickal rites twice a year at the site of an outdoor temple on Sentinel Hill. Lovecraft alludes to incantations and some magickal materials in the course of the story, referring to the Dho formula, the Dho-Hna formula, the Voorish sign, and the powder of Ibn Ghazi, but Lovecraft doesn't provide concrete details about any of these things. At the end of the story, Armitage and his companions perform a rite on Sentinel Hill to send Wilbur Whateley's monstrous brother back to the alternate dimensions. The locals, who are able to view the rite by telescope, observe the three men as they chant, waving their arms and using the powder of Ibn Ghazi, which makes the creature visible to human eyes. But the locals are too far away to observe exactly what the three men are doing.

In his final published story, "The Haunter of the Dark," Lovecraft focuses on the last few months in the life of Robert Blake, an artist and writer from Milwaukee, who takes up residence in Providence. Blake finds himself drawn inexplicably to a huge, old, deserted church in the Italian quarter of the city. Blake discovers that this church had formerly been the headquarters of a group known as the Starry Wisdom cult. Blake visits the church and breaks into it. In the tower, he discovers a chamber that had obviously been used for magickal rites. There is a stone altar in the center of the room, surrounded by seven megaliths. On the top of the altar is a box that contains a shining Trapezohedron, which Blakes takes with him. This polyhedron was used to call up a creature that lived in darkness, the "Haunter" mentioned in the title of the story, and by taking the crystal, Blake has inadvertently summoned the creature into existence again. Blake ends up coming face to face with this creature, and he dies of heart failure. As with his other stories, in this last tale Lovecraft doesn't provide the reader with any clear description of the types of practices that must have taken place in this desecrated church; he only hints that the members of the Starry Wisdom cult used the trapezohedron in their rites.

3

THE SPURIOUS NECRONOMICONS

From a strictly magickal standpoint, the Lovecraftian magickian uses ritual to contact the Great Old Ones. As demonstrated in previous chapters, Lovecraft didn't believe in magick and his scholarship did not extend very deeply into the Western magickal tradition. Understandably, then, he didn't provide any actual ritual texts, other than a few phrases and an occasional symbol or magickal sigil. The actual rituals are embodied in a number of magickal, mystical, scientific, historical, and occult treatises and grimoires alluded to by Lovecraft at various points in the Mythos stories. Some of these are real books, while others are fictitious. The real books include *The Story of Atlantis and the Lost Lemuria*, published in 1896 by Scott-Elliot; Joseph Glanvil's *Sadducismus Triumphatus* (1681); the *Daemonolatreiae* of Nicolas Remy, printed in 1595 at Lyons; and *The Book of Dzyan* (1888), an English translation of the Sanskrit Rig-Veda published by Helena Petrovna Blavatsky, the founder of Theosopy, who claimed that the book was written originally in Atlantis in the lost Senzar language. The fictitious books include the *Liber Ivonis*; Comte d' Erlette's *Cultes des Goules*; the *Unaussprechlichen Kulten* of Von Junzt; Ludvig Prinn's *De Vermis Mysteriis*, *the Seven Cryptical Books of Hsan*; the *Pnakotic Fragments*, or *Manuscripts*, as it is sometimes referred to in individual stories; and, most importantly, the Necronomicon, which is the most famous of Lovecraft's fictitious texts, and the principal grimoire of the Mythos.

The Necronomicon is a book of spells for summoning the Great Old Ones. In a small sketch titled *A History of the Necronomicon* (written in 1927; published in 1937), Lovecraft created a pseudo-history of this book. The original title of the book was *Al Azif*, a word which, according to Lovecraft, was used by Arabs to refer to a nocturnal sound made by insects, and meant literally "the howling of demons."[78] The Necronomicon was originally written by a mad Arab poet named Adbul Alhazred in Damascus in AD 730. Lovecraft's "history" is fairly well developed and shows acuity of thought not usually associated with conceptions of this nature:

> Original title *Al Azif*—*Azif* being the word used by Arabs to designate that nocturnal sound (made by insects) supposed to be the howling of demons. Composed by Adbul Alhazred, a mad poet of Sanaa, in Yemen, who is said to have flourished during the period of the Ommiade Caliphs, circa AD 700. He visited the ruins of Babylon and the subterranean secrets of Memphis, and spent ten years in the great southern desert of Arabia—the Roba El Khaliyeh or "Empty Space" of the ancients and "Dahna" or "Crimson Desert" of the modern Arabs, which is held to be inhabited by protective evil spirits and monsters of death. Of this desert many strange and unbelievable marvels are told by those who pretend to have penetrated it. In his last years Alhazred dwelt in Damascus, where the *Necronomicon* (*Al Azif*) was written, and of his final death or disappearance (AD 738) many terrible and conflicting things are

told. He is said by Ebn Khallikan (twelfth-century biographer) to have been seized by an invisible monster in broad daylight and devoured horribly before a large number of fright-frozen witnesses. Of his madness many things are told. He claimed to have found beneath the ruins of a certain nameless desert town the shocking annals and secrets of a race older than mankind. He was only an indifferent Moslem, worshipping unknown entities that he called Yog-Sothoth and Cthulhu.[79]

Regarding the various editions of the Necronomicon, Lovecraft offers this summary:

1. *Al Azif* written circa AD 730 at Damascus by Abdul Alhazred.
2. Translated into Greek as *Necronomicon*, AD 950 by Theodorus Philetas.
3. Burnt by Patriarch Michael AD 1050 (i.e., Greek text)—Arabic text now lost).
4. Olaus [Wormius] translates Greek into Latin, AD 1228.[80]

Although Lovecraft leaves no doubt that the Necronomicon is fictitious, a number of actual texts bearing the name "Necronomicon" have surfaced over the last fifty years, most of which have subsequently been revealed as hoaxes. In my opinion, only one of these texts is credible, at least from a purely magickal standpoint. But it is important to examine all of these "recensions" (as Kenneth Grant refers to them) before attempting to understand exactly what Necronomicon magick is all about and how it works.

THE OWLSWICK PRESS NECRONOMICON

The earliest scholar who presumably acquired a copy of Lovecraft's famous book was L. Sprague de Camp, Lovecraft's biographer and author of a large number of fictional and nonfictional works. De Camp's version is written entirely in Duriac, which is an obscure Semitic language associated with the village of Duria in northern Iraq, and which is not easily susceptible to translation, according to de Camp, despite its similarities to the other Arabic and Syrian languages. The book was attributed to Abdul Alhazred and published under the title *Al Azif* (*The Necronomicon*) by Owlswick Press in 1973 in a limited edition of 348 copies.

In his preface to *Al Azif,* de Camp provides a rather stirring account of how he came by the manuscript. In 1967, de Camp and a friend were traveling to India and stopped over in Baghdad for a few days. De Camp was approached by a member of the Iraqi Directorate General of Antiquities, who sold him the manuscript in question. De Camp learned later, from another friend, that one of Iraq's foremost archaeologists, Ja'afar Babili, disappeared while engaged in translating the manuscript, and his subordinate, Ahmad ibn-Yahya, who took over the translation, also disappeared. The same thing happened to the next person who tried to translate the Duriac text, Professor Yuni Abdalmajid, a scholar attached to the University of Baghdad. De Camp then concluded (probably half-humorously, though it is hard to tell how firmly his tongue is embedded in his cheek in this preface) that the book had been sold to him to satisfy the anti-American sentiments in Iraq, since "the manuscript [will] wreak its woe upon American scholars . . . as but a just requital for . . . America's crimes against the Arabs."[81] At the end of the preface, de Camp advises any prospective translators to beware, particularly if they are the types of readers who mumble as they read, since they might inadvertently recite spells that evoke entities from the alternative dimensions.

An examination of the untranslated manuscript does yield some interesting things. The book is meant to be read from right to left, as with other Semitic languages such as Hebrew, Arabic, and Syrian; for the most part, it consists of rows of very neat, rather artistic characters. The writing seems more hurried (or harried, as the case might be)—and even slovenly—as the writer reaches the end, lending credence to the argument that the author, Abdul Alhazred, was aware that his days were numbered and felt the need to complete his task. Despite these interesting features, however, de Camp's *Al Azif* has been shown to be a hoax. De Camp didn't actually acquire the manuscript; this was produced by a man named Robert Dills, who simply repeated a sequence of sixteen pages over and over again, altering this sequence only at the beginning and end. The script was written in a style of calligraphy that mimicked ancient Arabic texts. As John Wisdom Gonce III argues, George Scithers of Owlswick Press asked de Camp to write the preface in order to lend authority to the hoax.[82] The fact that the book is a hoax is also apparent just from a cursory look at the physical nature of the manuscript. Magickal grimoires invariably share one common trait: the manuscripts are always punctuated with diagrams, charts, talismans, sigils, incantations, and chants. De Camp's manuscript, however, is clean and neat from start to finish, with the exception noted above. Owlswick Press adopted a marketing policy that ensured that readers who were inclined to take the manuscript seriously were, at the very least, reimbursed for their credulity. As Gonce notes:

> Owlswick proved to be much more conscientious in its marketing of the book than later publishers of hoax Necronomicons. As George Scithers told me, he received orders from people who clearly thought the book was real. In each case, the person's check was returned. At one point, a student wrote them stating that he thought the book contained real spells and that he was writing a thesis that would prove the book authentic. Failing to make the student believe that it was a fake, Scithers was forced to write the young man's thesis advisor and tell him what was going on. Few people have ever considered this to be the "real"

Necronomicon—but the fact that it is often kept under tight control in the special collections department of libraries has shocked more than a few.[83]

THE NECRONOMICON:
THE BOOK OF DEAD NAMES

A few years after the Owlswick Press edition of *Necronomicon*, *The Book of Dead Names* appeared on the occult scene. This book, published by Neville Spearman in Great Britain in 1978, is the product of a group effort. *The Book of Dead Names* is edited by George Hay, introduced by Colin Wilson, researched by Robert Turner and David Langford, and appendixed by L. Sprague de Camp, Christopher Frayling, and Angela Carter. In the rather rambling, and somewhat inconsequential Introduction, Wilson cites a statement by a certain Dr. Hinterstoisser, who argues that this version of Lovecraft's fictitious grimoire not a stand-alone book, but rather part of a larger work from the Middle East.

> The Necronomicon is not a single work by one man—Alhazred—but a compilation of magical material from Akkadia, Babylonia, Persia and Israel, probably made by Alkindi [Ya'kub ibn Ishak ibn Sabbah al-Kindi, who died about AD 850]. It claims to contain the remnants of a magical tradition predating mankind.[84]

According to Wilson, Robert Turner, investigating various manuscripts in the British Museum with the intent of writing a book on Dr. John Dee, the famous Elizabethan magickian, discovered the *Liber Logaeth*, or *The Book of Enoch*, a cryptic sixteenth-century manuscript written by Dee, which, in Turner's estimation, was actually an encoded copy by Dee of the Alkindi treatise alluded to by Dr.

Hinterstoisser. The *Logaeth* manuscript, consisting of sixty-five folios containing 101 complex magickal squares, each letter of which represented either a Latin or Arabic character, was then subjected to computer analysis by David Langford for translation purposes; the nature of this complex process is outlined in a rather overblown and confusing chapter in the book by Langford. The results of the analysis, according to the editor, yielded an English fragment of some 7,000 words. Subsequently, under the ministrations of George Hay and the others, *The Book of Dead Names* was set up in the form of eighteen small chapters.

The first half of *The Book of Dead Names*, comprising nine chapters, demonstrates very quickly that this recension is also spurious, and certainly, not even remotely linked with any possible document or scroll unearthed in ancient Akkadia, Babylonia, Persia, or Israel. Without exception, the entire text has been very obviously and rather clumsily derived from themes and images in the works of Lovecraft himself, spiced up with some general information drawn from European magickal practices and grimoires. The first chapter, "Of Ye Old Ones and their Spawn," provides a description of the principal entities of the Lovecraftian pantheon; most of this has been taken almost verbatim from Lovecraft's works, particularly from the Necronomicon excerpt in "The Dunwich Horror." The second chapter, "Of Ye Times and Ye Seasons to be Observed," offers the reader information regarding the best times and seasons to conjure the Great Old Ones. This material, again, represents a literary pilfering on the part of the editors; the appropriate seasons to perform rites associated with the Great Old Ones coincidentally occur on the same days and nights as the major Sabbats and Esbats of the Wiccan religion, even though the information in this small grimoire supposedly derives from a magickal tradition pre-dating mankind itself. In addition, the editors refer to astrological data, particularly the movements of the planets, the signs of the Zodiac, and so on, which are specific to the

Western magickal tradition. The third chapter, "To Raise up Ye Stones," gives the reader instructions on how to construct a gateway using large stones; this gateway will serve as a point of entry for the Great Old Ones when they are called forth from the alternate dimensions. This chapter was, undoubtedly, inspired by Lovecraft's description of Sentinel Hill in "The Dunwich Horror," and by pictures of the rock formations at Stonehenge. The next series of chapters, "Of Diverse Signs," "To Compound Ye Incense of Zkauba," "To Make Ye Powder of Ibn Ghazi," "Ye Unction of Khephnes Ye Egyptian," "To Fashion the Scimitar of Barzai," and "Ye Alphabet of Nug-Soth," offer instructions on how to execute various gestures alluded to by Lovecraft in his works, i.e. such signs as the Sign of Voor, the Elder Sign, and the Sigil of Koth, and how to make some of the powders and materials mentioned by Lovecraft, such as the Powder of Ibn Ghazi, also referred to in "The Dunwich Horror." All of this information, in its entirety, is clearly inspired not only by Lovecraft's imagery and words, but also by information found in fourteenth, fifteenth, and sixteenth-century European magickal grimoires such as the *Key of Solomon the King*, *The Lesser Key of Solomon*, the *Grimorium Verum*, *The Grand Grimoire*, and the *Grimoire of Honorius*, among others.

The second half of *The Book of Dead Names*, at last, provides the student with actual magickal rites. However, in keeping with the preceding chapters, there is nothing original in these chapters that can't be traced directly to either Lovecraft's works or August Derleth's interpretations (misinterpretations?) of Lovecraft's works, or the material found in the previously mentioned grimoires. In a sort of four-part preamble to the rites, chapter 10, "Ye Voice of Hastur," chapter 11, "Concerning Nyarlathotep," chapter 12, "Of Leng in Ye Cold Waste," and chapter 13, "Of Kadath," the text provides general information about two major Lovecraftian entities, Hastur and Nyarlathotep, and two Lovecraftian environments, the Plateau of

Leng and Kadath in the Cold Waste, all of which paraphrase Lovecraft's own description of these entities and environments in his literary works. Then, the reader is provided with the texts of five rituals: there is a conjuration of Yog-Sothoth in chapter 14; a conjuration of the "Globes" of Yog-Sothoth in chapter 15; an adjuration of Cthulhu in chapter 16; a conjuration of Shub-Niggurath in chapter 17; and, finally, a ritual of Dho-Hna in the final chapter, which, we are told, will allow the magickian to "pass beyond ye Gates of Creation and enter ye Ultimate Abyss," where a being named "Lord S'ngac" (not referred to in any of Lovecraft's works) "eternally" contemplates the "Mystery of Chaos."[85] All of these conjurations and evocations are certainly adequately conceived and written, and the author has a good understanding of the various symbolic objects and stylistic settings of the black magickal tradition, referring not only to the medieval grimoires but also to more recent sources such as Crowleyan and Golden Dawn magickal practices. The conjuration of Yog-Sothoth makes use of the Pentagram of Fire, which can be found in Crowley's *Magick* and Regardie's two *Golden Dawn* volumes. Similarly, the ritual includes the signs of Caput Draconis and Cauda Draconis, both of which, as we have seen, were used by Lovecraft in "The Case of Charles Dexter Ward." The circle of evocation uses standard Zodiac symbols from the Western tradition, and the design is very similar to the numerous circle designs in the medieval grimoires. In the conjuration of the globes, the text identifies thirteen entities that personify the globes and represent the servitors of Yog-Sothoth. The descriptions of these entities are clearly based on similar images provided in traditional demonologies, such as the *Goetia*, a manuscript derived from London Papyrus 46 in the British Museum and translated by Mathers. In fact, entities such as Eligor, who appears as red man with a crown of iron, and Durson, who takes the shape of a raven, are so nearly equivalent to *Goetia* demons that these globes could very easily be included in Solomon's Vessel of Brass along with the others. The conjurations of Cthulhu and Shub-Niggurath, likewise, are heavily based on Western sources; Cthulhu is to be conjured on Halloween night when the sun is in Scorpio, while Shub-Niggurath is evoked when the sun is in Aries.

Langford, one of the primary researchers not "in" on the hoax, suspected at the time that the original manuscript was probably the result of a hoax perpetuated by Turner himself.[86] He noted that the rituals themselves were based closely on Lovecraft's work, which, of course, would not be the case were the manuscript an original product of ancient Semitic culture. The fragment, also, is too small to represent the central document of an actual magickal system. Wilson later confessed in *Fantasy Macabre* in 1980 that the whole book was, indeed, a "spoof."[87] Wilson gave a complete account of how this hoax was conceived and executed in an article written in the fanzine *Crypt of Cthulhu*.

> It began with Neville Armstrong, the founder of Neville Spearman Limited, a publishing company that reprinted the fiction of such Lovecraft contemporaries as Robert E. Howard and Clark Ashton Smith. Armstrong asked his friend George Hay to compile stories to create an authentic-looking Necronomicon. After collecting some material, Hay turned to the literary critic and occultist Colin Wilson for help. Wilson was unimpressed with much of the volume, and asked Robert Turner to write the actual text of the Necronomicon. An explanation of the volume's origins was still needed, but Wilson had his background in fiction to help him. He had a German friend write him a letter, addressing it from the fictional "Doctor Hinterstoisser." This helped him give the background; he filled in the rest with his imagination. Armstrong liked the book, and published it.[88]

THE CULTUS MALEFICARUM

A third Necronomicon recension, the *Cultus Maleficarium*, or Sussex Manuscript, was published by an obscure scholar named Fred L. Pelton as a large appendix to his book *A Guide to the Cthulhu Cult* (1996). According to Pelton, the *Cultus* was the work of an unidentified author in Sussex in 1598; the original manuscript, written in Latin, was "unearthed" by Pelton sometime before 1946 and then subsequently lost, but Pelton presumably managed to have the manuscript translated into English, since his published version is in English. The *Cultus* is not, strictly speaking, one of the Necronomicons, since it is not titled as such, but it is similar in tone, scope, and treatment to a number of the other recensions and so I have felt it necessary to include it my discussion of the Necronomicon texts. Despite the fact that Pelton's original manuscript is no longer extant, Pelton's motives in publishing the *Cultus* are made very clear in his *Guide*. Pelton seems to have viewed himself in a fashion very similar to Montague Summers, i.e. as a modern-day witch-finder who genuinely believed that the practice of black magick, particularly Necronomicon magick, represented a clear and continuing threat to the safety and the sanity of the modern world. As Pelton himself states it in part 4 of the *Guide*:

> The cult [of Cthulhu] is evil. The Gods of the Mythos are evil. The cult lives yet today for those gods. Only the eradication of this diabolic Satanism can alleviate the sufferings of untold numbers of hapless victims on bloody altars, and thus also prevent the perversion of otherwise useful minds.[89]

The *Cultus Maelficarum* is divided into four books, and the bulk of the text is devoted to an account of the general myth-pattern of the Cthulhu Mythos. The pattern involves three distinct stages: the creation of the universe; the conflict between the forces of good and evil on the planet Yuggoth (Pluto); and the conflict between the forces of good and evil on the planet earth. Although the unknown writer of the manuscript seems to acknowledge the first two stages, he is interested largely in recounting what transpired on earth after the Elder Gods banished Cthulhu into the outer reaches of space and sent the lesser evil gods and elementals to earth.

In the first book of *The Sussex Manuscript*, the author begins by describing the period of time in earth's pre-human eons known as the Cycle of Yog-Sothoth. This cycle represents a kind of golden age in the history of the Mythos. Azathoth, whose throne is located in the noumenal realms beyond ordered space and time, and Yog-Sothoth, who is the Guide and Guardian of the Gate leading to the noumenal realms, are the primary deities of the early civilizations on earth, and these two deities existed in harmony with the Elder Gods. In order to control the elementals and the evil, lesser gods, the Elder Ones sent a deity named Uldar, who served as a watcher; the *Cultus* refers to this deity as Ulthar, and, at times, speaks of Ulthar as a magickal "force" or "ritual," and even as a magickal "sign" whose existence keeps the forces of evil in thrall. The great, fabled empires and kingdoms of the earth at this stage are specifically identified, and these include all of the places referred to in Mythos literature: Sarnath, R'lyeh, Hyperborea, Carcosa, Chorazin, Kadath, Leng, and the rest. The priests and magickians who lived in these cities performed rites and gave sacrifices to Ulthar, and they possessed a device known as the Orb of Ulthar, which was nourished and recharged by the continuous sacrifices rendered by all the great kings and emperors of earth during the cyclical rites to Ulthar. However, the subjugated forces of evil on earth watched and waited to regain their dominion, just as they had watched and waited on Yuggoth. The resistance centered on the magickians of the tribes of Leng, who reserved a tiny portion of their sacrifices to Ulthar. These evil magickians created three shining black orbs, wherein they stored the droplets of their sacrifices. The black orbs grew over time, and slowly diminished the power of Ulthar. Ultimately, the three black orbs had grown in power to rival the Orb of Ulthar. The evil magickians placed these orbs on the high altar, and the divine incarnation Ultharathotep was replaced by the evil incarnation Nyarlathotep. At this point, the lesser gods, the elementals, and the evil kings and emperors of the earth had stored up sufficient power to call their Lord and Master, the great deity Cthulhu, from his exile in the outer realms, and Cthulhu came, re-establishing his dominion over the earth.

The second, third, and fourth books of the *Cultus Maleficarium* continue the account of the third stage of the Mythos myth-pattern. The period that began with the return of Cthulhu to earth was known as the Black Reign and was truly a dark period in the history of pre-human culture. During this period, the black orbs were enthroned in R'lyeh, the evil gods grew in strength and domination, and soon the entire earth was under their thrall. A dark tower was raised in ancient Arkand, and the city of R'lyeh became the central city of the evil gods. But two faithful acolytes kept the Orb of Ulthar hidden and secure. They migrated to the ruins of the city of Viryklu at the ends of the earth and there they set up a shrine to the Elder Gods. The Elder God Ulthar, inspired by this small renewal of his worship, caused a new race of beings to be born to wage war against the powers of Cthulhu and Nyarlathotep. Ulthar ordered his followers to bring the bodies of the faithful who had fallen in battle to the holy temple at Wyrkends; there, the pure essence of these bodies would be distilled into a "golden liquid" that would make the Orb of Ulthar more potent. Finally, the forces of good were strong enough to call the Elder Gods back to earth. The Elder Gods seized Cthulhu and imprisoned him in a death-like slumber in the sunken city of R'lyeh, and they stripped the elementals of their powers and banished them once more. The Elder Gods then returned to Yuggoth and there was peace on earth again. After untold eons, mankind appeared on earth and great magickians arose again. These magickians practiced their magick and witchcraft, but their practices were perceived as weak compared to the rites of the Great Old Ones—these magickians are described as "children playing beside a mountain for they behold ye mountain and seeth not that it is a pebble wherein standeth ye guardian of the gate."[90] Yet the magickians ultimately formed cults dedicated to the worship of the evil gods; they signed the book of Azathoth in their own blood; they denied all ties and claims to anyone outside the cults; they abandoned their families and friends; and they offered human sacrifices to Nyarlathotep and Cthulhu. At the end of the *Cultus*, Pelton makes it clear that the Cults of Cthulhu are still in existence today, and that the ranks of the black magickians devoted to Necronomicon magick are steadily increasing and continue to pose a threat to the safety and sanity of the world.

The *Cultus Maleficarium*, like the previous Necronomicons, is a hoax; there are no rituals and none of the elements characteristic of magickal grimoires. However, it is difficult to determine if this book was a deliberate hoax or just the result of some type of mental aberration on the part of Pelton. This latter view is suggested by the editor of the *Guide*, Pierre De Hammais,[91] and certainly, there is evidence in the *Guide* itself that Pelton may have experienced a mental breakdown. In his book, Pelton treats Lovecraft's fictional characters as though they are actual historical persons, and uses quotations from these "authorities" to support various aspects of his arguments. For example, in his discussion of signs and talismans, he quotes from Dr. Shrewsbury, a character in one of August Derleth's stories, and then supports this with a quote from Zadok Allen, a character in a Lovecraft story. He also refers to fictional places, such as Innsmouth, as though they are actual places.

While probably the Elder Signs belong to the Third Part concerning the actual magic of the cult and the Mythos, it is pertinent here to discuss it in some detail. It is beneath such signs that Cthulhu sleeps. These signs are variously referred to as "seals" and as "talismans" by which latter title they are more accurately described. Dr. Shrewsbury declares that these talismans are potent against the Deep Ones and the minions of the Old Ones (i.e. the Other Gods) but not against the Old Ones themselves, or their immediate servitors (whoever they may be). ... Zadok Allen of fabled Innsmouth gave a brief description of these signs which was recorded by Lovecraft: "In some places they was little stones strewed abaout—like charms—with somethin' on 'em like what ye call a swastika naowadays. Pro'ly them was the Old One's signs."[92]

It is important to note that Pelton uses the word "recorded" here in reference to a passage from Lovecraft's "The Shadow Over Innsmouth," suggesting that Lovecraft didn't write the passage, but was simply taking dictation. It is difficult to determine if Pelton is merely having some fun with his reader, and spinning some fictions of his own, or if he might possibly believe that Lovecraft and other Mythos authors really were recording the words of actual personages. If Pelton is, indeed, serious in this latter belief, then he really might have been suffering from some mental aberration. At the very least, however, this sort of thing certainly invalidates whatever pretense toward serious scholarship that the *Guide* might possess. There are, in addition, two other problems with the *Guide* and with the *Cultus Maleficarum*. First, Pelton interjects extraneous material from the fictional works of members of the Lovecraft circle into the actual text of the *Cultus;* for example, in book 1, he adds passages from Lovecraft's "The Dunwich Horror" that were taken verbatim from the text. Although an argument could be made that Lovecraft himself was responsible for plagiarizing a document from the sixteenth century, it is rather difficult to make an argument that the unknown author of a sixteenth-century document was plagiarizing from a short story written in the twentieth century. Secondly, Pelton is unable to present the original 1598 Latin manuscript of the *Cultus*, which makes it impossible to determine if the extant manuscript is, in fact, a genuine text.

NECRONOMICON:
THE WANDERINGS OF ALHAZRED

This book, published in 2004, is the most recent of the Necronomicon recensions. The "translator" of the book is the occultist Donald Tyson, who is, of course, actually the author, since this Necronomicon is as spurious as the others. Indeed, a close examination of *The Wanderings of Alhazred* makes it clear that it isn't a real translation at all; rather, it is a fictional account of the journeys and experiences of Lovecraft's character, Abdul Alhazred. Like the authors of the other specious texts, Tyson cannot provide the original Arabic text of the book, nor can he produce any of the Greek or Latin texts; indeed, he cannot even produce a transcription of any of these texts. In addition, Tyson offers no magickal rituals or evocations/invocations, other than a repetition of some incantations that Lovecraft himself provides in his fiction and two small invocations to Yig and Nyarlathotep, respectively. Tyson does give the reader photographs of seals that are meant to represent pictures of actual pieces of parchment, but which, in fact, are simply Tyson's own creations—he made them using the Aiq Bekr method for constructing magickal sigils. Thus, Tyson's recension is more of a tribute to the spirit of Lovecraft's mythos than a translation, and as such, it is not very useful from a practical standpoint either to the occult scholar or to the serious black magickal practitioner, though many black magickians, such as

Konstantinos, find this book to be inspirational. As Konstantinos describes it: "the book wonderfully captures the feel of someone seeing terrible, eldritch things by night in an ancient desert."[93]

The actual text of Tyson's *The Wanderings of Alhazred*, consisting of fifty-eight chapters, describes the early life and the experiences of Abdul Alhazred in Yemen, Egypt, Thebes, Memphis, Alexandria, Babylon, Damascus, and other places in the Middle East during the period of the Ommiade Caliphs circa 700 BC. In the first portion of the book, chapters 1–15, Alhazred visits Irem, a once fabulous city now buried beneath the sands of the vast desert known as Roba el Khaliyeh, or the Empty Space. In this city is a great chamber lit by colorless, faceted jewels that glow in the darkness and provide artificial light for the traveler. Alhazred refers to this chamber as the "starlit" chamber. There is a low, circular dais in the center of the chamber, and the walls are covered with curious paintings of different mythological times and places. At the perimeter of the dais is a series of raised metal pins that can be pressed down into the stone. These pins are used to magickally travel through seven different portals. To do this, the magickian sits with his legs crossed in the center of the dais and presses any of the pins; this causes particular jewels in the dome to be extinguished, so that only the paintings on the walls opposite the pins remain illuminated. After a short amount of time, as the magickian looks at the paintings, they begin to move and the magickian's astral body, or "soul," flies into the paintings. The portals afford access to various places, some of them fictional and some of them real. For example, the second portal leads to the fictional City of Heights, which Alhazred tells us is the original home of the Elder Ones, who are described in terms reminiscent of those used by Lovecraft in reference to the Great Race in his story "The Shadow Out of Time." Similarly, the fourth portal leads to the planet Yuggoth, "a world of ice and darkness beyond the sphere of Saturn, yet within the orbit of the fixed stars"; this planet is obviously Pluto, and the description here is, of course, based on Lovecraft's description of Yug-goth.[94] According to Alhazred, Yuggoth is inhabited by large creatures whose bodies are protected with horny armor, or shells, which, in turn, are covered with white fungus. These creatures worship the moon, and upon the face of the moon is a pattern of rings and lines that serves as a symbol of this race of beings. Among all of the portals, the seventh, which leads to Stonehenge, is the most important, since the barriers between our world and the other worlds are the thinnest at this location. Alhazred tells us that the ancient Druids were worshippers of Yog-Sothoth (which most occult scholars would dispute), and advises the black magickian to visit Stonehenge in his own body and, under the light of a waning moon, study the lunar hieroglyphs that are visible on the main recumbent stones of the temple, since these hieroglyphs, if inscribed on parchment, will assist the magickian in his dealings with the Great Old Ones.

The second portion of *The Wanderings of Alhazred*, chapters 16–24, is the most important section of the book, at least from a magickal standpoint—here, the author elaborates on the ontological nature of the Great Old Ones and then offers a number of chants and incantations that could be used for invoking these entities, though, as mentioned previously, there are no actual rituals. Alhazred identifies seven entities: five of these, Nyarlathotep, Azathoth, Yog-Sothoth, Cthulhu, and Shub-Niggurath, are integral entities in Lovecraft's pantheon, while two of them, Yig and Dagon, are not. For the most part, Alhazred describes these entities in a fashion not inconsistent with Lovecraft's own descriptions, though Alhazred's planetary attributions for each are largely inaccurate. However, a number of Alhazred's descriptions are startlingly original and do justify Konstantinos' effusive remarks about this Necronomicon recension. Alhazred speaks of Yog-Sothoth as "a shimmering array of ever-changing colors such as may be seen on the shell of a beetle or the wing of a dragonfly beneath the sun."[95] He also describes Cthulhu's body "as crystal or glass, and so soft that during his dreaming death it often breaks apart, but when it breaks it at once reforms itself."[96] Perhaps the most startling of these descriptions is that of Nyarlathotep; this description in particular does clarify nicely the distinction between Nyarlathotep and Azathoth. Nyarlathotep is perceived as a personification of the Void, an inside-out version of Azathoth: "As the face of Azathoth is darkly bright and radiates outward, so the face of Nyarlathotep his half brother is a void that draws inward both heat and light and never releases them."[97]

Along with his descriptions of the Great Old Ones, Alhazred includes magick sigils or "seals" for each of the Great Old Ones—all of which, Alhazred tells us, can be used in ritual workings. Tyson has conveniently designated that there are seven Great Old Ones, and thus he is able to associate each entity with one of the seven planets of our solar system. I say that this is "convenient" because it allows Tyson to use the magick squares of the seven planets as the basis for constructing the sigils. The construction is fairly straightforward, using the traditional Aiq Bekr methodology, and though Alhazred makes no reference to this technique or to the deletion of the zeros, it is nevertheless apparent that he is using this method.

> The magi likened Yig to the sphere of Saturn, for the reason that Yig is the most ancient of the Old Ones. . . . They gave to Yig the number square of Saturn as a sign and expression of his nature. It is a square of numbers having three rows and three columns, each with three cells that sum fifteen, and a total of nine cells that sum forty-five. From this square the seal of Yig is extracted, for the letters of the Hebrew script, most ancient among the writings still used by mankind, are also numbers, and the letters in the name of the god may be traced upon the square.[98]

Tyson's use of the Qabalah of Nine Chambers and the magickal squares of the planets affords the most objective evidence that this Necronomicon is a spurious document. According to Lovecraft, the Necronomicon was originally written in Arabic, or possibly Akkadian, in an obscure dialect that was, presumably, prevalent during the 700s BC. Yet Tyson has his character use Hebrew rather than Arabic as the basis for his talismans, even though the Hebrew language was not yet used in the ancient world for either magickal or mystical purposes. The use of Western planetary magick, particularly the magickal squares of the seven planets, likewise, is alien to the ancient Arabic or Mesopotamian civilizations. Indeed, the magick squares themselves appear in the *Grimoire of Honorius the Great*, a book purportedly written by Pope Honorius III that first appeared in the seventeenth century, and which is, clearly, unconnected with any of the magickal systems in ancient Mesopotamia or Babylon. The specious nature of the document is further confirmed when we take a look at the illustrations of the magickal seals. At first glance, they look impressive; the seals appear to be drawn with some kind of quill, the lines look authentically wavy and faint, and the material on which the seals are inscribed resembles torn and ragged pieces of parchment, with the types of creases and folds that one might expect. But upon closer inspection, these images are undoubtedly computer-generated; the actual cuts and tears in the "fabric" have the kind of matting that is characteristic of computer artistry, and the crumbled nature of the material and the occasional stains seem to be merely superimposed onto the surface of the images.

The remainder of the Tyson Necronomicon is much less impressive than the first two sections, and it seems clear that Tyson's creativity is waning a little as he brings his manuscript to a close. Alhazred resumes his wanderings, leaving the city of Irem and journeying to Memphis, the City of Mummies, and hence on up the Nile to the

Delta region. In a chamber under the Sphinx, Alhazred claims that there is a shrine dedicated to the true image of the Sphinx which, Alhazred informs us, has the head of Nyarlathotep rather than the head of Kephren; he further argues that this head resembles the hidden god Set. Alhazred visits the land of Khem, where the black races worship Yig and Tsathoggua, and he departs from Egypt through Alexandria. He explores Babylon, and describes the Watchers, or members of the Great Race, who are the subject of Lovecraft's great story "The Shadow Out of Time." Alhazred claims that the story of the fall of the Tower of Babel is an allegory for the story of the fall of the Great Race. The mad Arab's journey continues to the Far East and the river Tigris, and on to the Valley of Eden, where there is a wisdom seat that will confer the omniscience of a god and knowledge equivalent to that of the Great Old Ones. Near the river Tigris is a monastery of ancient magi who worship the Egyptian dog-god Sirius. According to Alhazred, the purpose of these magi is to study the history and nature of the Great Old Ones to ensure that these entities remain in the outer realms of time and space. The magi also take an active role in exterminating the black magickians and the priests who serve the Great Old Ones. In his commentary on these magi, Alhazred offers an interesting interpretation as to why the Old Ones are unable to re-establish dominion over the earth and its environs; he argues that each star has its own color, and that the changes in the colors of the stars over time, coupled with veils of cosmic dust, have effectively closed the gates between the noumenal and the phenomenal realms. Thus, the magi in this monastery make experiments with polished jewels of different colors in an attempt to create a "weapon of light" that will allow them to keep the gates closed for all eternity. Alhazred, leaving the monastery, travels next to Damascus, where he discovers a street called the Lane of Scholars that consists of rows of houses occupied by various black magickians and necromancers. The street affords these practitioners complete privacy in the pursuit of their profession. Tyson's Necronomicon concludes with Alhazred in Damascus, having made the decision to take up lodging in the Lane of Scholars and write his famous book.

4

THE SIMON/SCHLANGEKRAFT NECRONOMICON

The most ambitious text of the Necronomicon is a Sumerian/Babylonian manuscript that was acquired by a magickian known only as "Simon" in the early 1970s in Brooklyn Heights and first published by Schlangekraft, Inc. and Barnes Graphics, Inc. in 1977. Simon's identity is unknown, but in his writings he informs the reader that he is a priest of the Eastern Orthodox Church, ordained through uncanonical methods. According to Simon, the Necronomicon is purportedly based on the mythology and religious practices of ancient Sumer, the civilization that flourished in the area between the Tigris River and the Euphrates River in southern Iraq between 4000 and 3000 BC. In a chart of comparisons between the Cthulhu Mythos and the Sumerian tradition, Simon makes a convincing case that Lovecraft's primary deities are, indeed, based on their ancient counterparts. The word "Kutulu" (or Cuthalu), translated "Man of the Oceanic Underworld," "Satan," or "Set," is roughly equivalent to Lovecraft's "Cthulhu." The word "Azag-thoth," with "Azag" meaning

"Enchanter" and "Thoth" being the Egyptian for the god of wisdom, is similar to Lovecraft's "Azathoth." Shub-Ishniggarab, the Sumerian deity that answers prayers, is similar to Lovecraft's Shub-Niggurath. According to Sumerian mythology, there was a battle between the forces of light and the forces of darkness before man existed—the Ancient Gods, led by the serpent god Mummu-tiamat, were defeated by the Elder Gods, led by the warrior Marduk, and banished to the nether dimensions. This mythology, like the aforementioned barbarous names, accords remarkably well with the Derlethian myth of the struggle between the Elder Gods and the Great Old Ones, a myth that, it must be remembered, Lovecraft did not formulate nor perpetuate.

In his original introduction to the Necronomicon, Simon provides a sketchy account of how he came by the manuscript. He claims that he received the book from a priest, whom he refuses to name, and that the book was originally written in Greek, but then subsequently translated into English. Nearly thirty years later, Simon decided to flesh out this account and offer a fuller explanation for the genesis of the book. In *Dead Names: The Dark History of the Necronomicon* (2006), Simon describes his acquaintance with four key individuals who played a part in his acquisition of the Necronomicon. These were Andrew Prazsky, a bogus Archbishop of the Autocephalous Slavonic Orthodox Church; Peter Levenda, who was connected to the old Warlock Shop in Brooklyn Heights; and Michael Hubak and Steven Capo, both of whom were involved in stealing books from various libraries around the world. Among Prazsky's occult collection in his apartment in Brooklyn Heights, Simon and Levenda discovered a handwritten manuscript in a cardboard box labeled "the Necronomicon"; this manuscript was written in the Cyrillic alphabet, a Russian derivative of the Greek alphabet. Levenda recognized the title, for he was familiar with Lovecraft's works; at that time, Simon had never heard of Lovecraft, so he was initially unaware of the significance of the title. Simon recruited two members of his congregation who were familiar with Greek to translate the manuscript. Over the course of the translations, it was discovered that many of the incantations were written in Sumerian, and that the book itself was likely a Sumerian grimoire rather than a Greek workbook on magic. The translation was finished in 1974 and Simon made several copies of the manuscript; this turned out to be a good idea, since the original manuscript disappeared when Hubak and Capo were arrested for rare book theft. Shortly thereafter, Herman Slater, owner of the Warlock Shop, decided to move his business to Manhattan. He renamed it Magickal Childe. Simon left a copy of the Necronomicon with Slater to show to prospective buyers if and when the manuscript was eventually published. In 1976, Simon met Larry Barnes, a young drug addict whose father was a publisher. Barnes was enthusiastic about the Necronomicon and he convinced his father to form a special corporation, Schlangekraft Publishing, to publish the book in a special limited first edition of 666 copies (this number refers to Aleister Crowley, the Beast 666; Simon dedicated the book to the one hundredth anniversary of Crowley's nativity in 1975). A second hardcover edition of the Necronomicon was published in 1979, and the Avon paperback edition was published in 1980, making the book accessible to the general public.

The Simon Necronomicon has been widely criticized in occult circles almost from the first moment it was published. Most of the recent criticisms have appeared in various ephemeral online publications and postings over the years. The most ambitious critique is offered by John Wisdom Gonce III, a neopagan who claims to be a worshipper of the Sumerian deities, particularly the goddess INANNA, and co-author of the book *The Necronomicon Files* (2003). Gonce's criticism is threefold. First, he argues that the book's supposedly Sumerian origin is questionable, since the book reflects a flawed knowledge of Sumerian mythology and religious practices.[99]

Second, Gonce questions the actual existence of Simon, arguing that Herman Slater, along with some friends, actually created the book and then pretended that it was acquired by an obscure O.T.O. initiate named "Simon Peter."[100] And third, Gonce is bothered by the fact that the publishers of the Necronomicon are unable to exhibit the original Sumerian manuscript, and he questions whether there is, in fact, an original manuscript.

All three of Gonce's criticisms are unfounded; the last two are largely irrelevant. Gonce's view that the Necronomicon demonstrates flawed scholarship willfully ignores the fact that scholarship on Sumerian culture, religion, and belief systems is based on a paucity of actual data. Quite frankly, there isn't enough information about Sumerian civilization to enable any single scholar to make a judgment regarding which surviving artifacts of that civilization are genuine or not. In defense of his knowledge of Sumerian culture, Simon cites a reputable scholar whose viewpoint is very similar to his own: Michael Baigent, author of *From the Omens of Babylon: Astrology and Ancient Mesopotamia* (1994). Simon further discusses instances of Sumerian culture that did survive into modern times—the Toda tribe in southwestern India, and the Yezidi sect of northern Iraq—and provides examples of the cultural practices of these peoples that reinforce his own conclusions.[101] Simon also reminds Gonce and the other critics that the Necronomicon is not a pure Sumerian grimoire, and thus it cannot be dismissed because of imperfections in its references to the religion or mythology of Sumeria.

> The central issue of the Necronomicon that bedevils most of
> its critics is the fact that it is presented as a Sumerian grimoire.
> They point to inconsistencies between what the Necronomicon
> states and the actual practices of ancient Sumer. This is a "straw
> man" argument, for nowhere do we insist that the book is itself
> a pristine copy of an ancient Sumerian cuneiform text; instead,
> we point out that it was a Greek manuscript that appeared to

have been translated from an Arabic original. . . . Obviously, over thousands of years, much that was originally Sumerian would have been adulterated and distorted . . . [102]

Gonce's second criticism, that Simon himself is a fabrication, has been refuted by two reliable sources, both of which Gonce acknowledges. As Gonce notes, Robert M. Price, editor of Chaosium's *Call of Cthulhu* fiction series, relates that he met Simon in New York; he described Simon as "surprisingly young" with black hair and a beard. Khem Caigan, illustrator of the Simon book, likewise states that Simon is indeed a real person, and that he once offered classes on his Necronomicon at the Magickal Childe bookstore.[103] Even more importantly, it must be stressed that the principal members of the Necronomicon "gang" that Gonce claims perpetuated the myth of Simon are all dead now. Prazsky committed suicide in 1990; Herman Slater died in 1992; and Larry Barnes died in 2001; thus, virtually no one is left alive to have written the new Simon book other than Peter Levenda, who wasn't really part of the so-called "inner circle," and, of course, Simon himself. However, it doesn't really matter if Simon is actually the person he claims to be in the preface to the Necronomicon and in his recent books; or whether he is the Simon Peter alluded to above; or whether the name is wholly fictitious—*someone* discovered and edited the Necronomicon, and that is the important thing.

Finally, in response to Gonce's last criticism, if the publishers are unwilling or unable to exhibit the original manuscript, then that is their business; the fact that they do not exhibit it doesn't mean that the manuscript doesn't exist. In *Dead Names*, Simon reiterates the fact that he was never the owner of the manuscript, and thus, he didn't really have the authority or the opportunity to preserve the original manuscript; indeed, the best that he could do was to make copies, which he did. Furthermore, Capo and Hubak were indicted in 1973 and their stolen volumes were presumably all confiscated, along with any of the questionable books from Prazsky's library; thus, it is very plausible that the original manuscript was simply lost in the confusion or even inadvertently destroyed. Certainly, skeptics might find the disappearance of the original manuscript to be rather suspicious, but suspicion cannot be used as justification for making an argument that there was no manuscript in the first place. It is more sensible to maintain an open mind and simply examine the text of the Necronomicon as it is. If the text does bear a reasonable level of intellectual scrutiny, and if the rites and practices do, indeed, work, then it is equally reasonable to accord a certain degree of validity to the Necronomicon system as a whole.

Undeniably, the rituals in the Simon Necronomicon do, in fact, work, and the book is efficacious, at least from a purely magickal standpoint. The most famous of the black magickians who have tested the Simon Necronomicon is Kenneth Grant. In *Hecate's Fountain* (1992), Grant cites from the Simon recension; later, in *Outer Gateways* (1994), he refers to Simon's text numerous times, leaving no doubt in the minds of his readers that this text is, in fact, authoritative. The black magickian Konstantinos, likewise, admits that Simon's version of the Necronomicon works; he states this in general terms in his *Nocturnicon*,[104] and, in *Summoning Spirits* (2005), he even goes so far as to advise the novice magickian to try evoking a few of the fifty spirits listed in chapter 9 of the Simon text, *The Book of Fifty Names*.[105] In fact, Gonce recounts the experiences of several magickians who have had success while working with the Simon rites, but because his view of the text is mostly negative, he dwells on the negative experiences rather than the positive ones. Yet, by doing this, Gonce is indirectly undercutting his basic premise that the Simon Necronomicon is a hoax; indeed, if the book is nothing more than a hoax, then how can he explain the fact that it contains magickal rituals that really work?

THE NECRONOMICON'S MAGICKAL SYSTEM

The Simon Necronomicon provides a complete magickal system for contacting the Great Old Ones and utilizing their energies for knowledge and power. The author of the book identifies himself only as the "Mad Arab"—the name Abdul Alhazred does not appear in this recension of the work. In book 1, "The Testimony of the Mad Arab," the author explains how he came by the information in the book. The son of a shepherd, he is traveling alone in the mountains east of Mesopotamia, an area known as the Masshu by those who lived there. He discovers a great rock with three mystical symbols on it and decides to rest there for the night. He witnesses a ritual performed by devotees of the Great Old Ones and he understands that the gray rock represents a gate to other dimensions. From that night onward, the Mad Arab dedicates himself to discovering the key to the secret knowledge of the Ancient Ones, and he actively seeks out this knowledge. The fruits of this knowledge are then recorded in the book that follows, the Necronomicon, or the "Book of the Black Earth."[106] At the conclusion of his testimony, the Mad Arab tells the reader that he fears for his life; he has the sense that the ancient gods are displeased with him and are seeking to destroy him, and though he doesn't understand exactly why, he speculates that he may be guilty of having made mistakes in his magickal practices.

> For indeed, it appears as though I have failed in some regard as to the order of the rites, or to the formulae, or to the sacrifices, for now it appears as if the entire host of ERESHKIGAL lies waiting, dreaming, drooling for my departure. I pray the Gods that I am saved. . . . My fate is no longer writ in the stars, for I have broken the Chaldean Covenant by seeking power over the Zonei. I have set foot on the moon, and the moon no longer

has power over me. The lines of my life have been obliterated by my wanderings in the Waste, over the letters writ in the heavens by the gods. . . . I fear for my flesh, but I fear for my spirit more.[107]

Following the initial testimony, in book 2, "Of the Zonei and Their Attributes," the Mad Arab identifies the gods and goddesses of the seven stars (i.e. the seven planets). "Zonei" is a Greek word that refers to the "zoned" heavenly bodies, the planets that have set courses and regular, chartable orbits.[108] The identification and description of the zonei follow the progression of the seven middle sephira on the Qabalistic Tree of Life in an ascending order, beginning with Yesod, the ninth sephiroth, and ending with Binah, the third sephiroth.

The first of the zonei is NANNA, or SIN, the god of the Moon, who is clearly to be associated with Yesod. NANNA is described as the "Father" of the rest of the zonei. In this magickal system, the Moon, thus, is seen as the primary deity rather than as a lesser or lower deity—i.e. a mere reflection of the Sun, Tiphareth, as the Moon is understood in the Qabalistic tradition. The second deity of the zonei is NEBO, the god of Mercury. This entity is attributed to Hod, the eighth sephiroth. As the Mad Arab states: "His Gate is the second you will pass on the Ladder of Lights."[109] The god-form of NEBO is reminiscent of the god-form of Mercury, or Hermes, as pictured in Greek and Roman mythology. He is a bearded man, guardian of the sciences and messenger of the gods. The third entity of the zonei is the female deity INANNA, or ISHTAR, as she was referred to by the Babylonians. INANNA is the goddess of Venus and as such she is clearly to be associated with Netzach, the seventh sephiroth. The magickal image of INANNA is a beautiful woman who appears in the company of lions. The fourth deity of the zonei is SHAMMASH, the god of the Sun, who can be attributed to Tiphareth, the sixth sephiroth. The image of SHAMMASH is identical to all the sun gods in Egyptian, Roman, and Greek mythologies; a golden being, seated on a throne of gold, bearing a flaming disk that emits beams of brilliant light. The fifth entity of the zonei is NERGAL, the god of Mars, who is attributed to Geburah, the fifth sephiroth. Unlike the other zonei, this deity is more zoomorphic than anthropomorphic. NERGAL has the head of a man and the body of a lion, and he bears a sword and a flail. The fact that the lion is a "royal" beast, like the hawk or the ibis, places NERGAL in the tradition of the great Apollonian gods and goddesses of ancient Egypt. The sixth entity of the zonei is one of the primary deities of the Sumerian pantheon, the great god MARDUK, who was the son of ENKI, one of the supreme Elder Gods, and who, in turn, was entrusted with the task of slaying TIAMAT, the Great Serpent of Chaos. MARDUK manifests in the material planes as a mighty warrior with a long beard and a flaming disk in his hands. He also bears a bow and quiver of arrows and "treads" about the heavens, keeping watch so that Chaos cannot gain a foothold in the cosmos. The last of the zonei is NINIB, the god of Saturn. He can be assigned to Binah, the third sephiroth on the Tree of Life. NINIB shares the characteristics of Saturnian deities; he wears a crown of horns, like many of the Elder Gods, and he bears a long sword, but he is associated with blackness, decay, and death. NINIB has the fullest understanding and knowledge of the ways of the Ancient Ones and the practices of their worshippers and thus he can be rightly seen as a transition between the zonei and the azonei, or "unzoned" entities.

The next series of chapters, books 3, 4, 5, and 8, "The Book of Entrance and of the Walking," "The Incantations of the Gates," "The Conjuration of the Fire God," and "The Book of Calling," are centered on the ritual needed to achieve contact with the Elder Gods. There are seven variations on the initial ritual, one for each of the zonei. This ritual is strongly reminiscent of the type of planetary magick that has been part of the Western Apollonian magickal tradition since the thirteenth century. In the *Grimoire of Honorius the Great*, a seventeenth-century work purportedly written by Pope Honorius III, the magickian is provided with a wealth of data about the seven planets of the solar system and the spirits associated with each of these planets; the names and characters of the major spirits, demons, and angels are provided, along with talismans, stones, incenses, metals, etc. associated with these entities. The magickian is given full instructions on how to conjure these spirits, and the best times of day and night for performing the conjurations. In the *Key of Solomon*, the pentacles of each of the planetary spirits are provided, along with instructions with regard to the types of material that these talismans must be engraved on, and the proper hours of the day and night for making the engravings. Given these parallels, an argument could be made that Simon, in constructing a "bogus" grimoire, simply adapted the Mad Arab's seals and instructions from the medieval grimoires; this argument is implicit in John Wisdom Gonce III's "refutation" of the Simon Necronomicon in *The Necronomicon Files*. However, it is equally possible that the type of planetary magick used in both the Necronomicon and in the aforementioned grimoires derive from a common pre-Sumerian source; thus, planetary magick could have been part of the Mad Arab's repertoire. To his credit, Gonce does acknowledge this possibility.

> The correspondences in the Simon book make it obvious that these seven Gates are openings into planetary spheres—magickal worlds of the seven "philosophical" planets and of the gods—or Zonei—associated with those planets. This would seem to be a good choice for writing a supposedly ancient grimoire, since planetary magick is one of the oldest systems of magic and is foundational to most systems of Western magick, from the Qaballah to esoteric herbalism. Occult scholar Donald Michael Kraig believes planetary magick is at least as old as Babylon, and forms a bridge between natural magick (like

Wicca) and ceremonial magick (like the Golden Dawn), and between ancient and modern systems.[110]

According to the Mad Arab, the practitioner must "walk" the gates of the zonei in the proper, chronological sequence, i.e. from the bottom of the Tree of Life to the top. Thus, the magickian must start with the Gate of NANNA, the Moon, and then, once he has mastered this experience, he must then proceed to the Gate of NEBO, or Hod, and so on, concluding at the Gate of NINIB, or Saturn. Three days before the Walking proper, the magickian invokes the Great Elder Gods, ANU, ENLIL, and ENKI, whom Simon, in a supplementary table to his Necronomicon, associates with the Ain/Ain Soph/Ain Soph Aur, Kether, and Chokmah. Then, on the first night of the Walking rite, the magickian approaches the Gate with "awe and respect."[111] He begins by exorcising the temple. The magickian ignites a fire in the brazier and performs the Conjuration of the Fire God, which comprises the fifth book of the Necronomicon. He symbolically associates himself with ENKI, Master of the magickians, and MARDUK, the entity who pre-existed the Elder Gods, exhorting all the fiery powers of the Elder Gods to assist him, and to destroy any evil sorcerers who might be allied against him. After the Fire God is conjured, the magickian lights the four lamps and throws incense in the brazier. He then proceeds to invoke each of the four watchtowers. The Mad Arab is not specific about what these invocations are, but in book 8, "The Book of Calling," there are separate invocations to the four gates—the North, East, South and West—and a fifth, general invocation of all the gates. These are, no doubt, the invocations that the Mad Arab is referring to. Once the gates are invoked, the magickian must then evoke a being known as the Watcher.

In book 6 of the Necronomicon, "The Conjuration of the Watcher," the Mad Arab introduces an element into the text which is relatively unique in the annals of Western occultism. Most of the occultists and scholars who have studied the Simon text have called attention to the fact that the practitioner is virtually unprotected against the forces invoked during the course of the rites. There are, in fact, no specific instructions in the book about the casting of a protective circle, and this does run counter to the practices outlined in the majority of the Apollonian and Dionysian systems that precede or follow the Necronomicon system. Even more significant, this runs counter to other ancient Mesopotamian practices. As Gonce notes, Simon's text "contravenes" other Mesopotamian texts of like origin and age.

> Mesopotamian magickal texts ... routinely instruct the magician to demarcate a circle on the floor or ground by sprinkling flour (the Akkadian word zisurru literally means "flour which makes a boundary"). Rituals were carried out from inside the circle where the magician was protected from certain types of demons. Other circles were cast in whitewash or blackwash beside doors or around figurines of deities. There are even ancient commentaries that explain how the circle is symbolic of certain protective deities.[112]

This criticism of the Simon Necronomicon is further underscored by Simon's own warning in a preparatory note to his own text, in which he mentions that "there are no effective banishings for the forces invoked in the Necronomicon."[113] Yet, the Necronomicon does, in fact, offer adequate protection to its magickians. The Conjuration of the Watcher involves the drawing of a double circle of flour; thus, the magickian is as safe as any of the Akkadian magickians alluded to by Gonce. Although the magickian is not required to draw a circle again when he undertakes any of the Walking rituals after the invocation of the NANNA gate, nevertheless, the circle exists symbolically in the Place of Working, and thus the magickian is still protected. In addition, the Necronomicon offers a variety of other, mostly verbal protections for the magickian. In the seventh book, there are a variety of exorcisms and banishings that the magickian can utilize for personal protection during the course of any rite: there is the Barra Edinnazu exorcism, which is effective against any entities that attack the circle; the Zi Dingir exorcism, to be used against any type of malevolent magick; and a number of lesser exorcisms against any possessing spirits. It must be remembered, also, that the magickian is protected by the three signs of ARRA, AGGA, and BANDAR.

The Watcher itself represents the supreme protection for the magickian, and this being is one of the most fascinating aspects of the Necronomicon magickal system. As Gonce observes, there is some precedent for this kind of entity in the Western magickal tradition. He refers to an astral entity that is described by D. J. Conway in her book *Astral Love*. This creature is referred to by Conway as the "Terror of the Threshold" (an oddly Lovecraftian-sounding name). This is an astral creature composed of the deepest fears of the practitioner. If the practitioner can meet the Terror and face it in the proper manner, he or she can turn it into a powerful ally. One duty of the Terror is to guard the body of the astral traveler from harassment by astral entities.[114] According to the Mad Arab, the Watcher is not an astral entity; nor is he one of the Elder Gods or Ancient Ones. The Watcher is not a man, either, or a lesser entity like an elemental or spirit. He is descended from a race of beings that allied itself with the armies of MARDUK against the minions of TIAMAT. The progenitors of the original race were the three great Watchers of the cosmos, ANU, ENLIL, and ENKI, who preceded MARDUK and the race of the Elder Gods. In their manifestation as Watchers, these three entities are known as MASS SSARATI, MASS SSARATU, and KIA MASS SSARATU. The descendants of these entities, the Watchers in the zonei realms, manifest on the physical plane in three forms: a great dog, a noble spirit, or a frightening, evil, priest-like figure. As the Mad Arab describes it:

> And the Watcher appears sometimes as a great and fierce Dog, who prowls the Gate of the Circle, frightening away the idimmu who forever lurk about the barriers, waiting for sacrifice. And the Watcher sometimes appears as a great and noble Spirit, holding aloft the Sword of Flames . . . [and] sometimes the Watcher appears as a Man in a Long Robe, shaven, with eyes that never lose their stare.[115]

The magickian begins the Conjuration of the Watcher after he has conjured the Fire God. When he finishes, he thrusts the sword into the ground. At this point, the Watcher appears, in one of the forms previously mentioned. The Watcher will remain in the vicinity of the Place of the Walking until the License to Depart is given. In the Necronomicon, the Mad Arab provides another invocation of the Watcher, which he refers to as the "Normal" invocation. This particular invocation can be used during the course of any ceremony when the magickian deems it necessary to fortify his circle. The Mad Arab, however, is very clear about the nature of the Watcher; the Watcher is a threat to anyone, even the magickian himself, who leaves the safety of the Place of Working: "Thou mayest not depart thine sacred precincts until the Watcher has been given this license [i.e. to depart], else he will devour thee. Such are the laws."[116]

Once the Watcher is successfully evoked, the magickal practitioner moves on to the next phase of the Walking ritual, using the appropriate Incantation of the Gate in question, all seven of which are given in book 4, "The Incantations of the Gates." The practitioner takes up the seal of the planet in his right hand and whispers its name softly upon it. Then he recites the appropriate Incantation of the Walking in a clear voice, while walking about the Gate in a circular manner, beginning at the north, then moving east, south, and west, respectively. The number of times he walks is equal to the number of the planet. For example, the number of NANNA is thirty, so the magickian must walk thirty times around the Gate of NANNA. Each incantation follows the same pattern; they begin by exhorting the spirit of the planet to remember the covenant sworn between mankind and the race of the zonei. Then, the magickian exhorts the particular deity to hear his invocation, and then, finally, to open the Gate. Each incantation concludes with a series of sentences written in the Sumerian/Akkadian language; these phrases are clearly meant to be vibrated. After the incantation, the magickian, having arrived back at the center of the Gate and standing in front of the altar, must fall to the ground. He is warned against looking to the right or left; if he does so, he might be distracted by elementals, larvae, and demons that are characteristically drawn to magickal operations. As the magickian waits, he will presently perceive the Gate opening in the air above the altar. The magickian is then caught up in the vision of the Gate. The spirit-messenger of the planetary sphere will greet the magickian in a clear voice, and will give him a name which he is requested to remember, since he must use this name each time he passes the Gate in subsequent rites. Once the name has been received, the magickian is released by the spirit; he falls back to the earth. He rises and recites his thanks to the gods. He then strikes the sword of the Watcher with his left hand, pronouncing the formula that allows the Watcher to depart: BARRA MASS SSARATU! BARRA![117] Before concluding the rite, the Mad Arab advises the magickian to recite the incantation of IANNA, which celebrates how this entity conquered the realm of the underworld and vanquished KUTULU—this incantation is provided in the MAGAN text. This final incantation causes all the IDIMMU to vanish. The magickian can then extinguish the fire and depart from the Gate.

John Wisdom Gonce III, continuing his general critique of the Simon/Schlangekraft recension in *The Necronomicon Files,* focuses particularly on the Gate Walking rites. Gonce states unequivocally that these rites are "bogus,"[118] and he offers two arguments in support of this statement. First, Gonce notes that the Babylonians never conceived of the planets orbiting earth in the pattern laid out in the Necronomicon; therefore, Gonce concludes, the Necronomicon is a hoax, since it reflects a non-Babylonian, or perhaps more accurately, unorthodox Babylonian cosmology. Gonce does admit that there is a slight parallel between the Gate Walking procedure and the mysteries of Etana in ancient Mesopotamia, wherein Etana, a King of Kish, passes through seven gates to ask a favor from INANNA, but he demonstrates that the seven gates refer to a different set of deities. His list is as follows:

Etana/Necronomicon
Anu/Nanna (Sin)
Enlil/Nebo
Ea (Enki)/Inanna (Ishtar)
Sin (Nanna)/Shammash
Shammash/Nergal
Adad/Marduk
Ishtar (Inanna)/Ninib

There is certainly a discrepancy here, and Gonce's reasoning might be justified if the Mad Arab were propounding a traditional or "orthodox" Babylonian or Mesopotamian magickal system. But this is not the case. In his initial testimony, the Mad Arab informs the reader that his system has been gleaned from his travels in various countries, suggesting that the cosmology and magickal practices outlined in his Necronomicon are outside the orthodox channels. Therefore, there is no reason why the Necronomicon system should be judged on a strict Sumerian or Mesopotamian standard. As long as this system shares some of the general characteristics of magickal systems common in these regions, then it is worthy of acceptance.

And, as Peter Levenda, who did research for the Simon book, argues, the Necronomicon certainly does satisfy this requirement.

> Yes, much of what passes for Sumerology in the Necronomi-
> con is at variance with what has been generally disseminated
> in public forums. I feel that the confusion is the result of two
> factors: in the first place, so few of the Sumerian texts have
> been translated and made readily available to the public; at best,
> much of this has been left to technical journals inaccessible to
> non-academics . . . In the second place, the Necronomicon—
> while incorporating many Sumerian motifs in its pages—is
> work of a much later magician or magicians . . . yet it does seem
> to remain loyal to a Sumerian cosmology.[119]

Gonce's second argument is that the Gates in the Walking rites should be understood as the seven gates of the underworld, or the realms of ABSU, rather than as gateways to the seven planets. Specifically, Gonce implies that the seven-gated levels refer to the Tunnels of Set—the habitat of the demonic entities that inhabit Grant's Tree of Death.

> Some occultists have connected the seven-gated levels of the
> Babylonian underworld, the seven Hells of Hebrew Qaballism,
> the first seven Qlipphoth—the demonic "shells" or shattered
> realms of a former creation—of the Qaballah, Grant's Tunnels
> of Set, and the hellish lower astral realms described by both
> modern occultists and Tibetan and Indian yogis. What if these
> Gate Walking rituals of the Simon Necronomicon are engi-
> neered, either by accident or design, to take the practitioner
> into these infernal spirit realms?[120]

Apparently, Gonce is subtly trying to turn the reader against the Simon/Schlangekraft recension by suggesting that the Walking rites are deliberate traps engineered by Simon to trick innocent magickal practitioners into exploring the Tunnels of Set. But there is no evidence to suggest that the Mad Arab is attempting to do anything of the sort. And Gonce's argument ignores the fact that Simon's Gates, like most of the symbolic objects used in occult practice, are susceptible to a variety of different interpretations. The Gates do, indeed, refer to planetary portals, or heavenly gateways. But they can also refer to the gates in the underworld, if the magickal practitioner feels inclined to interpret them in that light. In fact, as we will see shortly, Simon himself devises an alternative interpretation of the Gates that adds another dimension to the Walking rituals. It is important to stress the fact that the Necronomicon magickian must be prepared to explore the realms of life *and* death in order to gain full knowledge and power.

The latter portion of the Necronomicon, books 9, 10, and 11, "The Book of Fifty Names," "The MAGAN Text," and "The URILLA Text," moves away from its central focus on the Rites of the Walking, and becomes more like the standard magickal grimoires characteristic of the Western magickal tradition. The Book of Fifty Names provides the magickal practitioner with the fifty names of MARDUK, who, as mentioned previously, was instrumental in the defeat of the Ancient Ones. The Mad Arab postulates that the magickian may only use these names after he or she has ascended to the Gate of MARDUK. The MAGAN Text is a long poem describing the war between the Elder Gods and the Ancient Ones. This poem appears to have been based on the ancient Sumerian *Enuma Elish*, in which a full account of this struggle between the forces of good and evil is given. The URILLA Text is the most interesting book of the latter part of the Necronomicon. This chapter alone is closer in substance to the popular image of the Necronomicon as a thoroughly wicked book, used solely by evil magickians for the purpose of opening the Gates between this world and the world of the Great Old Ones and bringing about the destruction of mankind. The Mad Arab refers to the URILLA Text as the "Book of the Worm,"[121] and he makes it clear that this worm is, in fact, the god TIAMAT, the great serpent of the Abyss. The book contains rituals that can be used to summon the Ancient Ones. The principal deities described in the URILLA Text are HUMWAWA, the Lord of Abominations; PAZUZU, Lord of Fevers and Plagues; AZAG-THOTH, the Mad, Idiot god of Chaos; KUTULU, the Sleeping Lord; GELAL and LILIT, the original Incubus and Succubus; and XASTUR, a demoness beloved by the Ancient Ones. The magickian is provided with sigils for each of these deities, and is given three conjurations to evoke any (or all) of the Ancient Ones.

In the final chapter of the Necronomicon, book 12, the Mad Arab offers his concluding observations. He reiterates his belief that his days are numbered, and he offers advice to future magickians, arguing that they must take care to protect themselves against the minions of the Ancient Ones.

> Remember to keep to the low ground, and not the high, for the Ancient Ones swing easily to the tops of the temples and the mountains, whereby they may survey what they had lost the last time. And sacrifices made on the tops of those temples are lost to them. Remember thy life is in running water, and not still water, for the later is the breeding place of the LILITU, and her creatures are the offspring of Them and do worship at their shrines. . . . Remember to carve the signs exactly as I have told thee, changing not one mark lest the amulet prove a curse against thee that wear it. . . . Remember that the Essences of the Ancient Ones are in all things, but that the Essences of the Elder Gods are in all things that live, and this will prove of value to thee when the time comes.[122]

The last passages are rather poignant; the Mad Arab tells us that the sign of XASTUR is looming over him, "casting a shadow over these pages,"[123] and that his own personal Watcher is not responding to him, suggesting that the Watcher is cowed by the impending fate that appears to be waiting for the Mad Arab. In his final words, the Mad Arab asks the reader to always strive to make sure that the Gate between our world and the outer realms is closed, and that, furthermore, the magickal practitioner should always be aware that the Ancient Ones are continually waging war against mankind. The Mad Arab then begins to succumb to his dark fate.

SIMON'S 2006 "RECENSION" OF THE SIMON/ SCHANGEKRAFT NECRONOMICON

Nearly thirty years after the initial publication of the Necronomicon, Simon decided to revise his thinking with regard to certain aspects of the text. Since these are fairly important revisions, they can be considered a new recension of the original material. These revisions appear in Simon's *The Gates of the Necronomicon*, which he describes as a companion volume to the original manuscript. There are, in effect, three basic revisions, the first of which is relatively minor. As Simon describes the discovery and publication history of the Necronomicon and the theft of rare books by Capo and Hubak (both of whom are not named), he explains how he found the manuscript of the Mad Arab. This time around, however, he refers to himself as an "Abbot," and he tells the reader that he was deliberately infiltrating the Capo-Hubak book-stealing operation on behalf of the Eastern Orthodox Church. Thus, or so Simon claims, he was acting as an agent for the Church. In making this claim, Simon does not seem to understand that this recasting of his role in the whole affair does not endear him to either his readers or his critics. Rather, the general impression garnered from all of this is that Simon is not only something of a thief himself, since he is pilfering books just as Capo and Hubak had done, but also an informant, i.e. a snitch, and thus is not to be trusted, even by his own peers. The end result of Simon's recasting here is that Simon has added to the general negativity surrounding himself and his manuscript and provided additional fuel for condemnation on the part of those who might otherwise have been predisposed to give his Necronomicon gnosis the benefit of the doubt.

Simon's second revision is much more consequential than the first. As the title of *The Gates of the Necronomicon* makes clear, Simon's general thesis is focused on the seven gates referred to in the Mad Arab's text. Specifically, what Simon is now arguing is that the Gates, though overtly associated with the traditional seven planets, refer actually to the seven visible stars in the constellation known as Ursa Major, the Great Bear, or, as this constellation is known commonly, the Big Dipper. Consequently, the gates are all part of this larger, general gate to the heavens. In developing this thesis, Simon devotes the first portion of his book to the argument that the Big Dipper was regarded as a "celestial gate" by a number of ancient cultures, including the Vedic Indians, the Daoist Chinese, and the Egyptians. With regard to the connection between the traditional underworld and the celestial gate symbolized by the Big Dipper, Simon explains that the Walking rites are not merely an exploration of the "divine" realms, but also an exploration of the chthonian realms; consequently, the black magickian must gain control of the forces of death as well as the forces of life. In a very revealing statement, Simon actually ends up agreeing with his biggest critic, John Wisdom Gonce III, in identifying the seven gates with Kenneth Grant's Tunnels of Set.

> The Dipper—or Celestial Gate—was uniformly regarded by the people of antiquity as the domain of beings who were already ancient, long before the founding of Pharaonic Egypt or Vedic India or Daoist China. [There] are ... the Seven Stars of the Big Dipper or Celestial Gate, according to Hindu tradition

... [These are] also eerily reminiscent of the Qabalistic tradition that the qlippoth, the "shells," are the demonic remainders of previous attempts at creation, the shards of the Sphere of Mars, which was not strong enough to contain the Divine Light and therefore shattered into myriad fragments.[124]

Simon's third and last important revision of the Mad Arab's magickal system is basically philosophical, or perhaps more accurately metaphysical. The magickal practices outlined in the original recension make it clear that the Necronomicon represents a genuine black magickal system, and this applies to all aspects of the Mad Arab's work, including the Calling and the Gate Walking portion of the text. The Necronomicon magickian, like the practitioners of the other black magickal systems discussed in subsequent chapters, practices his craft primarily for knowledge and power; he is not interested in the "white" magickal goal of spiritual attainment and perfection. The fact that the Necronomicon magickian is interested solely in knowledge and power is evident when we examine all of the statements and pronouncements of the Mad Arab in the original text of the Necronomicon; there is no suggestion of spiritual perfection, spiritual attainment, or an afterlife. A characteristic passage occurs near the beginning of "Of the Zonei and Their Attributes."

> The passing of the Gates gives the priest both power and wisdom to use it. He becomes able to control the affairs of his life more perfectly than before, and many have been content to merely pass the first three Gates and then sit down and go no further than that, enjoying the benefits that they have found on the preliminary spheres. But this is Evil, for they are not equipped to deal with the attack from Without that must surely come, and their people will cry unto them for safety, and it will not come forth. Therefore, set thy face towards the ultimate goal and strive ever onward to the furthest reaches of the stars,

though it mean thine own death; for such a death is as a sacrifice to the Gods, and pleasing, that they will not forget their people.[125]

However, in *The Gates of the Necronomicon*, Simon deliberately shifts the Necronomicon gnosis away from its roots as a black magickal system toward a white magickal orientation. Initially, Simon sets up his argument by accepting the Derlethian modification of Lovecraft's Cthulhu Mythos, i.e. the view that the Ancient Ones represent the forces of evil while the Elder Gods represent the forces of good (nowhere is this view sanctioned by Lovecraft, who was an atheist and didn't accept the Christian/Manichean view of the cosmos as a struggle between God and the Devil). Following this, Simon continues in the tradition of the proponents of the "alien-astronaut" theories of the 1970s and early 1980s, particularly Erich von Daniken (*Chariots of the Gods?*, published in 1971) and Robert Temple (*The Sirius Mystery*, published in 1976), and makes the claim that the Ancient Ones colonized the earth before the evolution of mankind and were put to rout by the Elder Gods. In Simon's estimation, there was blood spilled on both sides, and humankind actually evolved from the genetic code in this blood, which was mixed with natural elements such as carbon, nitrogen, and hydrogen.[126] Millions of years after human beings evolved, the Elder Gods returned to earth to check on the status of their human progeny. In their efforts to help mankind, the Elder Gods provided humanity with a series of rituals that would allow certain individuals to perfect themselves and become gods themselves. These rituals, which Simon refers to as remnants of the Elder Gods' star-traveling methodologies, are, in fact, the Calling and the Gate Walking rites provided by the Mad Arab in the Necronomicon. Specifically, Simon argues that the Necronomicon magickian, using the rites of the Calling, and "walking" each of the Gates in the proper sequence, succeeds in building up his or her astral body and purifying it, so that he or she can ultimately conquer death and attain immortality. This goal, in Simon's estimation, represents the true "quest" of the Necronomiconian magickian, one that is equivalent to the central quest of all the white magickal systems—a quest which has been described variously as the rising on the planes, the ascending of the ladder of lights, or, in Crowley's system, the attainment of the knowledge and conversation of the Holy Guardian Angel.

> The experience of rising on the ladder of light, of strolling among the seven stars of the Northern Dipper, is called the Pace of Yu. The "Pace of Yu" refers to another . . . gift to humanity: the method by which one walks among the stars. In the Necronomicon, this is known as the Walking, and is concerned with entering the Seven Gates. In China, this is also a Walking ritual designed to pace the seven stars, or gates, of the Northern Dipper. In this way the two rites from completely different cultures help to clarify and explain each other . . . As we can see, the methods varied but the goal was always the same: the creation of an "astral" body, a body composed of the same pure substances as the stars, and rising from the earth to the heavens, to that specific constellation.[127]

In making this argument, Simon is clearly showing his "white magick" roots; in effect, he is whitewashing the black magickal system of the Necronomicon. It is unclear why Simon felt the need to do this. Perhaps he really did come to believe that the Mad Arab's Walking rites can be interpreted as a system of attainment and spiritual fulfillment. More likely, he took to heart some of the criticisms of occultists such as Gonce, who assert that the Necronomicon is "bogus," and reasoned that the book might seem more legitimate if it were more squarely aligned with the Western magickal tradition.

5
THE GREAT OLD ONES

Lovecraft's Cthulhu Mythos presupposes the existence of a race of extraterrestrial entities, referred to as the Great Old Ones, or the Ancient Ones, who once ruled the earth before the advent of mankind. At present, the Great Old Ones no longer dwell on earth, but exist on other worlds and in other dimensions. However, as the Mythos indicates, they are attempting to regain control of earth, and are contacted by humans either directly on the physical plane, or through the use of magickal workings and dreams. These entities are unquestionably Dionysian in nature. They dwell in alternate dimensions, i.e. shadow-matter dimensions, and are seen by Lovecraft as being inimical to the human race—as evil beings, in effect. However, whether or not these gods should be viewed as evil is another question, one which Kenneth Grant addresses in his *Typhonian Trilogies*. Grant argues that these types of entities are, in fact, only archetypal patterns characteristic of the New Aeon and not really evil at all, only that Lovecraft, in his dreams, was terrified by these archetypes and thus concluded that they were "instinct with horror and evil."[128] In the Mythos, Lovecraft's attitude toward the Great Old Ones is rather unusual from both a fictional and a metaphysical standpoint. In some of the Mythos stories, the Great Old Ones are presented from a strictly science fiction perspective, i.e. as invaders or visitors from other worlds. In this form, the Great Old Ones can be accessed directly on the physical plane. In some of the other stories, the deities are transcendent, quasi-divine extraterrestrial beings, accessible via magickal practices. L. Sprague de Camp discusses Lovecraft's dual approach to the Mythos. He begins by pointing out that imaginative fiction usually falls into two separate fields, science fiction and fantasy. The distinction between the two is that fantasy, on the one hand, is based on supernatural assumptions, i.e. the existence of gods or demons that can be accessed through magick. Science fiction, on the other hand, presupposes the existence of extraterrestrial entities that dwell on another planet, or in other dimensions, and can be accessed through technological devices, i.e. spaceships, time machines, and so on. According to de Camp, the Cthulhu Mythos, in a sense, reconciles both genres:

> Whereas Lovecraft's Dunsanian stories are fantasy, the Cthulhu Mythos stories fall on or close to the border between science fiction and fantasy. Some can be classed as either or as both, since there is no sharp boundary. "The Dunwich Horror" is mainly a fantasy, since Yog-Sothoth is evoked and banished by magical spells. "The Whisperer in Darkness," however, is science fiction; the powers of the aliens, while unearthly, are still limited by natural law.[129]

Fritz Leiber refers to Lovecraft's temperament in this context as "mechanistic supernatural," and from a metaphysical standpoint, Lovecraft's portrayal of his extraterrestrial entities in this dual fashion allows him to have the best of both worlds. He is able to present

H. P. LOVECRAFT AND THE BLACK MAGICKAL TRADITION

his black magickal entities in conventional, magickal terms and yet relate them to the newest discoveries in the fields of modern science.

There are two levels of entities in Lovecraft's fiction. The first level consists of the Elder Gods. Presumably, these entities are benign; occultists and scholars often mistakenly interpret them as protectors of the human race, and therefore at "war" with the less benign entities in Lovecraft's pantheon. However, Lovecraft does not devote any significant attention to the Elder Gods in his works; thus, they are not important to the Cthulhu Mythos. Indeed, Lovecraft only identifies one of the Elder Gods by name—Nodens. In "The Strange High House in the Mist," Nodens appears in a vaguely anthropomorphic form strongly reminiscent of the Apollonian sea-gods of Greek mythology, i.e. deities such as Poseidon and Neptune. Lovecraft's treatment here is so vague that it isn't clear that Nodens is one of the Elder Gods at all.

As for this second level, these are the Great Old Ones themselves. The principal entities in the Mythos are Nyarlathotep, which Lovecraft describes as the "soul" of chaos; Azathoth, the blind, idiot god who dwells at the center of chaos; Yog-Sothoth, co-regent of Azathoth, the Gateway to the Outer Void; Cthulhu, Lord of the Deep Ones; and Shub-Niggurath, the Great Black Goat of the Woods with a Thousand Young.

Nyarlathotep is the most amorphous and complex of the Lovecraftian entities. According to de Camp, this name is a hybrid—a combination of the Egyptian word "Hotep," which means contented or satisfied; and the word *nyarlat*, which, de Camp speculates, is probably an echo of the African place name, Nyasaland.[130] This entity originated in a dream, as did most of the other deities. Lovecraft gives an account of this dream in a letter written to correspondent Reinhardt Kleiner on December 14, 1920.[131] In the dream, Lovecraft receives a letter from a fellow writer, Samuel Loveman, who informs him about an itinerant showman named Nyarlathotep who travels from city to city, staging an exhibition that consists of a prophetic film and then a terrifying electrical display. Lovecraft attends the performance and ends up experiencing first-hand a vision of ultimate chaos. Lovecraft embodied the details of this dream into one of the first of his Cthulhu Mythos stories, "Nyarlathotep," and the poem by the same name, which appeared in his thirty-six-sonnet sequence, "Fungi From Yuggoth" (1930). The narrator of the story, like Lovecraft himself in the dream, attends Nyarlathotep's electric show. Nyarlathotep is described first as human, or at least humanoid—swarthy, slender, sinister, vaguely oriental. But this is shown to be a guise. The electric show ends with the narrator and the rest of the audience exiting the theater into a blizzard that quickly disintegrates into chaos, the "soul" of which is revealed to be Nyarlathotep in his noumenal, otherworldly manifestation:

> And through this revolting graveyard of the universe the muffled, maddened beating of drums, and thin, monotonous whine of blasphemous flutes from inconceivable unlighted chambers beyond Time; the detestable pounding and piping whereunto dance slowly, awkwardly, and absurdly the gigantic, tenebrous ultimate gods—the blind, voiceless mindless gargoyles whose soul is Nyarlathotep.[132]

Here, Lovecraft defines precisely the veils of Negative Existence beyond the phenomenal world of manifested existence. This is also the realm of the Abyss, the area between the phenomenal and noumenal that Grant refers to as the Mauve Zone. Thus, Nyarlathotep, as the "soul" of the Abyss, is a chaos within chaos itself. Lovecraft offers a similar description of Nyarlathotep in sonnet XXI of the sonnet cycle "Fungi From Yuggoth." The sonnet is titled simply "Nyarlathotep." In the octet, Lovecraft describes the incarnate form of Nyarlathotep; this description is similar to Lovecraft's depiction of the swarthy, oriental character in the former tale.

And at the last from inner Egypt came
The strange dark One to whom the fellahs bowed;
Silent and lean and cryptically proud,
And wrapped in fabrics red as sunset flame.
Throngs pressed around, frantic for his commands,
But leaving, could not tell what they had heard;
While through the nations spread the awestruck word
That wild beasts followed him and licked his hands.

But in the sestet, the mask drops away, and Nyarlathotep is revealed as the "soul" of chaos. Nyarlathotep becomes faceless and formless, and his tangible outfit of red, "sunset flame" becomes a juggernaut of chaos, destroying manifest existence.

Soon from the sea a noxious birth began;
Forgotten lands with weedy spires of gold;
The ground was cleft, and mad auroras rolled
Down on the quaking citadels of man.
Then, crushing what he chanced to mold in play,
The idiot Chaos blew Earth's dust away.[133]

Despite his manifestation as the "crawling chaos," however, Nyarlathotep is able to visit earth in various forms and guises. For, unlike Cthulhu, Nyarlathotep was not imprisoned in time or space and he seems thoroughly capable of resisting the "poisonous" stars that hold Cthulhu in thrall. As a result, Nyarlathotep is often perceived as an intermediary between mankind and the Great Old Ones, but it would be a mistake to interpret Nyarlathotep as merely a messenger of the gods, as Kenneth Grant suggests. In Mythos literature, Nyarlathotep is spoken of as having a thousand forms, or avatars, and in these guises he was worshipped by a large variety of cultures and civilizations.[134] In the Congo, Nyarlathotep appeared as a being named Ahtu, a huge mound of viscous material with golden tentacles sprouting from its central mass. In Egypt, Nyarlathotep was worshipped by the Stygians under the name "Nyarlat," but it is said that the Egyptians grew afraid of Nyarlathotep and struck all references to him from their records and monuments and reassigned some of his attributes to Set and Thoth. Among the Celts, Nyarlathotep took the shape of the Green Man, a possessed effigy of a man made of the leaves and stems from various plants; the Celts also worshipped Nyarlathotep in the shape of a human male with the horns of a stag. Among the Aztecs, Nyarlathotep appeared as Tezcatlipoca, a man with dark skin and with a smoking mirror in place of one of his feet. In Britain, Nyarlathotep was often perceived in the form of the Black Man who presided over the Witches' Sabbat. Some of the forms taken by Nyarlathotep are very strange, even outrageous. For example, in China, Nyarlathotep has manifested as the Bloated Woman, an obese woman with five mouths and a multitude of tentacles. In Turkey, Nyarlathotep appeared as the Skinless One, a flayed corpse worshipped by a particularly noxious cult. One of the most chilling avatars can be found in Tyson's Necronomicon and *Alhazred*. Here, Nyarlathotep prowls the desert known as Roba el Khaliyeh, or the Empty Space, which is located southeast of present-day Iraq. He is human in form, wearing a black cloak, a hooded robe, and a black silk wrap across his face. His skin is black, his nails long and pointed. When he removes his silk wrap, there is no face—only a blackness filled with the same stars that shine behind him in the night sky.

Azathoth appears in "The Dream-Quest of Unknown Kadath" in a very similar fashion to Nyarlathotep, except that Azathoth is slightly less amorphous. Grant argues that the word *Azathoth* is derived from *Aza*, which refers to "the evil mother of all demons," and the Egyptian god Thoth. Furthermore, Grant argues that this entity is the feminine aspect of Choronzon.[135] In contrast to Grant, Simon argues that the word is derived from a Sumerian and Coptic root, "Azag," a Sumerian word that means "enchanter," and "Thoth," the name of the Egyptian god of magick—thus, Azag-thoth can be translated roughly as "Lord of Magicians."[136] Azathoth is described by Lovecraft as the primal chaos that dwells at the center of infinity. He is vague and undefined for the most part, but is spoken of as a "boundless, demon sultan":

> [No] man had ever suspected in what part of space it may lie; whether it be in the dreamlands around our own world, or in those surrounding some unguessed companion of Fomalhaut or Aldebaran ... There were, in such voyages, incalculable local dangers; as well as that shocking final peril which gibbers unmentionably outside the ordered universe, where no dreams reach; that last amorphous blight of nethermost confusion which blasphemes and bubbles at the centre of all infinity—the boundless daemon sultan Azathoth, whose name no lips dare speak aloud, and who gnaws hungrily in inconceivable, unlighted chambers beyond time amidst the muffled, maddening beating of vile drums, and the thin, monotonous whine of accursed flutes; to which detestable pounding and piping dance slowly, awkwardly, and absurdly the gigantic Ultimate Gods, the blind, voiceless, tenebrous, mindless Other Gods whose soul and messenger is the crawling chaos Nyarlathotep.[137]

In this passage, the relationship between Azathoth and Nyarlathotep is clearly specified. Azathoth is the primal chaos, while Nyarlathotep is the "soul" of chaos, indicating that Azathoth is on a slightly lower plane than Nyarlathotep. Azathoth is the antithesis of creation, a prime mover in the void, formless and unknowable, even in dreams; thus, Azathoth is appropriately assigned to the antithetical Kether on the Tree of Death (see chapter 8). Interestingly, some Lovecraft scholars associate Azathoth with the modern scientific theory of the "Big Bang"; this association captures both the creative and the chaotic aspect of this Great Old One, and, as Daniel Harms observes, links the Mythos creation myths with "the Greek and Norse creation myths, which hold that the universe was created out of primal chaos."[138] Donald Tyson, elaborating on this chain of reasoning in both his own Necronomicon recension and his *Grimoire of the Necronomicon*, argues that Azathoth's flute playing both creates and maintains the cosmos; thus, Azathoth functions in the same capacity as Vishnu, who, in the Hindu Mythos, maintains the continuing existence of time and space.

Lovecraft provides another description of Azathoth in his "Fungi From Yuggoth" sonnet cycle. In sonnet XXII, "Azathoth," which, significantly, follows the sonnet on Nyarlathotep, Lovecraft offers the following description of Azathoth, referring to this dark entity as a "vast Lord."

> Out of the mindless void the daemon bore me,
> Past the bright clusters of dimensioned space,
> Till neither time nor matter stretched before me,
> But only Chaos, without form or place.
> Here the vast Lord of All in darkness muttered
> Things he had dreamed but could not understand,
> While near him shapeless bat-things flopped and fluttered
> In idiot vortices that ray-streams fanned.

In the following sestet, the servitors of Azathoth are described; the realms of chaos are likewise delineated, and it is clear that Azathoth is, indeed, an antithetical prime mover in the formless void beyond the power-zones on the Tree of Death.

> They danced insanely to the high, thin whining
> Of a cracked flute clutched in a monstrous paw,
> Whence flow the aimless waves whose chance combining
> Gives each frail cosmos its eternal law.
> "I am His messenger," the daemon said,
> As in contempt he struck his Master's head.[139]

One of the earliest Lovecraft scholars, George T. Wetzel, acknowledges that Azathoth is, indeed, the prime mover, while Nyarlathotep, described elsewhere in Lovecraft as the "crawling chaos," is on a higher (deeper?) level than Azathoth. Wetzel focuses on the similarity between the alchemical term for the essence of life, Azoth, and the name Azathoth, but essentially his interpretation doesn't differ too much from my own.

> The god Azathoth in the Mythos . . . does seem to have some connection with Nyarlathotep. Collate the similar spellings of the Mythos god, Azathoth, and the alchemic term, Azoth, meaning "the primogenic source-essence of life." The god existing at the centre of Chaos which in the Mythos seems to have been the centre of the universe and life, then consider that chaos was a god in the sonnet "Nyarlathotep" and consider the epithet given Nyarlathotep as "the crawling chaos": what is seen is part of the Mythos still not quite formed but in the slow process of gestation.[140]

Yog-Sothoth is spoken of as the Gateway to the Void, the outer manifestation of the primal chaos. Grant argues that this name refers to the union of the Egyptian gods Set and Thoth, "yog" meaning "union" and "So-Thoth" meaning "Set-Thoth." Alternate names for Yog-Sothoth include Umr-at-Tawil, the "Prolonged of Life," and the "All in One and One in All." Yog-Sothoth guards the gate between the world as we know it and the outer worlds. This entity also presides over a group of ancient wizards who are immortal and who sit on stone pedestals in a place out of space and time, dreaming and brooding on the future of the universe. A number of Mythos scholars argue that Yog-Sothoth was, in fact, imprisoned by the Elder Gods at a point where space and time converge, and that consequently, this entity is unable to leave this area due to gravitational effects. Other scholars argue that Yog-Sothoth dwells in an alternate dimension and appears only when a wizard wishes to open a gate between the noumenal and phenomenal realms. According to Mythos literature, Yog-Sothoth was a spawn of the Nameless Mist (the latter of which was created by Azathoth) and he shares rule of the earth with Azathoth. Yog-Sothoth, in turn, is the "father" of Cthulhu, Hastur, and an entity named Vulthoom; also, he has spawned two lesser gods: Nug and Yeb on Shub-Niggurath. There is an interesting theory, which is generally not accepted by scholars, that Yog-Sothoth was imprisoned beneath Mount Sinai in ancient times, and that Moses freed him from the bondage of the Elder Sign—thus, Yog-Sothoth was actually the Yahweh that Moses communed with on the mountain.[141] Qabalistically, Yog-Sothoth can be equated to Tiphareth on the Tree of Life, albeit this is a Qliphothic, anti-Tiphareth form of the archetype. According to Crowley, the spider is associated with Tiphareth.

> The Spider is particularly sacred to Tiphareth. It is written that she "taketh hold with her hands and is in king's palaces" . . . She has six legs and is in the centre of her web exactly as Tiphareth is in the centre of the Sephiroth of Ruach.[142]

The spidery quality of Yog-Sothoth is likewise brought out by August Derleth, founder of Arkham House Publishers, in his collaborative story "The Lurker at the Threshold" (1945):

> Not stars, but suns, great globes of light . . . and not these alone, but the breaking apart of the nearest globes, and the protoplasmic flesh that flamed blackly outward to join together and form that eldritch, hideous horror from outer space, that spawn of the blackness of primal time, that tentacled, amorphous monster which was the lurker at the threshold, whose mask was as a congeries of iridescent globes, the noxious Yog-Sothoth, who froths as primal slime in nuclear chaos beyond the nethermost outposts of space and time.[143]

This description is much more tangible than the descriptions of the other two primary gods, suggesting the shape of a vast, glowing, spidery creature. It reinforces the Tiphareth association as well, since Tiphareth on the Qabalistic Tree of Life is attributed to the sun. In "The Dunwich Horror," Lovecraft provides a vivid description of the child of Yog-Sothoth, a description which is comparable to the above depiction of Yog-Sothoth. This child has been locked up by Wilbur Whateley, a black magickian, and his grandfather, but upon the death of the former, it escapes and ravages the countryside. Ultimately, Dr. Henry Armitage, librarian at Miskatonic University, uses some incantations from the Necronomicon to send this monster back to the alternate dimensions. But before this happens, one of the backwoods inhabitants of Dunwich, Curtis Whateley, catches a glimpse of this entity:

> Oh, oh, my Gawd, that haff face—that haff face on top of it . . . that face with the red eyes an' crinkly albino hair, an' no chin, like the Whateleys . . . It was an octopus, centipede, spider kind o' thing, but they was a haff-shaped man's face on top of it, an' it looked like Wizard Whateley's, only it was yards an' yards acrost.[144]

Cthulhu is described in the main story of the Cthulhu Mythos, "The Call of Cthulhu." He is the Lord of the Deep Ones, the Initiator of Dreams, and is clearly associated with Yesod on the Tree of Death. Both Grant[145] and Simon[146] agree that the Sumerian deity Cutha, or Kutu, the "Man of the Underworld," is the prototype of Lovecraft's Cthulhu. Cthulhu is the most popular of the Cthulhu Mythos entities, a popularity that stems, no doubt, from the fact that the Mythos was "named" for him by August Derleth. Many fantasy and horror writers have fleshed out the biography of Cthulhu in their own works and traced his background in detail. Apparently, he originated on the world of Vhoorl in the twenty-third nebula and traveled to the green double star of Xoth, where he coupled with an entity named Idh-yaa, resulting in the birth of Ghatanothoa, an earth elemental, and two other entities, Ythogtha and Zoth-Ommoog (the latter of which appears to be a water elemental).[147] From Xoth, Cthulhu then traveled to Yuggoth, and then to earth, where he built the mighty city of R'lyeh. Later, after some sort of cosmic struggle, R'lyeh sank beneath the Pacific Ocean for reasons that are unclear. Unlike the other deities in the Lovecraft pantheon, Cthulhu was not banished to an alternate dimension when the Great Old Ones were vanquished. Rather, Cthulhu was imprisoned in a death-like trance and left sleeping in R'lyeh, accessible to black magickians only through the dream state. According to Pelton, Cthulhu is connected with Huitzilopochtli, the war god of the Quichua-Ayars Indian tribe in ancient Peru, and he is also linked with the Aztec war gods. Certainly, Cthulhu must have been warlike in nature, since the lesser gods on earth summoned him to lead the battle to overthrow Uldar, an event that led to the Black Reign spoken of in the *Cultus Maleficarum*.

In the first part of Lovecraft's "The Call of Cthulhu," the narrator, heir and executor of George Gammell Angell, Professor Emeritus at Brown University in Providence, Rhode Island, discovers a disturbing bas-relief that represents the principal deity of the Cthulhu Cult. The bas-relief depicts a monster reminiscent of an octopus, a dragon, and a human being. As the tale progresses, Inspector Legrasse, a New Orleans police officer, confiscates a similar object from a Vodou cult. This statuette of Cthulhu is described as follows.

> The figure . . . was between seven and eight inches in height, and of exquisitely artistic workmanship. It represented a monster of vaguely anthropoid outline, but with an octopus like head whose face was a mass of feelers, a scaly, rubbery looking body, prodigious claws on hind and fore feet, and long, narrow wings behind. This thing, which seemed instinct with a fear-

some and unnatural malignancy, was of a somewhat bloated corpulence, and squatted evilly on a rectangular block or pedestal covered with indecipherable characters. The tips of the wings touched the back edge of the block, the seat occupied the center, whilst the long, curved claws of the doubled-up, crouching hind legs gripped the front edge and extended a quarter of the way down toward the bottom of the pedestal.[148]

Later in the story, the narrator discovers in a newspaper an account of the finding of a ship in Norway with one sailor on board. The narrator reads the sailor's memoir describing how the ship found the lost city of R'lyeh, which an earthquake has heaved up from the depths of the ocean. As the Norwegian sailors explore the city, Cthulhu awakes from his sleep. He kills all of the crew except two men, Johansen, who escapes, and Briden, who is driven mad by the sight of this eldritch entity and dies before the ship is found adrift at sea. The appearance of Cthulhu is very frightening; he resembles the statuette previously described, only now this monstrous shape is a living, breathing juggernaut of destruction. At the end of the story, the city of R'lyeh sinks back into the ocean and Cthulhu returns to his watery abode. But he is still accessible via the dream state and it is possible that R'lyeh will rise again—if the stars are right and the devotees of the cult perform the rites properly.

Most of the fictional treatments of Cthulhu associate this entity with the element of water. But there is some dispute among occultists as to whether Cthulhu should be viewed as a watery being. In *Grimoire of the Necronomicon*, Donald Tyson asserts that it is a mistake to associate Cthulhu with water—that Cthulhu is basically an earth being, and is only associated with water because he has been imprisoned beneath the sea. Tyson writes: "It is only misadventure that cast them [Cthulhu and his spawn] below the waves of the sea, which they loathe and despise with a passionate hatred."[149] But there are two problems with this reasoning. First, there is no indication anywhere in Mythos literature that Cthulhu and his spawn "despise" the water. Cthulhu was, indeed, placed in a death-like trance and imprisoned in the city of R'lyeh, but this doesn't mean that Cthulhu despises the water or even R'lyeh itself. After all, Cthulhu was living in and presumably ruling this city before his imprisonment. The fact that Cthulhu ended up beneath the sea might have been merely a matter of expediency; whoever or whatever imprisoned him in R'lyeh picked a location where Cthulhu was most easily accessible and vulnerable. Second, Tyson's assumptions about Cthulhu are clearly disputed by all of Lovecraft's physical descriptions. As described above, Cthulhu certainly resembles a water being; earth entities, or air and fire entities for that matter, would usually not manifest as green and scaly, with heads like an octopus. But then again, in "At the Mountains of Madness," Lovecraft refers to a land race of octopus-shaped entities that he associates with the spawn of Cthulhu—so the question of Cthulhu's elemental association is certainly an open one.

More recently, a second issue has arisen with regard to Cthulhu, centered on the belief that Lovecraft's Cthulhu is equivalent to the Egyptian deity Set-Typhon. Aleister Crowley's *Liber Cordis Cincti Serpente Vel LXV* (1907), book 4, verses 34–5, offers the reader a particularly unpleasant vision of a god-form that Peter Levenda, in *The Dark Lord*, seems inclined to identify with Set-Typhon. As Crowley writes: "On the threshold stood the fulminant figure of Evil, the Horror of Emptiness, with his ghastly eyes like poisonous wells. He stood, and the chamber was corrupt; the air stank. He was an old and gnarled fish more hideous than the shells of Abaddon. He enveloped me with his demon tentacles; yea, the eight fears took hold of me."[150] Although Crowley does not specifically identify this god-form with Set-Typhon, Levenda does just that, and then goes so far as to argue that this god-form represents not only Set-Typhon, the so-called

"Hidden God" that Kenneth Grant discovered in Crowley's works, but also Lovecraft's own Cthulhu.

> It is possible that the same forces of which Lovecraft himself writes—the telepathic communication between followers of Cthulhu and the Great Old Ones—was what prompted him to write these fictional accounts of real events. Either Lovecraft was in some kind of telepathic communication with Crowley, or both men were in telepathic communication with . . . this Dark Lord [Set-Typhon] of the Holy Books . . . one of the gods— perhaps the most important god—of the Crowley pantheon. In the Crowley line of succession, this god is at the junction of Egyptian and Sumerian religion and is thus pre-Judaic. In Lovecraft's succession, Cthulhu is a high priest of the Great Old Ones who came to the planet from the stars aeons ago, long before humans walked the earth.[151]

Levenda, like his mentor, Kenneth Grant, has discovered an- other "hidden god." In support of his assertion, Levenda notes that Crowley received by divine inspiration the text of *The Holy Books* in 1907, and though Lovecraft wrote his own story in 1926, Love- craft dated the action of "The Call of Cthulhu" to 1907. And so, Levenda concludes, both men were dealing with the same subject matter, i.e. the same god. It seems scarcely necessary to observe that this sort of reasoning is specious at the very least, and perhaps even laughable—certainly it is unworthy of Levenda, both as a scholar and as an occultist. If Levenda could put forth evidence that Love- craft and Crowley had received their inspirations on the same day, or even the same month, then his theory might be worthy of some minimal level of credence. But not otherwise. And in fact, Levenda himself makes it clear elsewhere in his book that he knows better than to make arguments of this sort. While criticizing the Thelem- ites for trying to blend gods and goddesses from different religious systems and practices, Levenda alludes to the "dangers" of such "facile comparisons."[152]

It might be useful to note, in this context, that the actual physical descriptions of Lovecraft's pantheon of gods and goddesses matter relatively little. As previously explained in chapter 2, Lovecraft's conceptions are closer in alignment with the findings of modern quantum physics than with the anthropomorphic, or even zoomorphic, images of Western occultism and religion. Thus, although Cthulhu clearly bears some affinity to the element of water due to his physical appearance, the actual physical appearance of this Great Old One is about as unstable as any transient, human-centric image in the vast cosmic scheme of things. The image of Cthulhu can be understood as an image that is essentially "writ in water," and this holds true for all of the Great Old Ones as well as the lesser, Other Gods. As Donald Tyson sensibly observes: "The gods are described by the poets in ways that allow human comprehension. [But] the mind of man cannot conceive their true shapes, which extend beyond our reality into higher and lower planes."[153]

Shub-Niggurath, the last of the traditional Great Old Ones, is the earthly component of Lovecraft's pantheon and the most tangible of all his preternatural entities. Simon notes that the word Shub-Niggurath is similar phonetically to the Sumerian word "Ishnigarrab," which refers to the Sumerian deity that functioned as the "Answerer of Prayers," though Simon is unable to ascertain what exactly is meant by this combination of syllables.[154] There is, of course, no evidence that Lovecraft was familiar with Sumerian mythology, and it is likely that he derived the name "Shub-Niggurath" from Dunsany, since Dunsany refers to a god named "Sheol-Nugganoth" in one of his fictional god cycles. In a letter to Willis Conover, Lovecraft describes Shub-Niggurath as female—Yog-Sothoth's wife, a hellish cloud-like entity.

Yog-Sothoth's wife is the hellish cloud-like entity Shub-Niggurath, in whose honor nameless cults hold the rite of the Goat with a Thousand Young. By her he has two monstrous offspring—the evil twins Nug and Yeb. He has also begotten hellish hybrids upon the females of various organic species throughout the universes of space-time.[155]

This definition has been fleshed out considerably by subsequent Mythos literature. Most occult scholars agree that Shub-Niggurath, in her noumenal version, does take the form of a noxious cloud (a cloud that, at times, produces hoofed feet and tendrils). But there is dispute about exactly where this cloud-like entity resides; some claim that Shub-Niggurath lives beneath the surface of the planet Yaddith; others argue that Shub-Niggurath dwells in a cavern beneath the ground in Arabia; while still other scholars assert that this being dwells in another dimension entirely. It is clear, however, that Shub-Niggurath does manifest on earth as a black, goat-like creature, and that this entity is summoned to the phenomenal realms by magickal rites—particularly the Rites of the Goat with a Thousand Young.

Shub-Niggurath is mentioned in a number of stories, notably "The Whisperer in Darkness," and bears a remarkable resemblance to Eliphas Levi's famous 1861 drawing of the God of the Witches. This drawing, in turn, is based on the classical image of Dionysus that served as the prototype for the Sabbat Goat and the Horned God of the Witches. Shub-Niggurath has the head and lower extremities of a goat, and her upper body has female breasts. She exists outside phenomenal existence, but can be evoked on the material plane by her devotees. Thus, she is closest in conception to the primary goddesses of a number of the other black magick cults, particularly the totemistic cults of ancient Africa. Indeed, as Daniel Harms observes, Shub-Niggurath serves as the central deity to a variety of different cults.

Shub-Niggurath's cults may be the most widespread of any Mythos entity. It is known to be worshiped by the Tcho-tchos, Hyperboreans, Muvians, Greeks, Cretans, Egyptians, Druids, and the people of Sarnath, as well as by the fungi from Yuggoth, the dholes, and the Nug-Soth of Yaddith. Sicily was a stronghold of Shub-Niggurath's cult during the ninth century, and the secrets rites performed to it in its guise of Artemis of Ephesus are matters of legend. Others worshipped it in the guise of the Norse Heid and the Greek Hecate, and it may also have been propitiated in the guise of the Great earth Mother around the world.[156]

THE "OTHER" GREAT OLD ONES

Lovecraft's Cthulhu Mythos has attracted the attention of a number of writers of weird fiction and horror stories, and these writers have incorporated elements of the Mythos into their own original compositions. The more imaginative of these writers have added their own deities and constructs to the Mythos, a process that has both enriched and, in some cases, weakened the archetypal efficacy of the Mythos.

This process began when Lovecraft was still alive. Lovecraft had a habit of circulating his manuscripts among his friends and fellow writers before submitting them for publication, and his correspondents tended to reciprocate by sharing their manuscripts and ideas with him. Of course, Lovecraft himself eked out a scanty living by doing revision work for his clients, but often he freely offered his correspondents valuable editorial suggestions and in some instances even revised the works of his fellow writers. Most of the original contributions to the Mythos are imaginative constructs only, and are not linked with the archetypal reality of Lovecraft's own visionary experiences; thus, these contributions are not any more efficacious in terms of magickal practice than the imaginative constructs of any other disparate writer or artist. However, Lovecraft did set his seal of approval on some of the concepts of his fellow *Weird Tales* writers, and I would argue that these constructs can be used in actual magickal workings. Lovecraft's "seal of approval," as defined by Lin Carter in *Lovecraft: A Look Behind the Cthulhu Mythos* (1972), is his acknowledgment of an entity or concept by referring to it in one of his own tales. Carter himself asserts that Lovecraft good-naturedly accepted any genuine contribution from a fellow writer, whether or not he actually set his seal of approval on it, using the example of August Derleth's contributions and revisions to the Mythos as an example.

> Lovecraft, as we have seen, frequently set his seal of approval on some of his friends' contributions to the apparatus of the Mythos by using the new additions in one of his own Mythos stories: It may or may not, be significant that he did not in any future story mention [Derleth's] theme of the Elder Gods v. the Great Old Ones; neither did he incorporate references to [Derleth's] Hastur, Zhar, or Lloigor in any story of his ... I think it rather likely, though, that this failure to use Derleth's then newly coined apparatus in one of his stories was just an oversight on Lovecraft's part. Lovecraft did not take the Mythos at all seriously and vigorously encouraged his friends to use it as they liked in their own stories, so it can be safety assumed that whether or not he approved of Derleth's simplistic cosmic war theme, he did not really care.[157]

It is true that Lovecraft was extremely good-natured when it came to the productions of his friends and fellow writers, but I disagree with Carter's view that Lovecraft did not take the Mythos seriously, and that he didn't care what the other writers did to it.

Admittedly, Lovecraft was a materialist, which meant that he did not think that the Mythos entities were more than fictional constructs. But, as I have shown, Lovecraft did acknowledge the unconscious, archetypal validity of the Mythos. He also recognized that the Mythos represented, in effect, his bread and butter. In these two important senses, Lovecraft did take the Mythos seriously. Consequently, I think that it is significant that Lovecraft set his seal of approval on the work of certain fellow writers, such as Clark Ashton Smith, and at the same time avoided doing this for the works of August Derleth and many of the other *Weird Tales* writers. In examining the "other" Great Old Ones, it is useful to look at the major contributors to the Mythos on an author-by-author basis, beginning with the contributors who garnered the Lovecraftian seal of approval and then moving on to those writers who received either a partial seal of approval or none at all.

The most important contributor to the Cthulhu Mythos (and, in my opinion, the best writer among all the contributors, excepting Lovecraft himself, of course) is Clark Ashton Smith (1893–1961). Smith lived most of his life in Auburn, California and initially devoted his immense creative energies to poetry, sculpture, and painting, the fruits of which invariably dealt with cosmic, otherworldly themes. Smith became a fiction writer rather later than most of the other *Weird Tales* authors; his first story was published in *Weird Tales* in 1928, but well before then, Smith had begun to correspond with Lovecraft and to share his unpublished manuscripts with Lovecraft and other members of the circle (the earliest surviving letter from Smith to Lovecraft is dated March 20, 1925). Smith contributed eight stories to the Cthulhu Mythos: "The Return of the Sorcerer" (1931), "The Tale of Satampra Zeiros" (1931), "The Door to Saturn" (1932), "The Nameless Offspring" (1932), "Ubbo-Sathla" (1933), "The Holiness of Azederac" (1933), "The Seven Geases" (1934), and "The Coming of the White Worm" (1941). The new entities that

Smith added to the Mythos are Tsathoggua, Abhoth, Ubbo-Sathla, and Atlach-Natcha. Atlach-Natcha, the Spider-God, appears in "The Seven Geases"; Abhoth, who, along with an entity named So-thoth, serves as one of the archetypal creators of the evil and uncleanliness of the physical world, likewise appears in the same tale; and Ubbo-Sathla, the archetype "soup" of evil and uncleanliness, appears in "Ubbo-Sathla." According to Fred L. Pelton, occult scholar and transcriber of the *Cultus Maleficarum*, Abhoth, Sothoth, and Ubbo-Sathla represent the three "creative" powers of the Old Ones, while the other three major entities (Nyarlathotep, Azathoth, and Yog-Sothoth, as Pelton tells us) are the "administrative, or ruling, powers."[158]

Out of all of Smith's creations, Tsathoggua, the great toad-like deity, is the most significant. In Mythos literature, Tsathoggua was the offspring of two entities named Ghisguth and Zstylzhemghi, all of whom migrated from a distant galaxy to Yuggoth. Tsathoggua alone made the journey to earth, where he made his home in the dark world of N'Kai beneath Mount Voormithadreth and then mated with a being named Shathak, spawning Ossadagowah.[159] Smith first describes this entity in "The Tale of Satampra Zeiros." The image of Tsathoggua is hideous and toad-like, and totally in keeping with the images of the other Great Old Ones.

> [Tsathoggua] was very squat and pot-bellied, his head was more like that of a monstrous toad than a deity, and his whole body was covered with an imitation of short fur, giving somehow a vague suggestion of both the bat and the sloth. His sleepy lids were half-lowered over his globular eyes; and the tip of a queer tongue issued from his fat mouth.[160]

In this tale, two Hyperborean thieves, Satampra Zeiros and Trirouv Ompallios, decide to visit the deserted desert-city of Commoriom in order to despoil the city of its treasures. Commoriom is reputedly haunted, and no one who has visited the city has ever returned alive, but the thieves are not afraid to make the attempt. In the city, they break into the temple of Tsathoggua, an ancient god who is no longer worshipped by mankind. They discover an idol of the deity, seated in front of a large, bronze basin. As they begin to search for jewels, Tsathoggua slithers out of the basin and begins to pursue them. The thieves escape from the temple and try to evade the creature by fleeing through the city, but the creature continues to chase them, and finally corners them in the temple. Ompallios is devoured by the creature; Zeiros manages to escape, but he loses his hand in the process.

Tsathoggua also appears in "The Seven Geases" and "The Door to Saturn." In the first tale, which occurs when Commoriom was a flourishing kingdom and not deserted, the Lord Ralibar Vooz, while on a hunting expedition, encounters a sorcerer named Ezdagor and insults him. The sorcerer puts a "gease," a type of curse, on Vooz, exhorting him to go unarmed into the bowels of a mountain and seek out Tsathoggua, presenting himself to the deity as a blood-offering. Vooz does so, but Tsathoggua is not hungry, so the entity sends Vooz on another gease, which leads to another gease, and so on. Eventually, Vooz manages to extricate himself from the subterranean worlds, but he plunges to his death from a cliff as he makes his escape.

In "The Door to Saturn," the sorcerer Eibon (author of *The Book of Eibon*, one of the mythical books of the Mythos), and a worshipper of Tsathoggua (or Zhothaqquah, as this entity is referred to in the story) escapes a death plot by using a doorway to the planet Saturn; Zhothaqquah's relatives and friends live on this planet, including Zhothaqquah's "paternal uncle," Hziulquoigmnzhah. Eibon and one of his pursuers, Morghi, spend the rest of their lives on the planet, living with a race of beings known as Ydheems. The description of Tsathoggua in both stories is very similar to the description given in "The Tale of Satampra Zeiros," as illustrated by the following description from "The Seven Geases."

> He [Ralibar Vooz] discerned in a dark recess the formless bulking of a couchant mass. And the mass stirred a little at his approach, and put forth with infinite slothfulness a huge and toad-shaped head. And the head opened its eyes very slightly, as if half-awakened from slumber, so that they were visible as two slits of oozing phosphor in the black, browless face . . . There was a sluggish inclination of the toad-like head; and the eyes opened a little wider, and light flowed from them in viscous tricklings on the creased underlids. Then Ralibar Vooz seemed to hear a deep, rumbling sound, but he knew not whether it reverberated in the dusky air or in his own mind. And the sound shaped itself, albeit uncouthly, into syllables and words.[161]

In "The Whisperer in Darkness," Lovecraft mentions Tsathoggua, and includes a sly pun on Clark Ashton Smith's name in doing so. In this story, Henry W. Akeley, a scholar living in Vermont, encounters a race of strange, crustaceous beings that dwell in the forest. These beings come from Yuggoth (Pluto) and are connected to the Ancient Ones in some vague, unspecified manner. Akeley corresponds with the narrator of the story, Albert N. Wilmarth, who finally visits Akeley and discovers that his scholarly friend's brain has been transplanted into a machine, while one of the crustaceous beings has disguised itself as Akeley. As Wilmarth and the pseudo-Akeley converse, Wilmarth learns about Tsathoggua and the realm in which this being normally dwells on earth.

> They've [the crustaceous beings] been inside the earth too— there are openings which human beings know nothing of— some of them in these very Vermont hills—and great worlds of unknown life down there; blue-litten K'n-yan, red-litten

Yoth, and black, lightless N'kai. It's from N'kai that frightful Tsathoggua came—you know, the amorphous, toad-like creature mentioned in the *Pnakotic Manuscripts* and the Necronomicon and the Commoriom myth-cycle preserved by the Atlantean high-priest Klarkash-Ton.[162]

Lovecraft also refers to Tsathoggua in "The Shadow Out of Time." In this story, three of the alien minds that Nathaniel Wingate Peaslee conversed with during his stint with the Great Race were "furry, pre-human Hyperborean worshippers of Tsathoggua."[163] Lovecraft likewise refers to Tsathoggua in two revised stories he did for his ghostwriting clients—Hazel Heald's "Out of the Eons" (1935) and Zealia Bishop's "The Mound" (1940). It seems clear, therefore, that Tsathoggua can be considered a viable member of the Lovecraftian pantheon, which is why occultists such as Kenneth Grant treat this toad-like entity as a genuine Great Old One.

A second important Mythos entity not directly created by Lovecraft in one of his own compositions is Yig, the serpent god. Yig is introduced in "The Curse of Yig" (1929), written by Zealia Bishop, who was one of Lovecraft's ghostwriting clients. In this story, the narrator, an American Indian ethnologist, visits Oklahoma to gather data on serpent worship among the Indian tribes. In an asylum, the narrator discovers a creature that is half-human, half-snake, and he learns from the physician in charge that this creature is the child of a woman named Audrey, who had been married to a settler named Walker. Her husband had been afraid of snakes and when she had slain a brood of young rattlesnakes to protect him, both she and her husband were put under the curse of Yig, the serpent god. The woman had been transformed into a half-human, half-serpent creature. When she died, she left three children, one of which survived. Unfortunately, there is no tangible description of Yig in this story, except for Audrey's brief mention of a nightmare, where Yig appears to her "in the guise of Satan as depicted in cheap engravings she had seen."[164] Nevertheless, Lovecraft mentions Yig in one of the same stories identified above, and thus puts his seal of approval on this entity as a member of the Mythos pantheon. In "The Whisperer in Darkness," the pseudo-Akeley discusses "The legend of Yig, Father of Serpents," with Wilmarth.[165] Lovecraft, also, in a revealing letter to Zealia Bishop dated March 9, 1928, acknowledges ownership of Yig in very unequivocal terms.

> The deity in question [Yig] is entirely a product of my own imaginative theogony—for like Dunsany, I love to invent gods and devils and kindred marvelous things. However, the Indians certainly had a snake-god; for as everyone knows, the great fabulous teacher and civilizer of the prehistoric Mexican cultures (called Quetzalcoatl by the Inca-Aztec groups and Kukulcan by the Mayas) was a feathered serpent.[166]

In the view of occult scholars and practitioners, Yig is usually understood as the "father" of all the serpents on the earth, as well as the progenitor of such creatures as the salamanders and the mythological dragon. It is believed that Yig was worshipped in the dark kingdoms below the earth, particularly in the subterranean kingdom of K'n-yan. More certainly, Yig does appear to have been the prototype for ancient serpent gods that were the focus of many of the ancient tribes of Africa. The worshippers of Yig make use of drums in their rites, for this sound is most pleasing to this god. These worshippers take care not to harm any serpent, since all serpents are, in a sense, the children of Yig, and Yig will punish any human who injures one. In Mythos literature, Yig reputedly came to earth from a world named Zandanua, and now this Great Old One dwells in the Pit of Ngoth in the caverns of the red-litten underworld of Yoth (some scholars argue that this dwelling place is actually in K'n-yan instead).

Three other *Weird Tales* writers developed entities and concepts that became part of the Cthulhu Mythos while Lovecraft was alive.[167] The first of these writers, Frank Belknap Long, was one of Lovecraft's closest friends. Long contributed four pieces to the Cthulhu Mythos: "The Space Eaters" (1928); "The Hounds of Tindalos" (1929); "The Horror from the Hills" (1931); and "When Chaugnar Wakes" (1932). The principal entity that Long created is Chaugnar Faugn, a vampire-like creature with tentacled ears, a trunk, and large, sharp tusks. Long also created the Hounds of Tindalos, creatures who dwell in alternate dimensions beyond time and space; these creatures seem to be of the same nature as the Qliphothic entities, or the unclean shells of the creation. A second *Weird Tales* writer, Robert E. Howard, was a correspondent of Lovecraft's and the creator of Conan, the famous swashbuckling hero of Hyperborea. Howard's Mythos stories include: "The Shadow Kingdom" (1929), "The Children of the Night" (1931), "The Black Stone" (1931), "The Thing on the Roof" (1932), "Arkham" (1932), "The Fire of Asshurbanipal" (1936), "Dig Me No Grave" (1937), and "The House in the Oaks" (1971). Howard created only one major type of creature, the Serpent-Men of Valusia, who lived in Valusia, a land in pre-glacial Europe that existed before the continent of Hyperborea rose from the sea.

The third *Weird Tales* writer who contributed to the Mythos was August Derleth. Derleth's work on the Mythos is fairly extensive, and can be broken down into two categories: his collaborations with Lovecraft, which basically consisted of Derleth's completion of various unfinished Lovecraft manuscripts; and his own Mythos compositions, some of which were written with a collaborator, Mark Schorer. The major Lovecraft collaborations are the following: "The Lurker at the Threshold," "The Survivor," "The Watchers Out of Time," and "Innsmouth Clay." Derleth's own work includes the following titles: "Lair of the Star-Spawn" (1932), "The Thing That Walked on the Wind" (1933), "The Return of Hastur" (1939), "Spawn of the

Maelstrom" (1939), "The Sandwin Compact" (1940), "The Horror from the Depths" (1940), "Ithaqua" (1941), "Beyond the Threshold" (1941), "The Trail of Cthulhu" (1944), "The Dweller in Darkness" (1944), "The Watcher from the Sky" (1945), "Something in Wood" (1948), "The Whippoorwills in the Hills" (1948), "The Testament of Claiborne Boyd" (1949), "Something from Out There" (1951), "The Keeper of the Key" (1951), "The Black Island" (1952), "The House in the Valley" (1953), and "The Seal of R'lyeh" (1957). Derleth decided to recast the Cthulhu Mythos in a more conventional religious structure, which is curiously reminiscent of the good versus evil dichotomy in Christianity. Derleth pictured the Ancient Ones as representatives of the forces of evil, while the Elder Gods, such as Nodens, represented the forces of good. The great archetypal entity Cthulhu was delegated to the status of a water elemental; Hastur, the half brother of Cthulhu, was perceived as an air elemental; Shub-Niggurath was seen as an earth elemental; and a new deity, Cthugha, became a fire elemental. The "lesser" deities in the Derlethean cosmos conspired to elevate Cthulhu to a dominant role on earth, and to overthrow the supporters of the Elder Gods. Derleth also added a few other entities to the Mythos: Ithaqua, also known as the "Snow Thing" and the "Wind Walker," a being Derleth equates with the Wendigo, celebrated in Algernon Blackwood's story of the same name; Lloigor, another air elemental; Lloigor's twin brother Zhar, likewise attributed to the air; and finally, the Tcho-Tcho people, who dwell on a high plateau in Central Asia and function as the earthly servitors of the air elementals.

Lovecraft was well aware of the contributions of these colleagues to the Mythos. In fact, he had read most of the earlier stories in manuscript before they were published by *Weird Tales*. In "The Whisperer in Darkness," Lovecraft mentions Long's Hounds of Tindalos in passing; he also briefly mentions the Serpent-Men of Valusia in both "The Whisperer in Darkness" and "The Shadow Out of Time." As for Derleth's contributions, Lovecraft mentions only the Tcho-Tcho people in a short passage in "The Shadow Out of Time." Of course, Lovecraft understood that Derleth was trying to apply a good versus evil dichotomy to his Mythos, but Lovecraft leaves no record of his view on this matter, so it is unclear whether or not he approved of this modification. In any case, it hardly matters. The contributions of Long, Howard, and Derleth are relatively minor, and Lovecraft's brief mention of the entities created by these three men certainly isn't an endorsement of their status as genuine ontological entities. Indeed, none of these minor entities ever seems to reach the magnitude of a Tsathoggua, or a Yig, even in the works of their own creators; they are basically imaginative creations only, and should not be taken as representative of any higher archetypes.

6

LOVECRAFT AND THE AFRO-HAITIAN VODOU CULTS

The Vodou cults (variant spellings of the word "vodou" include Voodoo, Vaudou, Vodu, and, more recently, in Haiti, Hoodoo) have expanded in the twentieth and twenty-first centuries into a complex magickal system that has become, in the opinion of scholars like Reginald Crosley, a full-fledged religious system. Contemporary Vodou practices do not merely incorporate the rich body of primitive African oral traditions and ancestral worship, but also include aspects of Western Catholicism, Native American Shamanism, Western Freemasonry and Apollonian magickal practices, and, as Crosley argues, elements of Judaism, Buddhism, and Islam as well. As such, Vodou can be understood as uniquely synergetic in a way that other magickal systems are decidedly not. Yet, like other black magickal systems, Vodou encourages its followers and initiates to pursue knowledge and power for its own sake as they venture beyond ordinary reality into alternate dimensions and universes.

As we have seen, H. P. Lovecraft's knowledge of black magick and witchcraft was scanty at best, and clearly did not extend to the Vodou cults or any other of the non-Western, non-European Dionysian cults. Although Lovecraft visited New Orleans on at least one occasion and likely engaged in his usual antiquarian explorations and pursuits, there is no evidence that he ever set foot in an establishment that offered Vodou products or paraphernalia for sale. And not surprisingly, there is no mention of Vodou or Vodou practices anywhere in Lovecraft's voluminous correspondence. Nevertheless, there are significant similarities between Lovecraftian magick and the magickal practices of the modern Vodou cults.

To begin with, there is the fact that the crisis of possession is central to both the Vodou cults and the Lovecraftian Mythos. In many of Lovecraft's major works, the protagonists are "possessed" by extraterrestrial entities and their bodies and minds are utilized for nefarious or alien purposes. Likewise, Vodou practitioners are "possessed" by extraterrestrial entities and the bodies and minds of those who undergo this experience are at least temporarily under the control of alien beings. Secondly, Lovecraft's philosophical and metaphysical views of the cosmos are remarkably in accord with the Vodoun theories of the pan-psychic field. Although Lovecraft, unlike the Vodoun thinkers, would not have acknowledged the likelihood of any type of personal immortality or the possibility of an afterlife, Lovecraft and the Vodoun thinkers share a view of the universe that is remarkably akin to the paradoxical discoveries of relativity theory and quantum mechanics that characterize much of contemporary scientific thought. Finally, certain key entities in the Cthulhu Mythos, particularly the serpent god Yig, are eerily similar to major entities in the three Vodou pantheons.

THE RISE OF THE VODOU CULTS

The Afro-Haitian Vodou religion is indisputably the oldest of the black magickal systems. The slave trade from Africa to Haiti began in the early sixteenth century when the island of Santo Domingo, the western part of which contains Haiti, was in the possession of Spain. In 1677, Spain ceded Haiti to France and retained the eastern part of the island, which became the Dominican Republic proper. Plantations were established in Haiti and they began to grow swiftly, increasing the demand for slaves. By around 1789, Haiti had roughly 465,000 slaves. Most of these slaves were taken from tribes in West and Central Africa, since these areas were nearest the coast where the first British and French settlements were established in the 1800s. There were basically three West African regions in play during this period. The first region was Dahomey, which was just east of Asante near the Gold Coast, bordering the Atlantic Ocean. The Dahomeyan kingdom had conquered all of the Abomey plateau in West Africa between 1650 and 1708, and by the turn of the century it had subsumed most of the minor Vodou cults and incorporated them into the Dahomeyan religion proper. The second region was located just east of Dahomey in Southwestern Nigeria. This region belonged to the Yoruba, one of the largest ethnic groups south of the Sahara Desert. The Yoruba, in particular, were among the original progenitors of the tripartite view of the soul, which is a characteristic feature of the modern Vodou religion. The third region of importance was located further east of Yoruba in Southeastern Nigeria, nestled between the Benin province and the Cameroun Mountains. This area was occupied by the Igbo clans. In Central Africa, the Bantu religious systems were equal in importance to the Dahomeyan, Yoruba, and Igbo clans. The Bantu systems came from the wide diversity of Bantu tribes, both western and eastern, inhabiting the Congo and Zaire just south of the equator. As a result, the Afro-Haitian Vodou religion can be viewed as the result of a syncretism between the Dahomeyan, Yoruban, and Igbo and Bantu religious systems, with the Dahomeyan influence predominant.

The Vodou cults expanded in Haiti to such an extent that, in 1792, the Governor of Louisiana, then under French and Spanish rule, prohibited the importation of slaves from Santo Domingo into America, fearing that the slaves would bring Vodou with them. But with the Louisiana Purchase in 1803, this ban was lifted and slaves were imported into America. Consequently, Vodou grew phenomenally in both America and Haiti, and continues to do so today. The key to this growth lies in three factors. First, the slaves were extremely tenacious about their religious beliefs, keeping them intact despite the harsh conditions of slavery and the stipulations against banding together imposed upon them by their white masters. Second, the slaves quickly established a secret network linking groups of slaves from one plantation to the next. Slaves were not allowed to assemble for any purpose whatsoever during the early days of slavery; if they were discovered in gatherings, their owners were fined heavily and the slaves were branded with fleur-de-lis, whipped, or even put to death. However, they were still able to meet secretly via an enormously efficient underground network. By the mid 1800s, it was finally recognized that slaves needed recreation and they were allowed to band together on plantations for weddings, dances, and publically staged Vodou celebrations. But these public celebrations were mainly ceremonial, designed not to offend the white onlookers. The real, Dionysian rites were still performed secretly. The final factor that kept the growth of Vodou consistent during the period of slavery was the syncretizing mindset of the original Dahomeyan tribal influence. Vodou, from the start, had a strong tendency to blend, harmonize, and reconcile various seemingly incompatible elements in religions and cults. Thus, Vodou could never be weakened, but only strengthened by foreign philosophical and metaphysical influences. Indeed, when Roman Catholicism went to work on Vodou in the nineteenth century, attempting to convert its practitioners to Christianity, Vodou incorporated Catholicism into its belief system. As a result, Catholic saints were added to the Vodou pantheon of deities.

The advent of modern Vodou is undeniably the work of two of the greatest Vodouns in New Orleans in the early to late nineteenth century. Marie Laveau (1797–1881) and her daughter, Marie II (1827–1897?), were free women of color who consolidated Vodou practices at a time when Vodou wasn't organized as a religion, per se. The first Marie Laveau was a mixture of Negro, Indian, and white. She was a tall, statuesque woman with curling black hair, hypnotic black eyes, Caucasian features, and reddish dark skin. Initially, Marie wasn't interested in Vodou or anything magickal; she was a daily worshipper at the St. Louis Catholic cathedral. In 1819 she married Jacques Paris, a carpenter, who left her shortly after they married and died five or six years later. Marie took to calling herself the "Widow Paris" and earned her living as a hairdresser, going into the homes of prominent citizens to ply her trade. She became privy to the secrets of many rich, powerful people, and applied this knowledge a few years later when she converted to the Vodou religion in the late twenties. At this time, Vodou practitioners, both free men and women of color and slaves, were allowed to practice their religion in public celebrations on Congo Street. There were also larger, private group rituals at the lake at St. John Bayou and at Lake Pontchartrain on the outskirts of the city. There were many Vodou queens, but Marie Laveau perceived that Vodou was not well organized and that, consequently, there was an opportunity to assume control of all the separate cults and consolidate them into a single body. She accomplished this end by disposing of her rivals one by one, using more powerful magick or else less intangible means, such as threats, physical violence, or blackmail. In a few short years, Marie Laveau was indisputably the Queen of all Vodou queens. She took charge of the Congo Square rites and the lake ceremonies. She also had a strong talent for self-promotion and publicity, and she knew how to manipulate politicians, policemen, and public figures. She acquired a house on St. Ann Street and this cottage became the center of her activities. Indeed, Marie extended her influence by operating as a procurer; she built a house near Milneburg, which was known as Maison Blanche, and which she used as a meeting place for pre-arranged appointments between white men and mulatto or quadroon women. There was a softer side to Marie, too; in the early 1950s, she nursed the sick during a yellow fever epidemic and regularly visited prisoners in the local jails, offering them comfort and support. In 1869, the *New Orleans Times* reported the last Vodou ceremony that Marie presided over as Queen. In 1875, she entered her home at St. Ann Street and didn't leave it until her death six years later.

Marie Laveau's daughter, Marie II, took over rulership of the Vodou conclaves slightly before her mother's death. She was as beautiful as her mother, though more light-skinned, and could have passed as a younger Marie I's twin. Because of the strong resemblance between mother and daughter, they were often confused for each other. This greatly enhanced the reputation of the Laveau Vodou dynasty, lending an aura of timelessness and personal immortality to the image of the Queen. Marie II continued her mother's work, presiding over the public and private rites at St. Ann's, Congo Square, and the lake areas. New Orleans was becoming increasingly cosmopolitan, and the Creoles were intermarrying with the Anglo Saxons; Marie II obtained clients among all the different cultural and ethnic groups, and made the Vodou religion even more profitable by charging high prices for her magickal services. She also charged admission fees to the public ceremonies. She had a better business sense than her mother—she printed out cards with her name and address, and short descriptions of her services, careful to term herself a "healer" rather than a Vodou Queen, thus making herself and the religion more palatable to a diverse clientele. Indeed, a tribute to the effectiveness of Marie II's methods was the simple fact that Marie II became one of the major tourist attractions in her day; newcomers and visitors sought her services, much in the same way that they dined in the famous restaurants, or attended performances at the French Opera House. Marie II died sometime in the late 1890s (the exact date is not known) and after her death, Vodou leadership was shared among a number of priests.

In retrospect, the most important contribution that Marie II and her mother made to the Vodou religion was to re-establish in the New World the matriarchal ritual framework of the ancient African rites. Janet and Stewart Farrar, in their comprehensive work on the principles, rituals, and beliefs of modern witchcraft, *A Witches' Bible,* define the relationship between the Wiccan priestess and priest, and their remarks apply equally well to the relationship between the Vodou priestess (mam'bo) and the Vodou priest (houn'gan).

> The senior working partnership is, of course, that of the High Priestess and High Priest. She is *prima inter pares*, first among equals; the High Priest is her complementary equal (otherwise their "battery" would produce no power), but she is the leader of the coven and he the "Prince Consort."[168]

Indeed, Marie Laveau and her daughter epitomize this definition. The reputation of the Laveaus was so high that they were, in fact, ultimate High Priestesses or "queens of queens," as Tallant phrases it, presiding over the group as a whole while less important mam'bos and houn'gans conducted the actual rites.[169] Due to the work of these High Priestesses and other less well-known houn'gans and mam'bos, Vodou became a viable religion among both whites and blacks at the turn of the century, not only on the islands and in New Orleans, but throughout the South and in great urban cities such as New York,

Chicago, Miami, and San Francisco. In fact, Reginald Crosley, in *The Vodou Quantum Leap* (2000), argues that modern Vodou is as much a religion as any of the traditionally recognized faiths such as Christianity, Buddhism, or Islam. According to Crosley, Vodou has a community of priests and priestesses, a body of faithful worshippers, a well-developed liturgy and belief system, and a complex, sophisticated, and thoroughly modern view of the afterlife.[170]

THE THREE VODOU PANTHEONS

Compiling a complete list of the gods and goddesses of the Vodou pantheon would be a monumental if not impossible task, since new gods and goddesses are created on an ongoing basis out of the spirits of dead Vodou initiates and ancestors who have satisfied the complex criteria for divine status. There are three main pantheons of deities. The Rada, or "greater" pantheon, contains the major loa of the Dahomeyan, Yoruban, and Igbo cults. This pantheon is the most "prestigious," according to Crosley, for two reasons.[171] First, it contains the central loa of the principal West African tribes. Second, the fundamental principles and rituals of Vodou are derived from Rada doctrines. For example, the Vodou initiation rites, the kanzo, are derived from the Rada tradition. Similarly, the dessounin rites originated in the Rada tradition. The "lesser" pantheons, the Petro and Congo, represent the darker aspects of the principal deities of the Vodou religion; these pantheons introduce new, different deities who partake more of the dark, chaotic elements of the universe than the Rada deities. Crosley describes it thusly: "The Petro pantheon manifests the tumultuous, bellicose, forceful, and dangerous aspects of the deities. The Congo pantheon also represents the nefarious, destructive, and dark magick aspect of the forces."[172] The distinctions between the three pantheons are essentially arbitrary, since, as Milo

Rigaud observes, a loa belongs to whatever rite it is "served" in and most of the major deities appear in each of the three subdivisions, distinguished only by minor changes in nomenclature.[173]

The Rada pantheon, the most important of the Vodou pantheons, contains the Dahomeyan loa. These are the major loa of the Vodou religion. Among the Rada loa are the Vodou trinity, Mawu, Lissa, and Danbhalah, representing the lunar goddess, the solar god, and the fire-snake. However, in Haitian syncretism, this trinity is generally known under the names Erzulie, Legba, and Danbhalah Wedo. The first deity, Erzulie, is the Moon goddess and the chief goddess of the Vodou pantheon. Erzulie is the shadow-matter Aphrodite, as Crosley refers to her.[174] The Erzulie name appears in the Rada lists as Maitresse Erzulie, Grande Erzulie, Erzulie Freda, Erzulie Dos-bas, and Erzulie Severine Belle-Femme (Fair Lady); she appears in the Rada-Dahomey mysteries again as Erzulie Freda and Erzulie La Belle Venus; and she appears in the Rada-Nago-Congo-Dahomey mysteries as La Sirene and La Baleine. These are all the relatively innocuous, daytime Erzulies, visualized in anthropomorphic terms as a beautiful, light-skinned woman who rules over the realm of feminine beauty and coquettish affairs. Erzulie is also visualized in zoomorphic terms as a small, python-like serpent. In the Vodou tradition, Erzulie fulfills several important functions. She is the loa of eloquence, of the spoken word, a function that she shares with Legba. Erzulie also serves as the loa of all aspects of love, including jealousy. Rigaud, in fact, equates Erzulie with Venus—he describes her brandishing two serpents, like Mercury, though she does so for the purpose of sowing discord and jealousy rather than harmony.[175]

The second Rada deity, Legba, is a solar entity equivalent to Lissa, or Ogou, in the ancient African religions, and functions in a fashion similar to the demiurge Ra of the ancient Egyptians by bringing order out of chaos. Legba, interpreter of the Vodouns, is equal in importance to Erzulie in the Rada pantheon. According to Crosley, there are about sixteen different Legba personalities in that pantheon; these include Atibon Legba, Legba Avadra (the wanderer), Legba Mait Calfou (guardian of intersections), Legba Mait Bitation (master of plantations and farms), Vie Legba (old Legba), Legba-Si, and Legba-Pied-Casse (the broken-leg Legba).[176] Rigaud adds the following god-forms to Crosley's list: Boco Legba, Lihsan Gba Dya, and Legba Adingban. Traditionally, Legba is the deity of the crossroads, and functions as a conduit to alternate levels of existence. At the beginning of a standard Vodou ceremony, an invocation to Legba is usually performed to open a channel of communication between the two separate realities. This is why Legba represents the houn'gan himself in his relationship to the High Priestess, just as Lissa represented the ancient African worshipper in his relationship with the goddess Mawu. It is important to note, in this context, that Crowley's view of the connection between Hadit and the goddess Nuit, as expressed in *Liber Legis,* mirrors exactly the connection between Legba and Erzulie; the magickian, assuming the mantle of Hadit, establishes a magickal connection with the High Priestess, who assumes the mantle of Nuit—the congruence of this connection brings about the generation of magickal power (Danbhalah).

The third and final member of the Haitian trinity is the firesnake Danbhalah Wedo, a being that is thoroughly zoomorphic, metaphysically as well as symbolically, and thus closer to its original prototype in ancient Dahomeyan culture than the other two deities are to their respective prototypes. Danbhalah is viewed as a great snake, reared up on its lower coils as though it were in the process of striking out. This image is reflected in the snake vertebras in the rattles, or assons, which are used by the Haitian Vodou houn'gans and mam'bos. The snake image is also represented by the poteau-mitan, or center-post of the Vodou temple (oumphor), and in virtually all of the Danbhalah veves used in ritual workings. In the Rada pantheon, Danbhalah is more than just a god-form; he is a state of being, an experience, or "beatitude," as Rigaud refers to it. Indeed, Rigaud describes the experience represented by Danbhalah as three separate beatitudes.

> Danbhalah ... appears always to "swim" in grace and to de-
> light totally in metaphysical and hyperphysical pleasure while
> seeming at the same time to be lost in active and contemplative
> joy. This phenomenon is due to the three types of beatitudes
> recognizing in theology: the active, the contemplative, and the
> joyful ... Danbhalah expresses geometric perfection because
> in his quality as a mystere he corresponds to the gifts of the
> holy spirit through his beatitudes ... Danbhalah is therefore
> aptly named Dan-(Gift) Bhalah We-Do. Hence his geometric
> expression is total and perfect ... namely, the ultimate end of
> rational nature.[177]

Clearly, this description of the fire-snake accords remarkably well with the image of the fire-snake in ancient African religions as the source of magickal power, or magickal ecstasy; the image of the fire-snake "swimming" in grace and delight emerges from Rigaud's rather Christian interpretation of this experience. It is equally clear that this magickal experience is generated from the conjunction of the High Priest (Legba, or Lissa) and the High Priestess (Erzulie, or Mawu). As such, there are distinct parallels between the archetypal Danbhalah in ancient African metaphysics and the modern Haitian Vodou cults, and Kenneth Grant's view of the dragon and the Kund-alini of Tantric Buddhism. The Rada-Dahomey mysteries list sever-al Danbhalahs; these include Danbhalah Wedo, Danbhalah Ye-We, Aida Wedo, Danbhalah Grand Chemin (the Highway), Dahbhalah to Can, and Ayidohwedo. In the Rada systems, Danbhalah Wedo is visualized as a small, non-venomous boa constrictor and is conse-crated to the goddess Aidowedo. The veve of the fire-snake usually depicts a serpent rearing up to the heavens in profile, with three forks projecting from its mouth, and the lower tail coiled slightly around the body. The symbol of lightning is also a common feature of veves associated with Danbhalah.

The Petro pantheon introduces a darker element into the Vodou mysteries and has, consequently, played a significant part in the popular view of Vodou as black magick. The Petro pantheon includes the great Vodou trinity, but here they tend to be more like the popular conception of the Dionysian gods and goddesses. They are demonic, even violent deities. The Creole loa, in particular, illustrate the darkest strain of the Petro pantheon. These loa are indigenous to Haiti, as might be inferred from their name. They are "made" rather than "born," being the shadow-matter part of deceased houn'gans who have been elevated to the status of loa by Vodou rites. One of the most important Creole loa is Don Petro, from whose name the pantheon itself is derived, a powerful houn'gan who lived in colonial times in Santo Domingo. He was psychic and clairvoyant and created a special dance which, when performed during the Vodou rites, helped facilitate the "mounting" of the participants by the loa. Generally, Don Petro is visualized as a non-anthropomorphic axionic force, which is evoked in the Vodou sanctuary by the detonation of cannon powder.

Two demonic Vodoun who are derived from Don Petro are Ti Jean Petro, the son of Don Petro, and Petro Je Rouge (i.e. the red eyes Petro). Both of these loa are visualized as dark, amorphous beings with glowing red eyes. Ti Jean Pie-Cheche, another important Petro loa, appears as a deformed, devilish midget with one leg. One of the most fearsome of the Petro loa is Marinette Pie-Cheche, or simply Marinette. She is female, but is represented in the zoomorphic form of an owl. In fact, when Marinette possesses the participant in a Vodou rite, the participant will invariably mimic the behavior of the owl. Marinette wanders the forests at night in search of evil deeds. Consequently, she is worshipped by the Vodou practitioner who enjoys shape-changing (assuming the form of animals and then roaming the forest). The Loa Taureaux, like Marinette, also appear in zoomorphic forms. They take the shape of fierce, bellowing bulls. They are very dangerous, savage beings, and, not surprisingly, are extremely rough to the Vodou practitioners whom they mount. Last, but certainly not least, are the wandering Baku loa, the Bakulu Baka or mischievous spirits. These loa do not limit themselves to one specific zoomorphic form, as do Marinette and the Loa Taureaux. They can take the appearance of cats, dogs, pigs, and bulls. They can also assume the shape of strange monsters. They do not attack humans directly; instead, they usually attempt to inspire terror with their weird appearance.

The Congo pantheon is similar to the Petro in that it represents the darker aspects of the Vodou religion. This pantheon, like the others, includes entities who were originally human, but who became loa after death. The pantheon is divided into two separate sets of loa based on the physical habitats with which they are usually associated—the grasslands and the seashore. The seashore loa are seen as more benign or civilized than the grasslands loa. They are usually portrayed as light-skinned black men and women. The Congo-Savane loa, on the other hand, are the more Dionysian entities. They are grouped under the generic name of Zandor or Zando. The Vodou trinity is evident in the role of these loa, as I have shown, but they are all dark, evil entities. The principal loa of this group is Prince Zandor, or Ti-Jean-Zandor, who is depicted as a demon. He appears as a frightening little mannikin dressed in scarlet who hops around on one leg and climbs trees to seek out human victims. The most fearsome of the Congo loa are the Mondongue-Moussai. These are amorphous, vampire-like entities with a predilection for the blood of canines. They attack dogs by biting the tip of the ear and then sucking the blood, but are not averse to attacking humans when canine victims are not readily available. Other notable Congo entities are Miss Charlotte and Dinclinsin, both accomplished Vodouns of white French ancestry. Miss Charlotte is a demanding, vaguely anthropomorphic loa who speaks perfect French and demands rigid observance to details in her rituals. Dinclinsin, a male houn'gan, is less demanding, and is propitiated by offerings of alcohol. He is very hard to understand when he mounts a particular participant, since he speaks Creole in a thick foreign accent.

Lovecraft, in the major stories of the Cthulhu Mythos (with the exception of his last story, "The Haunter in the Dark"), does not deal with lesser, elemental beings or anthropomorphic deities. Thus, entities such as the Guedes or the frightening members of the Zandor clan do not figure prominently in his work. But Lovecraft contributes the serpent god Yig to the Cthulhu Mythos, and this entity is very similar to Danbhalah, the most important extraterrestrial entity in the Rada pantheon. In a letter to the author of the story, quoted previously, Lovecraft associates Yig with the snake gods of the Native American civilizations of South America—the deities Quetzalcoatl and Kukulcan. He doesn't explore the origins of the snake god any further, but he does seem to recognize that this particular archetype is one of the oldest of ancient civilizations—in "The Whisperer in Darkness," he mentions that Yig is a "father" of later serpent deities, and therefore a primal entity in his own right. In this instance, Lovecraft's instinct is perfectly sound, for the serpent has always been among the oldest religious icons of mankind, and has figured prominently in the earliest recorded magickal and religious practices in Africa, Egypt, and the Middle East. As indicated in chapter 1, the Dionysian or black magickal practices have their roots in ancient Africa and ancient Mesopotamia between 4000 and 1000 BC; from there, they spread into ancient Egypt and Greece. At the root of these early beliefs was the cult of the serpent, which is evident from the fact that the earliest of the ancestor-deity beings in ancient

Africa was Danbhalah. Milo Rigaud, in his analysis of Danbhalah, the serpent god, explains exactly how the ancient Vodouns regarded this primal deity.

> The snake vertebras that adorn the assons of houn'gans and mam'bos represent Danbhalah, while the cephalo-rachidian axis, as well as the fertilizing seed which makes Legba a phallic mystere, are represented by the center-post of the peristyle. Da, in magic, represents the oldest of the ancestors, a fact that gives him the right to have the "cosmic egg" as his ritual instrument.[178]

One interesting aspect of Rigaud's analysis here is that he associates Legba, the solar part of the Vodou "trinity," with the serpent archetype. Erzulie, also, can manifest as a small serpent or python. Thus, it can be argued that all the entities in the basic Vodou pantheon are serpent-entities, and that the three primal entities can be "collapsed" into the single image of Danbhalah. With Yig, Lovecraft acknowledges and pays homage to the importance of this image for the black magickal systems of antiquity and modern times.

THE PAN-PSYCHIC FIELD

The Vodou religion is centered on the theory that the universe is essentially composed of energy—a pan-psychic field—characterized by the principle of ubiquity where sentient beings can exist both in a localized state and in disaggregated, alternate realities. This is precisely the way that many of the more speculative of the quantum metaphysicians view the universe, only they use the terms "energy" or "quanta" rather than "Vodou." Crosley, referencing the Dahomeyan tradition, describes the parallels between quantum metaphysics and the Vodou universe.

According to a Dahomeyan philosopher questioned by Melville Herskovits (1933), Vodou is an immaterial force existing everywhere. For modern parlance, it is a ubiquitous force, existing everywhere in space-time. This force can be actualized as space-time events—persons, objects, and physical matter such as urns, rocks, trees, or rivers. This force is not the product of simple imagination, like the Western world would like us to believe, but is an essence of non-ordinary realities or alternate realities, manifestation of invisible matter, and/or quantum dimension of reality that the African intelligence and sensitivity have learned to harness and control.[179]

The houn'gan, or Vodou priest, whose name means literally "master of the Vodouns," initiates contact between the congregation of the oumphor and the loa. The loa, being existentially equivalent to the psychionic nature of the alternate realities, are contacted principally by the use of dream control, the crisis of possession, and the OBE. In achieving this contact, the houn'gans, mam'bos, and members of the Vodou congregation who are "mounted" by the loa partake temporarily of the peculiar existential reality of the alternate dimensions.

In the modern Vodou magickal system, human beings are viewed as tripartite. The first part of the individual is the actual, material body, known as the corp-cadavre; this part of the human being perishes after death and thus has little connection with the pan-psychic field. The second part of the individual is the spiritual part, or "soul," which is known as the Ti Bon Ange; this part likewise is not linked too closely with the pan-psychic field because it essentially transcends that field. However, the third part of the individual, the Gros Bon Ange, is intimately connected to the pan-psychic field. In fact, this invisible body is clearly equated with the shadow-matter substance postulated by Fritz Zwicky in 1930, and the descriptions of this body are fairly consistent throughout all the separate Vodou traditions in Africa and Haiti. The concept of the Gros Bon Ange probably stems from ancient Egypt, where there is a fourth component of human nature, the shadow of the being, which, unlike the khet (the physical, mortal body), does not decompose after death, but remains in a half-and-half state. This body exists in permanent high-energy state, or high vibratory state, which, except for duration, is equivalent to the state induced by trance in the houn'gan who is "possessed" by the loa. During the first stage of its existence, this being behaves like a spectator, remaining in the immediate vicinity of the family and following their actions. At this point, the Gros Bon Ange partakes of the fullest freedoms accorded by the quantum physicists. It has ubiquity, being everywhere and nowhere at the same time, like the particle that exhibits particle and wave characteristics. It can communicate with a living person via the pan-psychic field, provided that the living person is psychically predisposed.

The next stage of the Gros Bon Ange's existence only occurs if this entity exists for a long time. Over time, it exhibits the very darkest qualities of the chthonian, and, like demonic loa such as Marinette or Marinette Pie Cheche, it often transforms into a dangerous, wandering demon. As its power grows, it is increasingly likely to become a full-fledged loa and thus exist permanently in the alternate dimensions. There are, in fact, a series of rituals, the dessounin rituals, which are performed by Vodou houn'gans to elevate the Gros Bon Ange to the status of loa. Technically, this functions as a rite of exorcism, separating the aspect of the Gros Bon Ange that can function as a loa from the rest of the entity. The dessounin rituals are usually performed for families that can afford to pay for them, or for deceased persons who were particularly noteworthy in life. Invariably, the Gros Bon Ange of celebrated houn'gans or mam'bos are given dessounin rites.

The Vodou concept of the afterlife, as far as the individual is concerned, is clearly centered on the eventual disposition, or "fate," of the Gros Bon Ange. As explained previously, the Ti Bon Ange, or "soul," transcends the pan-psychic field; this being represents the ancestor or original loa of the individual, and as such, it is not really an individual at all. At best, it is the prototype or "predisposition" that ultimately becomes the individual. The Gros Bon Ange, however, is the individual in every sense of the word. In effect, it represents a duplicate of the individual, the corp-cadavre, but only in the shadow-matter dimensions. Crosley refers to this component of the tripartite human being as a "clone."

> [The Gros Bon Ange] should be seen as a duplicate of the person in shadow-matter. It reproduces all the functioning of the visible physical body with its trillions of cell connections and their physico-chemical and wave-function reactions, coordinated signal processing and mental switching networks, in the dimension of shadow-matter. It is a clone of the individual in invisible matter . . . It . . . coexists and participates intimately in the functioning of the physical body . . . when the physical, visible body dies or decomposes, we continue to be in existence in the parallel "clone."[180]

The Gros Bon Ange is not the mind or consciousness of the individual. It is similar to the concept of the soul in the major religions of the world, except that it is not necessarily immortal—it has a potential to be immortal, and that potential is realized after the dessounin rituals are successfully performed. The Gros Bon Ange becomes one of the loa, just as the original Vodouns in ancient Africa became loa. If the dessounin rites are not efficacious, then the Gros Bon Ange becomes more like a ghost or an elemental than a deity. In *The Vodou Quantum Leap*, Crosley describes the Vodou afterlife, illustrating the affinity between Vodou concepts and the theories of the quantum physicists:

> The Vodou choice of afterlife realm has no prospect beyond space-time. The Vodouists opt to remain in the continuance of

visible and invisible sides of space-time. When alive, they are locked into a symbiotic arrangement with the spirits and spend a great deal of time, effort, and money to nurture the disincarnate reality. When dead, a dynamic existence is obtained through the rituals or services of the living. They depend largely or uniquely on the living to obtain physical currency or amplitude of their wave function through modulation by rituals ... Salvation in Vodouism is attainment of loa status.[181]

Lovecraft's view of the cosmos, as we have seen in chapter 2, is remarkably akin to the cosmic view of the Vodou cults. He believes that the universe is composed of energy, and that sentient beings exist in both a localized state and in the form of a disaggregated, alternate energy-state. However, Lovecraft always stresses the "cosmic" aspect of this worldview at the expense of the human aspect, making it clear that there is no such thing as individual immortality or life after death. Indeed, Lovecraft tends to view humankind in a disparaging fashion, arguing that human life is rather inconsequential when compared with the cosmos.

If we can trace man's beginning and finish, we can say absolutely (a) that what corresponds to our universe is not humanely subjective in essence, (although our sensory picture of it is wholly so) and (b) that man and organic life, or at least man and organic life on this globe (or any like it, if we find the law of temporary worlds common to the visible universe), cannot be a central concern of infinity ... We find a cycle of constantly shifting energy, marked by the birth of nebulae from stars, the condensation of nebulae into stars, the loss of energy as radiant heat and the radioactive breakdown of matter into energy ... [but] all stars are temporary in the long run ... [and] if the cosmos be a momentary illusion, then mankind is a still briefer one.[182]

Given this view of humankind, it is not surprising that Lovecraft would not have agreed with the Vodou concept of the Ti Bon Ange, which returns to the creator after death; he would have argued that the material body, the corp-cadavre, is the only "real" body, and that it begins to dissolve immediately after death. It is likely that Lovecraft would have argued that the Gros Bon Ange, or "invisible" body, was also an illusory concept. However, the Gros Bon Ange, partaking as it does in the ubiquity of the quantum universe, is very similar in substance to the creature known as the "Haunter of the Dark," an entity that appears in Lovecraft's 1935 story of the same name. The Haunter of the Dark appears to inhabit the shadow-matter dimensions, or the "black gulfs of chaos," and partakes equally of matter and energy, for it can traverse space and time when summoned by a magickian who knows how to use the Shining Trapezohedron. Yet it is highly vulnerable to light.

THE VODOU RITUALS

There are two types of Vodou rites. At the basic level, there are the simple, solitary workings that the individual can perform for certain specific, practical ends. This type of black magick is invariably "low" magick, and the practitioner doesn't need any specialized knowledge of magickal practices in general—or even a modicum of magickal acumen—to successfully accomplish the task at hand. Instructions for the performance of minor Vodou rituals and spells can be obtained in a number of ways. First, they can be purchased, along with the necessary materials, at various occult and novelty shops that specialize in Vodou paraphernalia. These products are generally known as "gris-gris" (pronounced gre-gre) and include a variety of candles, powders, roots, oils, and, of course, the Vodou doll. The shops that sell gris-gris proliferate in areas where Vodou has a foothold, such as South Rampart Street in New Orleans. Second, and more commonly, instructions for performing gris-gris are provided by the houn'gans and mam'bos to practitioners who are able to afford their services. Finally, there are many books available in the marketplace, such as Denise Alvarado's *The Voodoo Doll Spellbook* (2014), that offer complete, step-by-step instructions for the enterprising Vodou practitioner.

The "higher" Vodou rituals are the group rituals, which are presided over by the houn'gans and mam'bos. These are the rituals commonly associated with the practice of Vodou, and they are the primary conduits through which the entities of the Vodou religion are contacted. As I have argued previously, the basic pattern of the ancient Dahomeyan, Nigerian, and Congo rites served as a paradigm for the pattern of black magickal rites in Egypt and Greece, and this pattern is more or less preserved in the modern Afro-Haitian Vodou religion. The houn'gans and mam'bos assuming the role of Legba and Erzulie "awaken" the deep, Dionysian energies of Danbhalah, the fire-snake, by the magickal use of possession, adorcism, or channeling. The rites reach a climax when the loa take possession of the bodies of the priests, priestesses, and participants, riding their human hosts like "divine horsemen," as one authority phrases it. The crisis of possession, central to the practice of Vodou magick, offers full contact between the human "host" and the loa, the extraterrestrial entities that inhabit the shadow-matter dimensions in the Vodou pantheon.

There are three stages in the crisis of possession. The first stage is the seizure itself, which can occur at any time in the Vodou ceremony. The nature of this seizure varies depending on the nature of the individual undergoing the seizure. If the individual is an experienced houn'gan or mam'bo, then there is little or no reaction to the seizure. However, if the individual is not experienced or has not received proper initiation into the Vodou mysteries, then the seizure can resemble an attack of hysteria as the individual's nervous system struggles against the invasion. The point of origin for the possession is generally either the top of the head or the bottom of the feet; once the possession begins to take hold, the individual's body will contort or jerk spasmodically, and the arms and legs will flail. These sensations are usually accompanied by shortness of breath and sweating.

The second stage in the crisis of possession is the Vodou mask, as J. C. Dorsainvil calls it in his *Vodou et Nevrose* (1931). This is a complete change of face, accompanied by voice alteration. Here, the possessed individual is starting to fall into the trance state. In the metaphysical terminology of the Vodou religion, the Gros Bon Ange is overshadowed by the presence of the extraterrestrial loa and relinquishes control of the individual. The face of the possessed individual takes on the characteristics of the invading loa. The voice, too, assumes the timbre, range, and intonation of the entity. At times this can be very frightening and dramatic. If the Vodoun is possessed by Danbhalah, for example, her face will assume the contours and expressions of a serpent and her voice will transform into a hissing sound. She may even climb a tree like a snake and go through the motions of moving from branch to branch like an actual serpent. If, however, the Vodoun is possessed by the coquettish Erzulie Freda, then her face is transfigured by the beauty of this divine entity. Her eyes become sly, deceitful, and flirtatious.

The third and final stage in the crisis of possession is the trance itself. Here, the possessed individual loses consciousness and the loa takes control of the individual's body and mind. At this point, the Vodoun has attained full contact with the extraterrestrial entity, becoming a physical incarnation of the loa. As such, he or she is able to make use of the powers of the loa. At the very least, these powers include the modulation of the human physiology to a higher degree than normal. Examples of this include phenomenal muscle strength, increased flexation, (i.e. turning the head 180 degrees, *Exorcist*-style), physical desensitivity, and even levitation. The entranced Vodoun might develop precognition, telepathy, telekinesis, psychic healing, the lifting of magickal curses or death currents, the ability to converse with the dead, the power of invisibility, or metamorphosis. In its highest manifestation, the trance state of the Vodoun allows him or her to move back and forth from ordinary reality to the alternate realities and interpenetrating dimensions that are superimposed on our own.

This stage of possession resembles the types of magickal possession described in Lovecraft's major works, particularly "The Case of Charles Dexter Ward," "The Thing on the Doorstep," and "The Shadow Out of Time." In the case of the former stories, the major characters, Charles Dexter Ward and Edward Pickman Derby, are temporarily possessed by the energies or life forces of black magickians who have managed to survive their own deaths and who presumably dwell in the shadow-matter dimensions. These black magickians, Joseph Curwen and Asenath/Ephraim Waite, are very similar to the Vodou houn'gans and mam'bos who end up becoming loa after death. In effect, they are unwilling to sever their connection with the corp-cadavre; consequently, they exist in a "betwixt & between" state that straddles both the visible and invisible worlds. In "The Shadow Out of Time," Nathaniel Wingate Peaslee's mind travels across time and space to earth's Triassic period, while one of the members of the Great Race inhabits his body and experiences life in the early twentieth century for six years. Technically, the members of the Great Race are not extraterrestrial entities in the same sense that the loa are extraterrestrial; the Great Race have no true physical forms but rather take up residence in whatever bodies are available. For instance, before their migration to earth, they took possession of the bodies of an amphibian-like race and inhabited the world of Yith. Then they suffered some sort of unknown doom and fled to earth, where they promptly took control of the bodies of the immense, cone-like creatures that Lovecraft describes so vividly in his story.

7

LOVECRAFT AND THE WICCAN RELIGION

The Wiccan religion, like the Vodou cults, has its roots in the ancient black magickal rites practiced in Africa, Egypt, Greece, and Rome. It is, thus, one of the oldest religions extant today, unlike the relatively late magickal systems represented in subsequent chapters of this book. Many scholars, historians, and students of the occult have speculated about the origins of the words "witch," "witchcraft," and "wiccan," and the consensus is that all of these words are based on the Old English masculine noun-substantive "wicca," which, as Montague Summers observes, offers a "comprehensive definition" of a Wiccan practitioner: "A man who practices witchcraft and magic; a magickian, sorcerer, wizard."[183] The fact that "wicca" is, in effect, a masculine word has bothered many modern practitioners, since the majority of contemporary Wiccan covens are based on a matriarchal structure. Thus, there has been a certain degree of quibbling over the etymology of the term. According to Janet and Stewart Farrar, who are key figures in the development of the contemporary Wiccan covens in London and Ireland, both wiccan (masculine) and wicce (feminine) are derived from the common word "wiccian," which can be translated roughly as "to bewitch," while the Old English word "wicca-craef" is the root of the word "witchcraft."[184] The Oxford English dictionary is unable to trace any further permutations of the word, but Philip Emmons Isaac Bonewits, in *Real Magic*, finds a common root for both the Old English and Middle English derivatives, which, he argues, is based on a Indo-European word.

> The meaning of the word "witch" has changed several times throughout European history and there are numerous partisans around today to claim that each and every one of these varying meanings was and is the One True Right and Only Definition. My current conclusion is that the word "witch" is utterly useless for communication without qualifying adjectives to indicate which of the different kinds of witches it is that one is talking about . . . we can begin, as usual, with some etymology. I seem to have been the first modern occultist to point out that the Old English words wicce (feminine) and wicca (masculine) and wiccan (plural), from which the Modern English word "witch" derives (via the Middle English wycche and witche) are based on the Old English root wic-. This in turn seems to be based on the Indo-European root weik, some of the meanings of which involve (a) magic and sorcery, in general and (b) bending, twisting, and turning. Which of these meanings is the true origin of wicce(a) remains to be settled, but it is fairly obvious that those practicing wiccian (or wigle) were considered to be magicians and/or benders of reality (or ones who could "turn aside" as in the Old Norse vikja).[185]

Wiccan groups are generally organized in the form of covens. The word "coven" is derived from the Latin verb "convenire," which is formed from the root words *con* (with) and *venire* (to come); it is translated as "to come together." Traditionally, a coven consists of thirteen practitioners. When membership exceeds this number, one of the Third or Second Degree High Priestesses will form a new coven, taking members who wish to go with her. The spinoff of a new coven is known as "hiving off." Regarding the sex of the practitioners, the ideal polarity of a given coven is an equal number of men and women, functioning in terms of working partnerships. When this arrangement is not possible, the coven still tries to maintain the man-woman dichotomy, since, as we shall see, sexual polarity is one of the central doctrines of Wiccan philosophy.

Lovecraft had a working knowledge of the early witch-cults in Western Europe as well as in the US. As discussed in chapter 2, Lovecraft had read two important texts that focus on the witch-cults in Europe and America. The first text was Cotton Mather's *Magnalia Christi Americana,* a book that Lovecraft had inherited from his New England ancestors; the other was Margaret Murray's *The Witch-Cult in Western Europe*, which Lovecraft recommended to his friend Clark Ashton Smith. Lovecraft's allusion to the organization of witchcraft covens, and the dates of major Sabbats and Esbat, indicates exactly how closely Lovecraft had studied these volumes. In his antiquarian pursuits, Lovecraft visited Salem, Massachusetts and Salem Village (now Danvers) and conducted his own research. He describes one such visit to his friend and *Weird Tales* colleague Frank Belknap Long in a letter dated May 1, 1923. In particular, he visited a farmhouse that had been built by Townsend Bishop in 1636 and inhabited in 1692 by Rebecca Nurse, who was executed for witchcraft during the Salem crisis. Lovecraft's description indicates not only his academic knowledge of early witchcraft in New England, but also his emotional attachment and fascination with this aspect of American history.

There is eldritch fascination—horrible bury'd evil—in these archaick farmhouses. After seeing them, and smelling the odour of centuries in their walls, one hesitates to read a certain passage in Cotton Mather's strange old Magnalia ... after dark . .. Thick dust cover'd everything, and unnatural shapes loom'd on everyhand as the evening twilight oozed through the little blear'd panes of the ancient windows. I saw something hanging from the wormy ridge-pole—something that sway'd as if in unison with the vesper breeze outside, though that breeze had no access to this funeral and forgotten place-shadows ... shadows ... shadows.[186]

Lovecraft's research on witchcraft was also supported by communication with actual witches. After "The Dunwich Horror" was published, Lovecraft received a letter from an elderly lady in Boston who claimed to be a direct descendent of another Salem witch, Mary Easty, and who possessed a wealth of information about early New England witchcraft handed down to her from her ancestors. Lovecraft mentions this lady in a letter to Clark Ashton Smith on March 22, 1929 and in another letter on April 14, 1929. From this source, Lovecraft learned about a contemporary group of Marblehead witches. In spite of his readings and research, however, Lovecraft makes it clear that he did not believe that witchcraft covens still existed in Europe or America after the early nineteenth century; this is particularly evident in Lovecraft's long discussion of New England witchcraft in a letter to Robert E. Howard dated October 4, 1930. Here, Lovecraft states bluntly: "the witch-cult itself is probably now extinct, but no one can say just when it perished."[187] Lovecraft died before Gerald Gardner published his first books on witchcraft and before the advent of the modern Wiccan covens, so Wicca did not have any impact on early Lovecraftian magick, per se. Yet, as with the Afro-Haitian Vodou cults, there are theoretical and metaphysical similarities between Lovecraft's views of the magickal universe and the contemporary Wiccan Theory of Levels (these will be explored shortly). Also, Lovecraft's conception of Shub-Niggurath, one of the principal entities of the Cthulhu Mythos (see chapter 5), bears a striking resemblance to the Great Horned God of the Witches, a similarity that will also be examined below.

THE RISE OF THE WICCAN RELIGION

The origins of the black magickal tradition and the subsequent manifestations of the Dionysian have been discussed in chapter 1. However, exactly when or where Wicca distinguished itself from other pagan practices is not clear. The image of the Horned God made its first recorded appearance in the Paleolithic and Neolithic periods, embodied especially in cave paintings in Ariage, France. Clearly, there was a nature-based form of worship that was no doubt derived from African and Egyptian prototypes, and these practices were widespread in Western Europe from 3000 to 2000 BC. Gerald Gardner, speculating on the development of early paganism, associates the early rites with the daily activities of prehistoric communities, particularly hunting and the procurement of basic necessities for survival.

> It became lucky to do certain rites to induce good hunting and gain power over the game . . . man wanted magical rites for hunting; the proper rites to procure increase in flocks, to assure good fishing, and to make women fruitful; then later, rites for good farming, etc.[188]

Over time, village priestesses and priests took charge of the rites, and the practices became standardized among the diverse communities. By the time the people of the early Bronze Age started migrating into Britain, the magickal rites had evolved from being a series of disparate practices into a workable religion, though there is no credible evidence indicating where or when this occurred. As Gardner describes it:

> By now, I think, this body of primitive belief and practice had become a real religion. Whether they had only two gods, the old hunting god and the new god of death and resurrection, one cannot say; but there is a natural tendency to amalgamate gods, to regard two different gods as being really different manifestations of the same deity, and it appears to me that at some time the Great Hunter, and the god of Death and What Lies Beyond became one and the same. Also, the Great Mother became amalgamated with the witch-wife who brought her slain husband to life again, the personification of feminine allure and excitement.[189]

Margaret Murray, agreeing with Gardner, also argues that the witch-cult, or as she refers to it, the "Dianic cult,"[190] was the religion of Western Europe in pre-Christian times.

> The evidence proves that ... [the Wiccan religion] can be traced to pre-Christian times and appears to be the ancient religion of Western Europe. The god, anthropomorphic or thenomorphic, was worshipped in well-defined rites; the organization was highly developed; and the ritual is analogous to many other ancient rituals ... it was a definite religion with beliefs, ritual, and organization as highly developed as that of any other cult in the world.[191]

Scholars have challenged the claims of Gardner and Murray, but there are two factors that lend credence to their conclusions. The early Bronze Age was the period in which many of the famous outdoor temples were constructed, including Stonehenge (built around 1800 BC), the Avebury temple, and the "Chalice Well" at Glastonbury. The fact that these temples were used for religious purposes is evident from the reverence shown to these sites by the Middle Bronze Age communities. In addition, these sites were erected in the vicinity of richly endowed barrow graves, funerary urns, and other accouterments of death, which indicates that the pagan rites conducted at the temples were religious in nature.

The presence of the Druids also attests to the widespread prevalence of the witch-cult in Western Europe. In the fifth century BC, the Druids were part of the Celtic invasion in Britain. Druidism was basically a white magickal system, centered on a paternalistic priesthood and derived from Persia and Sumeria. Despite this, Druidism exhibited features common to the pagan nature cults and the Wiccan religion in particular. Both the Druids and the witches believed in the efficacy of the magick circle as a method of harnessing the occult forces of the cosmos; both venerated the sacred places where the seasonal rites were conducted; both believed in a future life and in the doctrine of reincarnation; and both observed the same four grand rites celebrated throughout the year—the traditional Sabbats observed by present-day Wiccans. Indeed, a number of scholars have argued that Druidism and Wiccan were essentially one and the same—except Druidism represented the gradual usurpation of the Dionysian by the Apollonian, mirroring the same development in ancient Egyptian, Greek, and Roman religious practices. Thus, the eventual fruition of Druidism was a microcosmic example of what had been transpiring all along throughout the whole sphere of Western civilization, i.e. the routing and conquest of the Dionysian, and once the Druids had been exterminated by the Romans in Britain, the remnants of the cult merged seamlessly with the pagan nature cults. Gardner describes this situation in a memorable passage from *The Meaning of Witchcraft* (1988).

I think some priesthood of the Proto-Celts (call them "Proto-Druids" if you like) had by 1200 BC converted the nation to a type of sun worship, as the outer circle of Stonehenge circa

1200 BC is oriented to the sun, this possibly only meant that there was a male sect who mainly worshipped the sun-god and a female sect who worshipped the moon-goddess, both being really of the same religion, as we to-day have a monastery of monks who are dedicated, say, to St. Joseph, and a nunnery which venerates St. Anne, both being Christian . . . Robert Graves and others have postulated the evolution of a male priesthood which gradually usurped the privileges of the ancient matriarchy, and took over the exercise of its powers. May the Druids have been such a priesthood, which, when it was destroyed in Britain by the Romans, left the priestesses of the older ways, who had been pushed into the background for that very reason, in possession of the field? [192]

Christianity became the official religion of the Roman Empire by decree of the Emperor Constantine in 324 AD, and in 597 AD St. Augustine brought Christianity to Britain. Initially, the early Church councils were too occupied with the survival of the Church to devote effort toward the extirpation of Wicca and the lesser nature-based cults in Europe. There were laws against heresy and witchcraft, but the penalties were relatively mild. In 1144, Pope Lucius II was uncertain about what penalties should be imposed against heresy and related practices, but by 1184, the Vatican started to adopt a stronger stance toward the nature-based religions. During that year, Pope Lucius III created the first Episcopal Inquisition, which ordered bishops to make systematic inquiries (i.e. "inquisitio," from which is derived the term "inquisition") into any deviation from the official teachings of the Church. These inquiries, however, proved to be ineffectual, because they were essentially localized. Thus, Innocent III, in a bull dated March 25, 1199, appointed inquisitions directly from the Vatican, with the authority to exterminate heretics. This bull was strengthened in 1233 by Pope Gregory IX. At first, the investigations were directed primarily against overt heretics; practitioners of

Wicca and the older pagan cults were generally left alone, as long as they were not openly heretical. But when Pope John XXII was elected in 1316, he authorized the Inquisition to investigate magick and sorcery, if these practices were coupled with heresy. In 1451, Pope Nicholas V allowed the Inquisition to investigate sorcery even when heresy was not involved. The key church document that is generally regarded by scholars as the "cause" of the witchcraft persecutions in Europe was the papal bull of Innocent VIII, which was issued on December 5, 1484. Here, for the first time, the practice of witchcraft was singled out as equivalent in scope and severity to the practice of heresy, and the inquisitors were given free authority to hunt down and exterminate witches.

This bull differed from other bulls, too, in that it was prefixed to the new textbook written to assist the witch-hunters and thus exceeded the circulation of the previous papal bulls. This textbook was the infamous *Malleus Maleficarum*, or "Hammer of Witches," published in 1486 in Germany and written by Jakob Sprenger, dean of Cologne University, and Prior Heinrich Kramer. The issue at the heart of the witchcraft persecutions was the pact with the Devil, i.e. the belief on the part of the inquisitors, demonologists, Church officials, and the populace that witches had an agreement to work with and derive their powers from the Devil for the purpose of denying and opposing against the Christian Church. As noted elsewhere, the link between witchcraft and the Devil was essentially non-existent, except in the minds of those who chose to see a link. But this link was essential as justification for the inquisitional methodology, as stipulated in the *Malleus Maleficarum*, which detailed in clear, unambiguous terms the techniques necessary to initiate legal action against witches, secure a conviction, and pass sentence.

Gradually, Episcopal and secular courts took over the work of the Inquisition across Europe as the witchcraft hunt progressed through the fifteenth and early sixteenth centuries. The inquisitional method ensured that an accused witch would be convicted, since he or she was presumed guilty until proven innocent. The accused were not allowed counsel, and no witnesses were permitted to testify on their behalf. Torture was sanctioned as a legitimate means of extracting a confession, and, once convicted, the property of the witch was confiscated and the witch was either burned at the stake or else (as in Britain and America) hanged. Due to this foolproof methodology, the ranks of Wicca were largely decimated, although it is clear that many of those convicted were innocent—the persecutions were linked to monetary gain, and the secular and religious authorities often used the witch hunts as a way to enrich their coffers. In Germany, which Rossell Hope Robbins refers to as the "classic" land of witchcraft persecutions, at least 100,000 individuals were burned at the stake between the late sixteenth and early seventeenth centuries, a punishment that was the preferred method of execution in Germany.[193] Scotland, likewise, was noted for the barbarity of its witchcraft trials. The parliament of Mary, Queen of Scots, passed a law decreeing death for witches in 1563; in 1597, James VI of Scotland published at Edinburgh his famous treatise on demonology and witchcraft, thus effectively giving royal patronage to witch-hunters. Gerald Gardner, quoting from MacKay's *History of Extraordinary Popular Delusions*, estimates that 17,000 accused witches were executed in Scotland in roughly the same period that Germany executed 100,000.[194] These numbers are similar to quantity of executed witches in France during the same timeframe. Belief in witchcraft as a serious, heretical practice was not generally accepted in France until 1500, but after that period, the witchcraft persecutions began to grow and, from 1575 to 1625, they reached their peak; an estimated 2,000 to 3,000 convicted witches were burned at the stake.

In England, a witchcraft conviction carried a relatively light punishment before 1563, particularly if the accused was outside court circles, as Wiccan was generally recognized as the religion of the populace. Indeed, it took some time for witchcraft to be considered a heinous crime. In 1541, during the reign of Henry VIII, the Witch-craft Act was passed, but this was repealed in 1547 under Edward VI. The convicted witch usually spent some time in the pillory for the first offense, and death wasn't even considered suitable punish-ment until the third conviction. However, in 1604, the Witchcraft Act of James I was passed, yielding the same results as the passing of the witchcraft law in Scotland. In 1644, Matthew Hopkins, the celebrated witch-hunter, started his career. A failed attorney with only a passing acquaintance with the classic works on demonology, Hopkins made a profitable career hunting witches, claiming twenty shillings a head for every witch discovered, as well as expenses from the civil authorities who retained his services. Despite the severity of the witchcraft law and the efforts of Hopkins, however, the number of witches executed in England was considerably smaller than on the continent—only 1,000 or so individuals were executed.

The final flowering of the witchcraft persecutions occurred in the New World, in Salem Village, Massachusetts. The witchcraft mania lasted for only a short period of time, from February 1692 to the following September; yet, nearly 150 individuals were arrested, thirty-one of these were tried and convicted by the court of Oyer and Terminer (i.e. "hear and determine"), and nineteen were hanged. In his book *Wonders of the Invisible World*, which he wrote as a partial justification of the witchcraft trials, minister Cotton Mather por-trayed witchcraft as both heresy and a type of conspiracy against the Christian Church. (Mather's views mirrored those of the early Vatican theologians.) However, by the end of the seventeenth cen-tury, belief in witchcraft was starting to be questioned. On January 15, 1697 in Salem, the jurors who had brought guilty verdicts in the trials made apologies for their actions and there was general day of fasting in the colony to show repentance for the deaths. In 1711, the last trial for witchcraft took place in England; a woman named Jane

Wenham was found guilty of the offense by a jury, but the judge disbelieved the evidence and released her. In the reign of George II, the Witchcraft Act of 1735 was passed, which stated that there was no such thing as witchcraft and that no one should be prosecuted for it. Yet, the original Witchcraft Act of 1604 was not formally repealed until 1951. Thus, until that date, Wicca still functioned more or less underground; witchcraft rituals could not be advertised or practiced openly, and even books advocating the use of witchcraft could not be released in Britain or Canada.

The rise of modern witchcraft can be attributed to four pivotal practitioners. The first of these is Gerald Gardner, who was born in 1884 in Blundellsands, London. Dr. Leo Louis Martello, in his preface to Gardner's fifth book, *The Meaning of Witchcraft*, describes Gardner as the "Grand Old Man of Witchcraft."[195] This description is apt, since Gardner's view of Wicca and the rituals he practiced served as the basis for all of the later derivatives. Indeed, according to Francis King, Gardner's writings were directly responsible for the phenomenal growth of the Wiccan religion in the 1950s and 60s in Europe and America.[196]

Gerald Gardner was a relatively late bloomer, however, as far as his involvement in neopaganism is concerned. He spent most of his early life in Malaya and wrote his first book on the history and folklore of Malayan weapons. He retired in 1936 and settled in the New Forest area of Hampshire, where he came into contact with a Rosicrucian organization headed by a man known as "Brother Aurelius" and Mabel Besant-Scott, the daughter of Annie Besant, the famous Theosophist. This organization, the Fellowship of Crotona, had links to witchcraft covens and Gardner was initiated into one of the New Forest covens in 1939 by a priestess named Dorothy Clutterbuck, who was known as "Old Dorothy" (though she was about the same age as Gardner). Gardner found witchcraft stimulating, and he described many of his own experiences with the New Forest coven in his second book, *High Magic's Aid* (1949). This book was largely non-fictional, but Gardner presented it as a novel; he was forced to do this because the 1604 Witchcraft Act was still in effect in 1949.

In 1946, Gardner was introduced to Aleister Crowley, who had retired to Hastings. The two "magickal colleagues" had quite a few meetings and Crowley made Gardner a Seventh Degree initiate into the O.T.O., which allowed Gardner to operate his own O.T.O. lodge if he so desired (something which he never did, however). At this time, Gardner had grown tired of working in a subordinate role in the New Forest coven and was planning on establishing his own coven. He was in the process of writing his Book of Shadows, the personal book of spells and rituals that every practicing witch is obligated to write, and, impressed with Crowley's knowledge, Gardner asked Crowley to help him write the rituals for his projected coven. Crowley did so, and shortly after, Gardner started his coven in 1951. As one might expect from Crowley, these initial rites were sexual, but Gardner too tended to favor the sexual aspects of magickal workings. However, Gardner later revised his rituals between 1954 and 1957 with the help of one of his own initiates, Doreen Valiente, and much of the Crowleyan material was written out. The revised rituals formed the basis of what has become known as the Gardnerian tradition in contemporary witchcraft. In 1954, Gardner published *Witchcraft Today*, his first non-fiction book about Wicca. This book gained substantial media attention and was responsible for the formation of numerous Wiccan covens all over Europe. Gardner moved to Castletown on the Isle of Man, where an occultist named Cecil Williamson had established the Museum of Magic and Witchcraft. Gardner bought the museum from Williamson and added to it his own collection of ritual tools and devices. In 1963, Gardner met Raymond Buckland, an Englishman who had moved to America, and Buckland was initiated into the Wiccan religion. Buckland later introduced Gardnerian witchcraft to the United States. Gardner died in 1964, while returning to England after a visit to Lebanon. He bequeathed his museum to his High Priestess, Monique Wilson, who ran it for a few years with her husband, then sold it to the Ripley organization.

A number of contemporary witches have questioned the legitimacy of the Gardnerian tradition, arguing that Gardner was never initiated into the Third Degree (the highest of the three grades of the Craft, which entitled the initiate to found his or her own autonomous coven). Consequently, or so the argument goes, Gardner lacked the authority to found his own magickal system, since there is only record of Gardner's First Degree initiation at the hands of Dorothy Clutterbuck. Nevertheless, most prominent occultists and practitioners would agree with Martello that, initiation requirements notwithstanding, the modern Wiccan movement would not be what it is today without Gardner.

> Gardner was the apostle of modern Witchcraft, whether he was ever given a third degree initiation or not. And many who have claimed to be "Traditional" or "Hereditary," as opposed to "Gardnerian," give themselves away by both the rites and the "tools" used in their ceremonies, traceable to Gardner's influence . . . Without Gardner there are many today, regardless of what they call themselves, who simply wouldn't exist . . . not as Witches or Pagans.[197]

The second important pioneer of the modern Wiccan revival was Alex Sanders. Sanders was born in Manchester in 1916. His introduction into witchcraft was rather unique—one day when he was seven years old, he visited his grandmother Bibby and was surprised to find her in her kitchen naked, performing a Wiccan ritual. She swore him to secrecy and then initiated him into the craft. Before grandmother Bibby died in 1942, she initiated Sanders into the Third Degree, thus qualifying him to establish covens of his own.

In 1967, Sanders married Maxine Morris, a young woman who had visions of becoming a Wiccan High Priestess. The couple moved to Notting Hill Gate, where they established their first witchcraft coven. Sanders had a talent for self-promotion and a certain media savvy, and he established himself as the leading witch in Great Britain, at least as far as the public was concerned. As Drury observes, a disparate group of 1,623 practitioners of Wicca endorsed Sanders as the "king" of the witches.[198] Sanders made a number of appearances on television, late-night talk shows on the BBC, and recordings of his rituals; he even allowed a movie, *The Legend of the Witches*, to portray him and his activities. Though the couple separated in 1973, Morris basked in Sanders' limelight, and was known as the "queen" of the witches. Sanders' main contribution to Wicca was his popularizing of the craft. He was also a Third Degree initiate, which satisfied many purists who were troubled by the fact that Gardner had only been initiated to the First Degree. Sander's work wasn't original—his Book of Shadows was virtually equivalent to Gardner's, an observation made not only by King, but also by Janet and Stewart Farrar as well. Yet, Sanders' brand of witchcraft has had a lasting appeal to modern practitioners, and Wiccan tradition refers to covens based on that brand as "Alexandrian covens." Sanders retired from active participation in the Wiccan religion in his last years, moving to Bexhill in Sussex, where he died in 1988.

The last two of the most influential Wiccan practitioners in modern times are Janet and the late Stewart Farrar, both of whom were initiated into Alex Sanders' coven, making them technically of the Gardnerian/Alexandrian Wiccan tradition. Janet Farrar (née Owen) was born in 1950, the product of a strict Christian upbringing. But she moved away from Christianity in her adolescence and explored some other options, including a stint with transcendental meditation. After she visited Alex Sanders' coven in Notting Hill Gate and decided that Wicca was exactly what she was looking for, she was initiated into the coven in 1970. Her future husband, Stewart Farrar, joined that coven around the same time. Stewart was thirty-four years older than Janet, and had a wider experience of the world as well—he had studied journalism at the University College in London in the 1930s, served as an anti-aircraft gunnery instructor during World War II, and produced radio drama scripts for the BBC. Indeed, Stewart first learned of Sanders' coven through his work as a journalist and he had been invited to visit the coven for the purpose of writing an article about it. He became a convert instead. Despite the large age difference, Stewart and Janet were drawn to each other and they left Sanders' coven a few months after their initiations, determined to set up their own brand of witchcraft. Sanders wasn't too happy about this, and he demanded that they rejoin his coven, but they ignored his order. Stewart and Janet married five years after the formation of their first coven, undergoing a traditional Wiccan hand fasting. In 1976, they moved to Ireland and ran a coven in a farmhouse located around Drogheda, north of Dublin. Many covens and individual practitioners were spun off (or "hived") from their Irish coven.

The Farrars returned to England in 1988, and continued to increase the growth and influence of their coven. The couple has been criticized by many lesser practitioners because the Farrars do not feel that the rites and practices of Wicca should be cloaked in secrecy. Indeed, they have demonstrated a nearly Crowleyan compulsion to publish the secret practices of their craft. Their books include *What Witches Do* (1971); *Eight Sabbats for Witches* (1981), and, most recently, *A Witches' Bible.* In these volumes, the Farrars have revealed nearly all there is to know about the practices of a traditional Wiccan coven. The books provide instructions on preparing and using magickal tools, setting up circles, and performing the Sabbats and the initiation rites. Justifying their breach of traditional Wiccan oaths to secrecy, the Farrars argue that Wicca represents an important alternative to current forms of religion, and that this alternative should be available to all who desire it.

> We hope it is no longer necessary at this late stage to defend ourselves against the charge of betraying secrets . . . with the publication of Doreen Valiente's *Witchcraft for Tomorrow*, the Wiccan situation has changed. On the principle that "you have a right to be a pagan if you want to be," she has decided "to write a book which will put witchcraft within the reach of all" . . . For ourselves, we welcome it wholeheartedly . . . The need is genuine, wide-spread and growing; and to leave it unsatisfied for reasons of alleged "secrecy" is negative and unrealistic.[199]

THE GOD AND GODDESS OF WITCHCRAFT

As noted previously, Wicca is a nature-based religion. Modern witches, like their descendants, perceive themselves to be in tune with the earth, which Wicca personifies as Gaia, the earth-organism. A central aspect of the natural as well as the human worlds is sexual polarity—the interplay between the masculine and feminine principles. This interplay is so important to the Wiccan religion that it has been articulated in the form of a bona fide theory, which is known simply as the Theory of Polarity. Janet and Stewart Farrar describe this theory in *A Witches' Bible*.

> The Theory of Polarity maintains that all activity, all manifestation, arises from (and is inconceivable without) the interaction of pairs and complementary opposites—positive and negative, light and dark, content and form, male and female, and so on; and that this polarity is not a conflict between "good" and "evil," but a creative tension like that between the positive and negative terminals of an electric battery. Good and evil only arise with

the constructive or destructive application of that polarity's output (again, as with the uses to which a battery may be put).[200]

The Theory of Polarity is derived from the metaphysical nature of the cosmos, and can be seen as a reflection of the relationship between the two god-forms of Wicca. The lesser of these entities is the Horned God, which personifies the masculine principle, and which, as Murray has shown, is derived from the Paleothitic period in human history. The prototype of this image was undoubtedly the African god Lissa, consort of Mawu, the Moon Goddess. After the Paleolithic and Bronze Ages, the Horned God was fairly common throughout the Western world. In Greece and Rome, of course, there was Dionysus himself, and lesser horned deities such as Bacchus and Pan. The Horned God was central to the pagan nature cults that flourished in Britain just after the Norman Conquest in 1066, and one version of this god-form was adopted by the newly established Wiccan religion. This god was known by his Roman name, Cernunnos. According to Murray, Cernunnos was the "supreme deity" of Gaul.[201] The earliest record of the worship of Cernunnos in Britain is in 1303, when the Bishop of Coventry was accused by the Vatican of paying homage to a Horned God (which the Church, of course, referred to as the Devil in the form of a sheep).[202] In fact, the Church characteristically labeled the Horned God as the Devil, or Satan. The pagan populace, however, never thought of Cernunnos as the Devil, or indeed, as anything other than a god-form that was separate from Christian theology. The modern Wiccan religion focuses on the role of Cernunnos as consort to the Moon Goddess, and his role is basically that of a sacrificial victim. In so doing, the Horned God is divided into two separate archetypes to capture the natural fertility theme in all of its complexity. These archetypes are known as the Oak King and the Holly King. Janet and Stewart Farrar provide a succinct description of the two archetypes and how they function in the ritualistic schemata of Wicca.

[Two] concepts of the God-figure [are] involved . . . the God, in both concepts, dies and is reborn . . . the god of the Waxing Year (who appears time and again in mythology as the Oak King) and the God of the Waning Year (the Holly King). They are the light and the dark twins, each the other's "other self," eternal rivals eternally conquering and succeeding each other. They compete eternally for the favour of the Great Mother; and each, at the peak of his half yearly reign, is sacrificially mated with her, dies in her embrace and is resurrected to complete his reign . . . This theme in fact, overflows into the Lesser Sabbats of Yule and Midsummer. At Yule the Holly King ends his reign and falls to the Oak King; at Midsummer, the Oak King, in turn is ousted by the Holly King . . . The Horned god [thus] is a natural fertility figure; the roots of his symbolism go back to totemic and hunting epochs. He is the Oak King and Holly King, the complementary twins seen as one complete entity. We would suggest that Oak King and Holly King are a subtlety which developed in amplification of the Horned God concept.[203]

The goddess archetype is more important and more fundamental to Wicca than the Horned God. The goddess, like the god, is one goddess, but Wicca views her in terms of her two aspects. The first aspect is the Earth Goddess, a deity with which both the male and female members of the coven must seek attunement. According to Wiccan teachings, Wicca is centered around the development and subsequent use of the "gift of the goddess"—the psychic and intuitive faculties of the human mind—as opposed to the "gift of the god," the Apollonian faculties such as logical thinking, reasoning, and intellectual domination.[204] It is the right and duty of every Wiccan practitioner to cultivate a working relationship with the Goddess. In fact, Janet and Stewart Farrar describe this duty as the requirement of every incarnate individual, pagan or otherwise, at this stage of human evolution.

The Earth Goddess in Greek mythology was known as Gaia. Originally, in the Neolithic, Sumerian, and Minoan periods, Gaia was the supreme mother of all living things; this included the creation of the heavens, since the god Ouranos (Uranus), heaven, was described as being one of Gaia's children. In their book *The Myth of the Goddess*, Anne Baring and Jules Cashford describe a bust of Gaia that had been fashioned in the late third or early second century BC in Paleokastro, Crete.

> In the face [of Gaia], the distinction of character is subsumed in the idea of origin; in modern terminology, the very absence of particularity makes her seem the most "archetypal" of all the goddesses. The flat and heavy stillness of her face evokes the Indo-European name for the goddess earth, Plataea, "the Broad One," and, despite the slow curls of the hair, there is an androgynous feeling, drawing us back to the pre-Hellenic sensibility and also into the land of beginnings, which is, of course, nowhere.[205]

The second aspect of the goddess is the Moon Goddess, and it is this aspect that is addressed ritually by the Wiccan religion. There are separate archetypes associated with the Moon Goddess, or perhaps more appropriately, separate "phases." However, unlike the god archetype, there are three phases rather than two, and these phases correspond to the phases of the moon in her waxing, full, and waning phases. As such, the Moon Goddess is known as the Triple Goddess among Wiccans. Janet and Stewart Farrar describe the Triple Goddess archetype.

> The concept of the Triple Goddess is as old as time; it crops up again and again in widely differing mythologies, and its most striking visual symbol is the Moon in her waxing, full

and waning phases. The fact that the Moon-cycle is reflected in the menstrual cycle of women touches on deep and mysterious aspects of the feminine principle, and of the Goddess herself ... All Goddesses are one Goddess—but She shows herself in many aspects, all of which relate to the three fundamental aspects of the Maid (enchantment, inception, expansion), the Mother (ripeness, fulfillment, stability) and the Crone (wisdom, retrenchment, repose). Every woman, and every Goddess-form contains all three—both cyclically and simultaneously. No woman who fails to grasp it can understand herself; and without grasping it, no one can understand the Goddess.[206]

The Triple Goddess appears in divergent sets of mythologies; the Greek or Roman names are the most commonly used among Wiccan covens. The first persona of the Triple Goddess is Artemis, the Maiden Goddess. Sometimes called Diana, she is the Greek goddess of the wild, virgin nature. She usually appears as a huntress, carrying a golden bow and accompanied by various nymphs (the forest divinities that dwell in brooks and flowers) and forest animals, particularly deer, stags, and hares. The second persona of the Triple Goddess is Demeter, the Greek goddess of the harvest and the fertility of the earth. Demeter is a perfect archetypal representation of the Mother-aspect of the Triple Goddess; the name Demeter is derived from the Cretan word for barley grains, "dyai."[207] The final and, in my opinion, most significant aspect of the Triple Goddess is Hecate, the Crone. Hecate personified the Dark of the Moon, the period when Demeter was searching for her daughter. In *The Myth of the Goddess: Evolution of an Image*, Hecate is described as follows.

Hecate—"Queen of the Night," as the poet Sappho calls her—wears a bright headband and carries two torches in her hands as the brilliant eyes of the dark, an image, perhaps, of intuition that sees the shapes of things not yet visible ... Dogs were her companions, animals who follow a scent blindly, recalling the jackal Anubis of the Egyptian underworld, who could distinguish good from bad, and the three-headed dog Cerberus, who guarded the underworld of Greece. Hecate has three heads, like Cerberus, as well as six arms, and appears as a formidable figure, reminiscent of the Hindu goddess Kali.[208]

Modern Wiccan covens tend to view Hecate as a wisdom figure, i.e. the older female goddess who has lost her youth and maternal qualities, yet, in the natural course of life, gained knowledge and experience. This aspect of Hecate is signified by the torches in Hecate's hands—she is able to see in darkness, to look into the after-world and understand the secrets of life and death. But the terrifying aspect of Hecate is perhaps played down by Wiccans, who are, after all, an extremely positive, pragmatic group of people. Hecate's frightening aspect has seized the imagination of poets, scholars, mystics, and historians since the Christian period. The picture of Hecate as Kali, three-headed, six-armed, is indeed a menacing figure. Both Hecate and Kali illustrate the stark reality that the female aspect of fertility is basically a double-edged sword. The goddess is creator as well as destroyer. The destructive or "gorgoneion" quality intrinsic to Hecate is explored by Kenneth Grant in his *Typhonian Trilogies*, particularly in *Cults of the Shadow* (1976). Grant argues that Hecate is derived from Hekt, the frog-headed Egyptian lunar goddess, who represents the power of magickal transformation and enchantment: "Hecate, the witch or transformer from dark to light, as the tadpole of the waters to the frog of dry land, as the dark and baleful moon of witchcraft to the full bright orb of magickal radiance and enchantment."[209] The transformation that Grant speaks of is the passage from the Tree of Life to the Tree of Death; the frog represents the act of leaping from the light to the darkness that is true magickal illumination. Grant's interpretation, thus, aligns the Wiccan Triple Goddess with the Typhonian tradition as he perceives it.

Lovecraft, in his Cthulhu Mythos, makes it clear that genuine extraterrestrial entities must necessarily be non-anthropomorphic, since they originate in dimensions outside our own space-time continuum and thus bear no resemblance to human conceptions of "being-ness." The closest that Lovecraft comes to an anthropomorphic entity is shown by Wilbur Whateley in "The Dunwich Horror," who is mostly human in form, as opposed to his thoroughly non-anthropomorphic twin brother, who partakes more of the "outside" than Wilbur. Yet, both Wilbur and his brother have a human mother; therefore, they cannot be considered genuine extraterrestrial entities.

Among the genuine extraterrestrial entities, Shub-Niggurath is the closest in shape and form to an anthropomorphic entity. On one level, Shub-Niggurath is non-anthropomorphic; she is described only as a "cloud-like" being, the "hellish" wife of Yog-Sothoth (see chapter 5). However, on another level, Shub-Niggurath is a tangible, goat-like being. Lovecraft refers to this latter form of Shub-Niggurath in "The Whisperer in Darkness" as the Great Black Goat of the Woods with a Thousand Young. Though Lovecraft doesn't actually describe the physical manifestation of Shub-Niggurath in any of his tales, it is clear that Shub-Niggurath, a female, likely has breasts, and the head, or at least the lower extremities, of a goat—Derleth refers to her as the "horrible travesty on a god or goddess of fertility" in "The Lurker at the Threshold."[210] Lovecraft was familiar with the works of Eliphas Levi, as previously discussed in chapter 2, and it is likely that Lovecraft based his conception of Shub-Niggurath on Levi's "vision" of the Devil, the Baphomet of the Templars, as presented in the frontispiece of *The Ritual of Transcendental Magic*. Levi, in turn, based his drawing on the image of "The Devil, Atu XV" of the major arcana of the Rider-Waite edition of the Tarot. However, Levi "Christianizes" the image of the Devil somewhat, replacing the down-turning pentagram on the brow with an up-turning pentagram, and introducing some Qabalistic symbolism to the picture, including a caduceus rising from the loins of the animalistic figure. Nevertheless, Levi leaves no doubt in the minds of his readers that this somewhat frightening figure is, indeed, the Devil, and equivalent to the Horned Gods of antiquity, and to the god of the witches.

> Yes, we confront here that phantom of all terrors, the dragon of all theogonies, the Ahriman of the Persians, the Typhon of the Egyptians, the Python of the Greeks, the old serpent of the Hebrews, the fantastic monster, the nightmare . . . the gargoyle, the great beast of the Middle Ages, and—worse than all these—the Baphomet of the Templars, the bearded idol of the alchemist, the obscene deity of Mendes, the goat of the Sabbath. The frontispiece to this "Ritual" reproduces the exact figure of the terrible emperor of night, with all his attributes and all his characters.[211]

When the Lovecraftian/Levi vision of Shub-Niggurath/Baphomet is compared with the catalogue of horned entities that were briefly examined in the first part of this section, the similarities between Shub-Niggurath/Baphomet, on the one hand, and Pan, Dionysus, Cernunnos, the Oak King, and the Holly King, on the other hand, are undeniable. According to Simon and Kenneth Grant, Shub-Niggurath, in the form of the Sumerian Shub-Ishniggarab, actually predated the Greek, Roman, and medieval versions of the archetype; this is, arguably, a justification for Lovecraft's inclusion of this earthly entity into the pantheon of the Great Old Ones.

THE THEORY OF LEVELS

Although the Theory of Sexual Polarity is central to Wiccan magickal practices, the Theory of Levels represents the basic foundation of Wiccan metaphysics. According to Janet and Stewart Farrar, the

Theory of Levels formally acknowledges the existence and validity of alternate realities.

> The Theory of Levels maintains that reality exists and operates on many planes (physical, etheric, astral, and spiritual, to give a simplified but generally accepted list); that each of these levels has its own laws; and that these sets of laws, while special to their own levels, are compatible with each other, their mutual resonance governing the interaction between the levels.[212]

The levels in question are essentially five: the physical plane, the etheric plane, the astral plane, the mental plane, and the spiritual plane. The first plane, the physical, includes the material body, i.e. the "outer shell" of existence; this shell perishes at the moment of death. The second plane, the etheric (which, according to the Wiccans, is a subtle "energy-web of near matter"[213]), links the physical body to the third plane, the astral; the etheric plane, thus, is more of a conduit between two planes than a plane in itself. As for the astral plane, this is interpreted by the Wiccans in a largely psychological manner; the human personality contains instincts, passions, and abstract desires and emotions, and these can be used to create magickal entities and perform magickal workings. The mental plane contains the concrete mind as well as human individuality, which, according to Wiccans, is the basic unit of evolution and the component of the human being that eventually undergoes the process of reincarnation. The last of the five levels, the spiritual plane, refers to the concrete spirit—the spiritual body—and the pure, or abstract spirit. This aspect of the individual is wholly macrocosmic, the "divine spark" from unmanifested realms.

When the Wiccan Theory of Levels is compared to the tripartite levels of existence postulated by Vodou, the similarities are striking, lending credence to many Wiccans' belief that Wiccan philosophy is directly descended from the pagan, polytheistic black magickal systems of the ancient world. In the Vodou system, humans are seen as tripartite beings, composed of a material body (the corp-cadavre), an invisible body (the Gros Bon Ange) and the spiritual body (the Ti Bon Ange). Similarly, Wiccans acknowledge the existence of the physical body, the astral body, and the spiritual body. The Vodou loa inhabit the alternate realities of the spiritual and the invisible realms, while the Wiccan gods and goddesses inhabit the alternate realities of the spiritual and astral realms. Unlike Vodou, however, Wicca adopts the Eastern doctrine of reincarnation. According to Wiccan doctrine, all individuals, pagans as well as non-pagans, undergo reincarnation after death. The reason that individuals are reincarnated is the same reason articulated by Eastern philosophy: the individual must work out the karmic imbalance of successive lifetimes until he or she attains a permanent spiritual equilibrium, a balance in which one's evil deeds are atoned for and one's good deeds are rewarded. At the moment of physical death, the outer shell of the physical body is cast aside, since the etheric link between the subtler planes and the corporal plane is severed. The focus of the individual's consciousness is then centered on the astral body. The person is, in essence, experiencing a continuous OBE. At this point in the process of reincarnation, the disincarnate individual is equivalent to the Vodou concept of the Gros Bon Ange, functioning as a shadow-matter being. Whether or not the individual continues his or her withdrawal up to the higher planes depends on the life the person lived. If he has been particularly evil or gross, then he might decide to remain a shadow-matter being, "haunting" the place where he died. Eventually, if the individual doesn't pursue further development, he will dissipate into oblivion, as does the Gros Bon Ange. The higher order of individual, i.e. the well-integrated and advanced being, will usually continue past the astral plane into the spiritual planes. The individual may need to be reborn again; if so, then reincarnation will take place and the spiritual being will gather the raw materials of existence again, fashioning a new personality. If the individual has achieved perfection, then the spiritual body (comparable to the Vodou concept of the Ti Bon Ange and the Christian concept of the soul) will pass into the godhead, and subsequent series of incarnations will immediately cease. The spiritual being may also experience an intermediate stage between detachment from the physical and the astral and complete withdrawal into the godhead. This intermediate stage is known to Wiccans as the Summer Land. The Summer Land, as Gerald Gardner points out, was seen as a type of earthly paradise by ancient Wiccans.

> The witches' own traditions simply tell them that they existed from all time; but that they came to where they are now from the Summer Land in the distant past. When you ask them where the Summer Land is they do not know, but it seems to have been a place of warmth and happiness, the earthly Paradise of which all races of mankind have some tradition, and which so many adventurers have risked their lives seeking. [214]

H. P. Lovecraft, being a materialist, would not have sanctioned the belief in reincarnation. However, he would likely have been intrigued by the Summer Land, since this is, in effect, an alternate dimension, or more appropriately, a glorified shadow-matter realm, similar conceptually to the dimensions postulated by modern quantum physicists. Indeed, in his article "The Materialist Today" (1926), Lovecraft envisions just such a transitory place positioned between the cosmic processes of expansion and contraction characteristic of the universe as an infinite whole.

> It seems, in the light of recent discoveries, that all matter is in a state of balance betwixt formation and disintegration—evolution and de-volution—and that the infinite cosmos is like a vast patch of summer sky out of which little cirrus clouds gather here and there, presently to be dissolved into blankness again.[215]

Lovecraft would also have been in agreement with two further stipulations that the Wiccan religion makes about the afterlife. First, the Wiccan view of the afterlife is very positive; there is nothing inherently evil in any of the earthly paradises, or indeed, in the cosmic processes. Thus, evil is not really a force at all, but rather a misconception or misdirection of energy. Though Lovecraft didn't believe in the possibility of an afterlife, he did believe that there was no good or evil in any ultimate sense, and the phrase "misdirection of energy" would have been particularly appealing to him. The second difference about the Wiccan concept of alternate realities is that the afterlife is something that is actively experienced by everyone after death; many individuals go to the Summer Land; others reincarnate; and others simply dissolve into nothingness. There is a bracing, democratic flavor here that Lovecraft would have endorsed. In contrast, in Vodou, in LaVey's Church of Satan, and in Grant's Typhonian system, afterlife alternatives are available to only select individuals, the strong-willed or the accomplished magickal practitioners.

THE WICCAN RITES

Wiccan rites can, of course, be performed by the solitary magickal practitioner. However, the Wiccan religion, like most other religions, tends to foster group worship. There are two principal "officers" that rule the coven. The natural leader is the High Priestess. She functions as the earthly focus and, at times, incarnation of the Moon Goddess, just as the High Priestess of the Vodou circle serves as the physical embodiment of the goddess Mawu. The second officer is the High Priest, the earthly representative of the Horned God. He is chosen by the High Priestess, and is usually her husband or lover. Since the Horned God is subordinate to the Goddess in the Wiccan pantheon, the High Priest is secondary to the High Priestess; thus, the High

Priest must acknowledge the superiority of the High Priestess and support and complement her in all things. Among the variety of rites and ceremonies that are customarily performed by the average Wiccan coven, one particular rite, Drawing Down the Moon, represents the core magickal working of Wicca. In fact, this rite (or an abbreviated version of it) is usually performed at the start of each Sabbat. Basically, during the Drawing, the High Priest invokes the power and majesty of the Triple Goddess into the High Priestess, who thus incarnates the Goddess, symbolically or in actuality.

In addition to this central rite, most covens also perform eight other rites over the course of a year. These rites are known as the Sabbats. The four Greater Sabbats are Candlemas, Bealtaine, Lammas, and Samhain; the four Lesser Sabbats, or "Esbats," are centered on the equinoxes and solstices. All the Sabbats celebrate the natural fertility themes of the yearly cycle. At the pinnacle of the cycle is the Goddess. Her aspect changes based on the season and the particular magickal working—she is the Earth Mother in her fecundity phases and the Queen of Heaven in her lunar phases. But she is eternal and timeless, above the cycles of birth and death, and presiding over the earthly changes. The cycle itself involves the two forms of the Horned God Cernunnos, which were examined previously. These are the Oak King, god of the waxing year, and the Holly King, god of the waning year. The Sabbats celebrate the career of each of these gods, tracing the birth, sacrifice, mating, resurrection, death, and rebirth of the god-forms. The changes of the god-forms are, thus, "reflected" in the changes of the seasons.

The first series of Sabbats revolve around the rise and fall of the Oak King. The initial Sabbat is the Yule, or Winter Solstice Rite, performed on December 22. This Sabbat marks the death and rebirth of the sun god, as well as the vanquishing of the Holly King by the Oak King. The second Sabbat is the Candlemas Rite (also known as Imbolg), performed on February 2. Candlemas celebrates the first, faint stirrings of spring in the womb of the earth, with the Oak King on the ascendant. In the modern Wiccan rite, the High Priestess invokes the god Cernunnos (in the form of the Oak King) into the High Priest. This action represents the desire on the part of the coven to banish winter and welcome spring. The third Sabbat is the Spring Equinox Rite, performed on March 21. At this time, light and darkness are in balance, with light on the increase. Thus, the Oak King is still on the ascendant, moving vigorously toward his eventual consummation at midsummer. The modern Wiccan rite makes use of a wheel symbol in this rite, which signifies the balance of light and darkness. A Maypole is often erected in the center of the circle, with innumerable cords attached to it. The members of the coven each take one of the cords and perform the Wheel dance. The fourth and final Sabbat associated with the reign of the Oak King is the Bealtaine rite, performed on Walpurgis Night, April 30. Here, the Oak King achieves his apotheosis; he mates with the Supreme Goddess and ends up being reborn. In the modern Wiccan rite, a bonfire is enkindled in the center of the circle to represent fertility. The Oak King takes up a green scarf and pursues the High Priestess. When he captures her, he falls dead at her feet and the fire is extinguished. But then, the fire is rekindled and the Oak King rises again.

The second series of Sabbats revolve around the rise and fall of the Holly King. The fifth Sabbat is the Midsummer Rite, or Summer Solstice Rite, performed on June 22. The symbolism of this Sabbat is fairly straightforward. On the summer solstice, the sun is at peak brightness and potency, and the Midsummer Rite is mostly focused on commemorating this fact. The Oak King, previously reborn, now falls into darkness and dissolution, giving way to the Holly King, while the Goddess, unchanging, separate and aloof from the process of death and rebirth, presides over his death. The sixth Sabbat is the Lammas Rite, performed on July 31. This Sabbat is also known as Lughnasadh, which is Scottish Gaelic for "the commencement of

Lugh." The god Lugh was a Sun god, similar to Baal; the root of "Lugh" was possibly the Latin word "lux," which means light, and which is also the root of Lucifer, the light-bringer. The similarity of Lugh to Baal, the god associated with Bealtaine, is significant, since the Lammas Sabbat is the autumn parallel to the Bealtaine Rite. Again, one theme of Lammas is the sacrificial mating and resurrection of the Holly King, and the modern Wiccan rite emphasizes the fertility aspect of the Sabbat. The seventh Sabbat is the Autumn Equinox Rite, performed on September 21. The autumn equinox corresponds with the spring equinox, except that the theme of the former rite is rest after labor. The harvest has been gathered and the sun has become mellower; waning, to be sure, yet still a potent force in the cosmos. The modern Wiccan rite celebrating the autumn equinox focuses on three themes: the completion of the harvest; the salute to the still vital, yet waning powers of the sun; and the universal themes of rebirth and reincarnation. Here, the Holly King is still on the rise, but this is a descent as well, since the dark is gaining. The final Sabbat is the Samhain Rite, or All Hallows Eve Rite, performed on October 31. This is the most important Sabbat, and is based on the Celtic harvest festival practiced over two thousand years ago in England, Scotland, Wales, and Northern France. In Celtic tradition, the veil between the human realms and the spirit realms was very thin during Hallowmass; thus, bonfires were lit and sacrifices made to not only propitiate malefic sprits but also to achieve contact with the spirits of dead friends and family members. Similarly, certain types of magickal rites and practices were more likely to result in successful outcomes when performed on the night of Samhain, a fact that Lovecraft acknowledges in "The Dunwich Horror" when he describes Old Wizard Whateley and Wilbur Whateley performing their evocation rites to Yog-Sothoth on the top of Sentinel Hill on Halloween night.

8

LOVECRAFT AND THE TYPHONIAN O.T.O.

The Typhonian O.T.O., now known as simply the Typhonian Order, is a black magickal system first developed by the late Kenneth Grant, a British occultist and associate of Aleister Crowley. The order began as the New Isis Lodge, an unauthorized branch of the O.T.O. headquartered in London at the start of 1955, until Grant renamed it the Typhonian Ordo Templi Orientis in 1962. According to Grant, the Typhonian tradition represents Crowley's own conception of what an initiated magickal system should be. Thus, Grant argues, the traditional O.T.O. should, in effect, realign itself to conform to Crowley's original vision. In *Aleister Crowley and the Hidden God* (1992), Grant makes it clear that in his estimation, the traditional O.T.O. is basically an Apollonian or white magickal organization, in which the initiate is trained to "ascend" the Tree of Life, either metaphorically or mystically, in order to achieve higher levels of visionary attainment. However, this type of organization is no longer viable and needs to be replaced with a genuine O.T.O. structured as a series of black magickal "cells" in which initiates attempt to establish contact with the dark denizens, or Qliphoth, that lurk in the "tunnels" of Set behind the Tree of Life.

> Elaborate ceremonial and the establishment of fixed Lodges in specific localities [should] . . . be superseded by a fluid and far-flung web comprised of Thelemic power-zones. These power-zones would form a loosely knit network of occult groups using the Ophidian Current to prepare human consciousness for intercourse with the denizens of other dimensions.[216]

In this same book, Grant argues (without any real supportive evidence) that Crowley wanted to restructure the O.T.O. along these lines. In Grant's new O.T.O., the goddess who serves as the centerpiece of the magickal universe is Nuit/Isis (or Nu-Isis, or Maat). Nu-Isis represents the unknowable concepts of nothingness and the shadow-matter dimensions, concepts that the early Qabalists were unable or unwilling to address and thus dumped into a general category of the unanswerable, known only by the ambiguous phrase: "The Three Veils of Negative Existence." Nu-Isis is equivalent to the Whore of Babalon, i.e. Binah on the Tree of Life, the same goddess whom we have seen in the previous Dionysian systems, the goddess Mawu, or Odudua, of the ancient Vodou cults, the biune goddess Typhon, prototype of Nuit in ancient Egypt, and the androgynous Dionysus in the Greek mystery cults. The magickian, by the use of certain practices, projects himself, either in the Body of Light or via the avenue of dreams, into alternate dimensions; Grant refers to this experience metaphorically as projecting oneself through the sphere of Daath on the Tree of Life and into the Tunnels of Set on the other side of the Tree. The other side of the Tree, known as the Tree of Death, represents an antithetical Tree of Life, a reversal and intensification of the sephiroth. With regard to the actual methodology of accomplishing this projection, Grant, throughout his published works, seems inclined to cloak the actual magickal practices in mystical, alchemical, or metaphorical terms; yet it is clear from passages like the following that Grant is referring to sex magick practices. Indeed, in the following passage, Grant directly associates Daath on the Tree of Death not only with the Goddess, but also with the human female as priestess, and in so doing, refers specifically to all the possible sexual orifices of the priestess, i.e. the "hole," or anus; the "mouth," or mouth, and finally, the "holy," or vagina.

> The one in eight is Daath or Maat—the Mouth of the Abyss, the hole in space that opens on to the other side of the Tree. Thus, ideas such as The Fool, the vacuous, the mouth, the holy, are all embodied in the image of Maat ... It is because the human female is the natural repository, temple, shrine, or sanctuary, of the alchemical elements of transmutation, that the Cult of Vama (i.e. Woman) re-emerges in the present aeon of the Child as the Shadow of the Vulture, the bird of prey that is the special symbol of Maat (the Mother-Mouth) ... the dark radiation of the human female whose vaginal vibrations deposit the red earth of reification. She is the Black Goddess, Khem-Isisx, Nu-Isis, the womb and birth-place of all manifested life.[217]

H. P. Lovecraft, as we have seen, had no deep knowledge of either Eastern or Western magick, and, consequently, was unacquainted with the O.T.O. or with Kenneth Grant. Indeed, the New Isis Lodge commenced its operations nearly twenty years after Lovecraft's death, and Grant had not begun publishing his *Typhonian Trilogies,* as he called them, until the 1970s. However, Grant was very familiar with Lovecraft and the stories in the Cthulhu Mythos canon, and links most of Lovecraft's Great Old Ones with various Qliphothic entities on the Tree of Death. In this chapter, I will concentrate almost exclusively on comparing and contrasting Grant's philosophical and metaphysical views of the magickal universe with the Lovecraftian view of the cosmos. In formulating his theories, Grant uses the phraseology of occultism and mysticism, along with some of the terms of earlier, pre-twenty-first-century science, while Lovecraft, despite the fact that he died in 1937, uses more contemporary, modern terminology. Nevertheless, there are significant similarities in the cosmologies of both men.

KENNETH GRANT AND THE TYPHONIAN O.T.O.

Kenneth Grant's association with magick started out as a fascination with the life and works of Crowley, whom Grant first became aware of at the age of fourteen. By the time Grant was twenty, he began a correspondence with Crowley, who by that time was in his decline and living in Netherwood, Hastings. The two men met in December 1944, when Grant moved to Hastings to become Crowley's disciple. Under Crowley's tutelage, Grant studied Eastern meditation techniques, ceremonial magic, astrology, and sex magic, and ultimately, Crowley, as the O.H.O. or Outer Head of the O.T.O., granted him the IX° of the O.T.O. Grant left Crowley in 1945, a few years before Crowley's death. Shortly after Crowley passed away, Grant asked the new O.H.O. of the O.T.O., Karl Germer, for a charter to set up a British branch of the order. Grant was given permission to work the first three degrees of the O.T.O. in London, and for a number of years, he ran the O.T.O. along traditional lines. But the more he studied Crowley's works and comparative religion, anthropology, and metaphysics, the more he was convinced that Crowley's system was Dionysian from the start; indeed, he argued that Crowley's Class A writings demonstrate this clearly, but that Crowley was personally unwilling (or unable) to accept it.

The seeds of it [the Dionysian] existed in Crowley's inspired writings, but he personally seemed unable to conceive a system of initiation outside the framework postulated by freemasonry. This is why he perpetuated the old and rigid system described in *The Equinox*, vol. III, No. 1., which was upheld by his unquestioning disciple, Karl J. Germer.[218]

In 1955, without Germer's approval, Grant transformed his O.T.O. lodge, which he named the New Isis Lodge, into a black magickal rather than a white magickal order. There are two basic aspects of Grant's new system, one of which involved a change in the traditional degree structure, and another of which involved a re-interpretation (or "re-alignment," as Grant describes it) of the metaphysical, magickal, and philosophical basis of the O.T.O. system itself. In a manifesto he sent to Germer, Grant proclaimed that the new degrees offered by the New Isis Lodge were based on secret magickal formulae implicit in Crowley's *Book of the Law*, but he explained that, to preserve secrecy, it wasn't possible for him to send the texts of the actual rituals. In fact, Grant never published any new grade rituals, even though he had promised to do so in one of his later books, *Hecate's Fountain*. Nevertheless, Grant makes it clear that the traditional O.T.O. rituals and other "Old Aeon" structures were no longer efficacious either for initiatory purposes or for magickal and mystical attainment.

> It is inevitable that during the process of a current's evolution, certain aspects found to be obsolete, impractical, or erroneous, have to be rejected in favour of more efficient means. This applies with particular cogency in the sphere of magical initiation as evolved in Orders such as the O.T.O., about which it is here necessary to say a few words ... The Old Aeon systems of masonry were based upon the Square, and founded upon a concept of male supremacy symbolized by Osiris, Solomon, and other

patriarchal figures. The new O.T.O. is founded upon the Circle, the Goddess, the Mother whose child is her symbol. It is thus a seeming revival of an earlier (in fact the earliest) ethos, in that it involves the worship of the Primal Goddess who, knowing no god, was later cast out as "godless," and therefore—by a mode of the same curious logic—"devilish."[219]

From this passage, and from others of a similar nature that were likely included in Grant's manifesto, it is quite understandable why Karl Germer, upon receiving Grant's manifesto, promptly sent a registered letter to Grant expelling him from the O.T.O. and withdrawing his authority to operate a lodge. But Grant, undaunted, continued his work with the New Isis Lodge. In spite of his expulsion from the establishment O.T.O., Grant's Typhonian O.T.O. was generally accepted by occultists, at least non-Thelemic occultists, as a viable, though unorthodox, version of the O.T.O., and even today, a large percentage of practicing occultists see Grant as one of the most original interpreters of Crowley's magickal system. Although the contemporary position of the orthodox lodges of the O.T.O. in the US, as expressed by former O.H.O. Frater Superior Hymenaeus Beta X° in a disclaimer inside the Skoob edition of *Aleister Crowley and the Hidden God*, still holds that Grant's magickal system "bears little or no resemblance to the O.T.O. as designed by Frater Superior Baphomet XI° (Aleister Crowley) and his predecessors," Grant continued his work with the Typhonian tradition. Among other published works, Grant completed his *Typhonian Trilogies*, three series of three books each, all nine of which deal with the Dionysian, Typhonian magickal tradition and the continuity of this current from Africa, Egypt, the Far East, Sumeria, and Greece up to its modern manifestation in the work of Crowley and other lesser known occultists.

In 2009, Grant moved away from exclusive association with any O.T.O. lodge, black magickal or otherwise, including his own Typhonian O.T.O. Grant subsequently served as an advisor and titular head of a number of undisclosed organizations, most of which were concerned with furthering the development of the Typhonian tradition, until his death on January 15, 2011. Previously, Grant, along with his wife Steffi, deputized Michael Staley, an associate of the Typhonian O.T.O., to continue operating the order, now known as simply the Typhonian Order. Concerning this newest permutation of Grant's organization, Staley, in a March 2009 statement in the journal *Starfire*, formally declared that the Typhonian O.T.O. had ceased to operate and that its functions and objectives had been taken over by the new Typhonian Order. At the present time, there is a great deal of secrecy about this new organization, but occultists and insiders claim that it has shifted even more dramatically from the formal O.T.O. hierarchies into a looser structure, making it closer in alignment with Grant's vision of a series of black magickal "cells" focused on achieving contact with the dark, preter-human denizens lurking behind the space-time continuum.

THE QLIPHOTH

According to Grant, the primal goddess Nu-Isis presides over the Qliphoth, the adverse power-zones, or kalas, which inhabit the Tree of Death. The twenty-two Qliphothic kalas are drawn from part 2 of Grant's *Nightside of Eden* (1994), "The Tunnels of Set."[220] These entities are similar in nature to the principal loa of Vodou. Grant also equates the Qliphothic entities with the Great Old Ones of Lovecraft's Cthulhu Mythos, though they bear little resemblance to any entities in the Lovecraftian pantheon, with the possible exception of the Haunter of the Dark, an elemental bat-like creature with a tri-lobed eye that is depicted in Lovecraft's last story, "The Haunter of the Dark." The names and magickal sigils representing the Qliphothic entities appear in *Liber CCXXXI*, a short, somewhat obscure Class A document published by Crowley in *The Equinox*. The magickal "experiences" associated with each of the Qliphoth are generally referred to by Grant as the kalas, and here, Grant is revealing the sexual aspect of the magickian's attainment of these experiences, since the kala is the "juice" or "essence" of magickal experience, and is usually associated with the magickally charged sexual fluids derived from the vagina of the priestess after sex magick operations.

There are four components to each kala. First, there is the guardian demon. Second, there is the sigil of the demon. Third, there are the lesser Qliphoth of the kala, each of which are enumerated by Crowley in *777* (1973), "Column VIII." Finally, there are the animals or other atavistic associations to the kala. It must be emphasized that this does not refer to actual animals, but rather to symbolic states of being that the black magickian may experience when he or she accesses the kala. All of the kalas are thoroughly non-anthropomorphic, in contrast to the anthropomorphic nature of the entities on the front of the Tree of Life. The kalas can be grouped according to their location on the Tree of Death.

The first eight kalas are associated with the Supernal Triad. They are Kether, Chokmah, and Binah, and these kalas comprise the eleventh through eighteenth paths on the Tree of Death. The guardians of each of these kalas are Amprodias, Baratchial, Gargophias, Dagdagiel, Hemethterith, Uriens, Zamradiel, and Characith, respectively. These guardians reflect in reverse the nature of the highest triad on the Tree of Life, and they serve various symbolic purposes, representing not only the Qliphoth, but also the goddess Nu-Isis and those who serve her. Baratchial, for example, is the deity of the dimension of the black brothers, i.e. the sorcerers, witches, and wizards who willfully dwell in the shadow-matter realms for their own evil purposes. The sigil of Baratchial shows two swords flanking a ghostly mask, which is surmounted by a crescent moon. The guardian Dagdagiel, on the other hand, lies behind the descending kala of Gargophias and personifies the Black Goddess herself, Nu-Isis, Mawu, or Odudua. Her sigil shows the Hebrew letter Daath reversed in the shape of a gallows from which hangs an inverted triangle. Under the triangle is the word AVD, which signifies the female serpent Od. The seventh kala, assigned to the seventeenth path, Zamradiel, is of interest as well. Zamradiel, according to Grant, manifests the energies of Choronzon, the Guardian of the Abyss, which Crowley and his partner Victor Neuberg evoked in the deserts of Algeria in 1909. Choronzon signifies dispersion and chaos, and is therefore a perfect representation of the Abyss.

The next eight kalas are associated with the Second Triad. They are Chesed, Geburah, and Tiphareth, and these kalas comprise the nineteenth through twenty-sixth paths on the Tree of Death. The guardians of these kalas are Temphioth, Yamatu, Kurgasiax, Lafcursiax, Malkunofat, Niantiel, Saksaksalim, and A'ano'nin, respectively, and the priest and priestess use the forms of these guardians along with their sigils to explore each of the cells of the Tree of Death. These eight guardians, like the first series, symbolize both the supracosmic and the microcosmic elements of Typhonian magickal workings. Grant rightly associates the tunnel of Temphioth, for example, with Danbhalah, the serpent deity, and the sigil of Temphioth vividly illustrates this association—it shows a lion-headed serpent, with four spermatozoa issuing from the belly. The tenth kala, Yamatu, assigned to the twentieth path, is the demon of the Black Brothers. The sigil of Yamatu shows an inverted cross at the end of a meandering, chaotic line. One of the most important of the middle pillar guardians is Malkunofat, which Grant associates with Leviathan, who is one of the four crowned princes of hell in LaVey's pantheon. The sigil of Malkunofat is, in essence, a portrait of the demon. The face is a strange, gelatinous, Lovecraftian creature, with the letters NVH descending beside a downward-pointing arrow. NVH is the Ain, or Not (Nuit), suggesting a connection between Not and the image of

Leviathan; an intimate association between the goddess symbolism and the gods and goddesses of the watery Abyss.

The last six kalas are associated with the Third Triad. They are Netzach, Hod, Yesod, and Malkuth, the tenth sephiroth. These kalas comprise the twenty-seventh through thirty-second paths on the Tree of Death, and the guardians include Parfaxitas, Tzuflifu, Quliefi, Raflifu, Shalicu, and Thantifaxath, respectively. Of these guardians, the nineteenth kala, Qulielfi, a female demon, is the most interesting. Quliefi represents Hecate, Queen of the Night, and the Lady of Transformation and Bewitchment. The sigil of Qulielfi illustrates the lunar associations. It shows twenty-two inverted lunar crescents, the three central crescents surmounting an eye raying downward. The twenty-first kala, attributed to the thirty-first path, is also significant; this kala is under the guardianship of the shadow-matter entity known as Shalicu. According to Grant, this demon manifests as Choronzon and extends the influence of Daath to Malkuth. The sigil of Shalicu is a magick square reminiscent of the door of a tomb, whose letters NON PAT EBO announce the formula of death, judgment, and resurrection.

THE MAUVE ZONE

The twenty-two cells of the Qliphoth are equivalent in nature to the alternate dimensions and the sub-parallel worlds envisioned by the quantum physicists of the Copenhagen School. Grant's treatment of his Dionysian system, as expressed in the *Trilogies*, makes use of the phraseology of earlier scientific theories, particularly the idea of anti-matter, or anti-existence, and the ancient Qabalistic theories about negative existence. In Grant's view, the Tree of Death is a metaphorical glyph for the chaotic, dark Dionysian forces on the "other side," i.e. in the dimensions outside our own space-time continuum.

[The Ain] . . . is symbolic of true being (i.e. non-being), as distinct from apparent or phenomenal existence, which, as the word implies, exists outside. That which is noumenal (i.e. within) is prior to that which is without (i.e. phenomenal). There is no objective reality, but there is the manifestation of nonmanifestation; the shadow of being that is cast by non-being. This current, when applied to the physiology of incarnation, produces the typhonic teratomas which became the types of the Qliphoth as symbolic of the influences emanating from the "other world"; in the terminology of qabalistic metaphysics, the other side of the Tree . . . The blind forces of chaos in the infinities of space preceded the planets and stars . . . [these] forces of the "other side," being timeless, were therefore chaotic and existed only in the spaces that were considered dark, disruptive, lawless, Qliphotic; they were the inverse spaces of the sephiroth, or cosmic emanations inclusive of the planets as representing phenomenal law and order in the form of time cycles.[221]

As this description makes clear, the Qliphoth inhabit the alternate dimensions outside the space-time continuum of phenomenal existence. The magickian accesses the Tunnels of Set by the use of magickal practices. According to Grant, there are three states of human consciousness, and these states are analogous to the guises in which the Qliphoth appear to mankind. There is the waking state; the subconscious, or dream state; and transcendental consciousness, which, for the non-initiate, is the state of sleep. In the waking state, the Qliphoth manifest in amorphous, zoomorphic shapes. In the subconscious state, the Qliphoth communicate with mankind via dreams. Grant refers to these manifestations as the Deep Ones, the denizens of inner space, or the subconscious. The principal zootypes are viscous, slimy creatures like the cuttle fish, the octopus, and the frog. In *Outer Gateways*,[222] Grant argues that the subconscious state is the primary mode of access to the Qliphoth for the artist, the poet, and the writer, and that Lovecraft made extensive use of dreams to contact the entities that appear in the Cthulhu Mythos. In transcendental consciousness, the Qliphoth exist in their natural state, i.e. in the alternate dimensions referred to above. Grant refers to the entities in this guise as the Outer Ones, denizens of outer space. The primary zootypes are those provided for each of the twenty-two shells, as described in the preceding account of the Qliphoth.

Grant also uses the rather poetic term "mauve zone" to designate the alternate dimensions on the backside of the Tree of Life. In Grant's system, the Tree of Life exists within the framework of conceptual thought, while the Tree of Death, situated in the mauve zone, exists outside that framework and serves as an outer gateway, via Daath, to the Voidness beyond the Abyss. As such, the Mauve Zone has a specific and less specific dimension; specifically, this zone represents an actual state between dreaming and dreamless sleep, while less specifically, it is a metaphor for in-betweenness in general (and is often interpreted as such by Typhonian initiates). In any case, however, there is no afterlife possible for the magickian, at least in a phenomenal sense. Since the noumenal realm beyond the Abyss is essentially inaccessible to the magickian while in an incarnate state, the magickian does not achieve any type of personal immortality after death. He simply merges into the Ain, where there is nothing— no concepts, no states of being, and no entities.

The similarities between Grant's view of the Ain, or Voidness, and Lovecraft's view of the cosmos are striking. Lovecraft believed that the universe contains different types of energy. In his estimation, sentient beings, for the most part, exist in a localized state that is usually described as being "in" space and time. This would be equivalent to Grant's view of phenomenal existence; the human being, in normal, wakeful consciousness, and, in fact, in subjective and transcendental consciousness, is invariably localized, since this human being still inhabits a physical body, and this body is attached to an actual mind, whether or not that mind is actually connected to the "spirit" or "soul" of the being in any mystical experience. Likewise, Lovecraft held that the human being can exist in the form of a disaggregated, alternate energy-state; this would be equivalent to Grant's view of the non-manifest, or noumenal, which Grant, elsewhere in his work, refers to as the Universe B (as opposed to Universe A, the phenomenal universe).

In addition, Lovecraft, like Grant, makes it clear that there is no such thing as individual immortality; once the individual magickian "passes" on, he or she must merge into the Ain, or the Emptiness. Both Lovecraft and Grant, then, would have rejected the Vodou concept of the Ti Bon Ange, and both would have argued that the Gros Bon Ange, or "invisible" body, was also an illusory concept. Of course, if one reads Grant's work in a superficial fashion, then it might appear that he is arguing that the human being *can* exist in a transcendental state after death. But a closer examination of Grant's philosophy demonstrates clearly that, in his view, no human being can survive the experience of crossing the Abyss, an experience which represents a passage from Universe A to Universe B. Thus, when Lovecraft makes the argument in his letters that the human being ceases to exist totally when "the chemical and physical process called life" is withdrawn, Grant would certainly concur.[223]

In spite of this concurrence, however, and in spite of Grant's constant allusion to entities and elements drawn from the Lovecraftian/Derlethian Mythos throughout the nine books of his *Typhonian Trilogies*, Grant's system doesn't really reflect either Lovecraft's grand conception of the cosmos or his profound insights into mankind's position in this cosmos, both of which are clearly at odds with the curious human-centric position articulated by Grant in his magickal practices and his works. Although Grant is fond of using the word "cosmic"—and variations thereof—in his writings, his focus is always on the human being, which he sees as the center of the cosmos and the central element in the universe. This view is exactly the same as the Crowleyan view of the cosmos, and it illustrates how closely aligned Grant really was to his mentor and to Crowley's Thelemic O.T.O., despite the restructuring of the New Isis Lodge described previously. According to Gnostic tradition, which Crowley himself adhered to, each of the cosmic aeons, corresponding to the twelve signs of the Zodiac, comprised about 2,150 years.[224] Thus, Crowley, receiving *Liber Legis* in 1904, instituted the new Aeon of Horus to replace the Aeon of Christianity. Magickally, then, the supposed next aeon, the Aeon of Maat, will follow after a period of roughly the same time span. But Grant and many of the former disciples of Crowley, following their mentor's egocentric, human-oriented concept of the cosmos, have been inclined to redefine and diminish the cosmic element of aeons and limit them to a period of human lifespans (specifically, their own lifespans), and then declare themselves prophets of the same caliber as Crowley. Charles Stansfield Jones, Crowley's "magickal son," proclaimed a new aeon, the Aeon of Maat, in 1948, only three years after Crowley's death. Following this, Grant forged a link with Aossic, an anthropomorphic entity equivalent in influence to Crowley's extraterrestrial Secret Chiefs, Aiwass and Lam. Then, in 1955, only ten years after Crowley's death, Grant channeled yet another aeon, the Aeon of Zain—the so-called "Aeon without a Word," as he refers to it in *The Ninth Arch* (2002).[225] This new aeon, curiously, is associated with the coleopterous race of futuristic beetle-creatures envisioned by Lovecraft in "The Shadow Out of Time" as the species that will supplant humanity in the future of the earth.

Grant further muddies the waters in the last three books of the *Trilogies* by associating Aiwass, Lam, and Aossic with the UFO craze that briefly seized the imagination of the general populace of the US from the late 1950s to the early 1980s. That fascination has now, in the twenty-first century, diminished in intensity and influence, having been effectively debunked by scholars, scientists, and experts as largely the product of a series of spectacular hoaxes operating in conjunction with a kind of mass "wish fulfillment" on the part of individuals who were seeking something, anything, to believe in the wake of the technological advances and overriding impersonality characteristic of our contemporary world.[226] Ignoring the fact that Lovecraft's vision of the Great Old Ones is magnificently free from the taint of the human-centric, Grant's conception of the Great Old Ones seems to reflect the distorted, angst-colored visions of the UFO contactees, as can be clearly seen when we examine the actual "portraits" of Grant's latter-day Secret Chiefs (the portraits of Lam, for example, scattered through the *Trilogies*, and a drawing of Aossic-Aiwass by Grant that appears in *Beyond the Mauve Zone*). In fact, Grant's images of the Great Old Ones closely resemble the traditional big-headed, tiny-bodied aliens envisioned by Hollywood producers and popular culture lovers during the early days of science fiction cinema and literature in the 1950s, the era of the so-called BEMs—bug-eyed monsters. These big-brained, bug-eyed, anthropomorphic images are clearly rooted in human concerns and motivations. In contrast, the Lovecraftian Great Old Ones, in their deepest nature, have very little, if any, connection with humanity. Lovecraft's extraterrestrial entities express much more correctly and competently the alignment between the contemporary scientific view of the cosmos and the current activities of black magickal practitioners.

The occultist Donald Tyson, who, in the opinion of many occult scholars, successfully recreates the atmosphere and the spirit of Lovecraft's best work in his own nonfictional and fictional works honoring Lovecraft, gives an account of the Fall of Barbelzoa, the daughter of Azathoth, in his *Grimoire of the Necronomicon*, which, in contrast to Grant's account of the same event, further underscores the human-centric basis of Grant's Typhonian system. Before beginning his account, Tyson is careful to observe that the Great Old Ones are not anthropomorphic, zoomorphic, or indeed, even material, in any way that human beings can comprehend; he does this so that his reader will not be deceived into thinking that he is trying to anthropomorphize the Great Old Ones as Grant invariably does. Following this, Tyson describes the creation myth. He pictures Azathoth as a shining king sitting on a white throne at the heart of creation, with his daughter, the goddess Barbelzoa, seated on a throne to his left. This Azathoth is not the blind, idiot god from the Mythos; he is more like the Christian God Jehovah, and he bears a scroll with the names of all the elect who will dwell in heaven, or the Summer Lands. Among the gods attendant on Azathoth is Nyarlathotep, who, also a shining being, is trusted by Azathoth, exactly as the archangel Satan was trusted by Jehovah. But Nyarlathotep has grown weary of the perfect realm in which he dwells and lusts after Barbelzoa. He casts a spell over Azathoth and then rapes Barbelzoa. This leads to the fall of the Goddess and the creation of the earth.

> While Azathoth slept and dreamed upon the white throne, Nyarlathotep descended from his place . . . He caught the sleeping Goddess up in his arms and raped her. This is not to be understood of the body, but in another manner of the spirit. When she awoke and saw what he had done, in shame she threw herself into the endless pit of stars and fell down and down for countless ages, wrapping her shining body ever tighter around herself as its outer shell turned to hard stone, and making salt seas upon its surface with her never-ending tears. When Azathoth cast off his unnatural sleep and saw that she had abandoned her place on the throne mount, he went mad with grief. He put out his own eyes with his fingernails . . . and the endless day around the throne transformed into endless night . . . Blind Azathoth squatted in his seat, neglected in his own filth and drool, [and] in disgust, Nyarlathotep assumed control over the blackened throne . . . The perfect summer land

of realized souls was transformed into a dark hell of torment and hunger.[227]

The importance of this description lies in the fact that the creation of the earth (which is actually the imprisoned, ravaged body of Barbelzoa) and the subsequent evolution of mankind is only an incidental by-product of cosmic activity among the Great Old Ones. Surely, this depiction is thoroughly in keeping with Lovecraft's pessimistic view of human life and of humanity's essentially minor role in the cosmos. However, the same claim cannot be made for Grant's own version of the creation myth. In *Beyond the Mauve Zone*, Grant, referring to an unnamed fragment of text held by an unidentified Tantric order operating in Assam in the present day, offers his readers a rather startling version of the same myth detailed by Tyson. According to Grant, an emissary of the Great Old Ones ends up living on earth and his presence leads to the diffusion of "alien propensities" among the primitive people of earth and the birth of magickal offspring by human women. Subsequently, this entity studies with a Tantric adept for many years in Assam and then withdraws back to outer space (or perhaps inner space; the document is not clear). After many years have passed, the entity returns, but then, inexplicably, becomes a reclusive scientist, who creates some sort of biomechanoid woman that further disseminates transmissions from the Great Old Ones.

> The entity . . . assumed the guise of an eccentric and reclusive
> scientist. In his laboratory an ever-burning flame flickered
> before an image of Nu-Isis, the only image of its kind on earth.
> It was wrought in substances condensed from vibrations em-
> anating from the transplutonic sphere. The image resembled a
> woman, suave, metallic, her body cast in vitrified ojas, with eyes
> lambent as the flame which flickered unceasingly within the
> cabinet that served as her shrine. At a well calculated time the

image stirred into life. It was fed with ojas discharged by the qliphotic creatures which were periodically sacrificed to it. The "scientist" cohabitated regularly with this alien embodiment of the Fire Snake after it had assumed the consistency of human flesh . . . Then a massive explosion destroyed the laboratory and the surrounding terrain was violently upheaved by the impact of a series of elemental disasters. Some time elapsed before it was realized by the Initiates of Nu-Isis that a daughter had sprung from this intercosmic union . . . [Her] name on earth is Lura and she is the Fire Snake in apparently human form, the vitalized image worshipped and nourished by the scientist in the secrecy of his laboratory.[228]

Grant asserts that this is not a magickal allegory, but rather an actual event that took place in the history of the earth—yet the account certainly reads like a standard creation myth. The "scientist" represents the Great Old Ones, Azathoth (Creator) and Nyarlathotep (Destroyer); the female biomechanoid is a glyph for Barbelzoa; the explosion serves as the cataclysmic event or "rape" that triggers the creation of the earth and the manifestation of Barbelzoa, as Lura, on the material planes. What is most revealing about this allegory, however, is that it is thoroughly human-centric. There are allusions to the cosmic power-zones and references to deep space and "stellar immensities," but the main focus is on the terrestrial, not the extraterrestrial. Indeed, the Great Old Ones that appear in the allegory are actual human beings, not extraterrestrial entities at all.

THE TYPHONIAN RITUALS

Grant's Typhonian O.T.O. was modeled on the Dionysian, or matriarchal, tradition of magick. The "Primal Goddess" is Nu-Isis, and is equivalent to Mawu, the goddess of the Draconian cults in ancient Africa, and Nuit or Typhon of the Star cults of ancient Egypt. The priestess in Grant's system holds the dominant position and is equivalent in scope and importance to the priestess, or mam'bo, in Vodou and the priestess in Wicca. Because of this shift in the sexual polarity between the priest and priestess, Grant recognized that the linear Tree of Life framework of the traditional O.T.O. would no longer suit the type of magick (and magickians) he hoped to train. The male magickian was not dominant; thus, all male magickians were on an equal footing as cogs in the workings of a gigantic matriarchal wheel. The three active degrees of Grant's O.T.O., the Eighth, Ninth and Eleventh Degrees, defined rather portentously in his analysis of the nineteenth Tunnel of Set in part 2 of the *Nightside of Eden,* instruct the magickal practitioner how to perform autosexual, or masturbatory, magickal workings, heterosexual magickal workings, and homosexual magickal workings. These techniques are derived from the East Indian Tantric texts, particularly the texts of the Sri Vidya sect, which Grant adapted freely for his own use in the Typhonian O.T.O. Instead of using the standard wand, cup, sword, and pentacle, the priest, working alone or with the priestess, engages in sexual activities that awaken the fire-snake, or kundalini, in the body of each participant; the fire-snake rises up the spines of both participants, charging the chakras and generating magickal power in the form of the kalas. Once magickal power is activated, the priest or priestess can actually enter the Qliphothic cells and achieve their magickal goals.

> In order to activate a particular cell, the magician is required to project his astral consciousness and to penetrate and permeate the cell with its subtle substance. To achieve this end, he assumes the form of the guardian whose sigil is inscribed in the appropriate colors, and whose name he vibrates, astrally, into the ear of the woman serving as the "door of power." The vibration should persist until the astral form of the woman assumes

that of the guardian. In other words, the magician—by a system of intense and super-sentient visualization—in penetrating the woman, enters in at the door of power ... and fully pervades the cell of subconsciousness typified by the sigil.[229]

In addition to these sex magick rites, Grant broadened the magickal curriculum of his dissident, "bend-sinister" order by staging elaborate group rituals at the New Isis Lodge, where the influence of Lovecraft played a key role, both in the selection of target entities and in the aesthetic design of the lodge itself. Grant, in his *Typhonian Trilogies*, doesn't provide the actual texts of any of the lodge rituals, arguing that these rites are too technical and repetitious to justify publication.[230] Nevertheless, Grant does offer enough description of the rites to show just how profound an influence Lovecraft had on the Lodge during the 1950s and 60s.

In *Hecate's Fountain*, for example, Grant describes the performance of a Nu-Isis group rite known as the Rite of the Ku. According to Grant, the Ku is a batrachian, ophidian entity that resembles a conglomeration of snake, centipede, and frog; of course, this is reminiscent of Lovecraft's half-human, fish-frog humanoids in "The Shadow Over Innsmouth." The priestess overseeing the rite is an Asiatic woman named Li, and the lodgeroom is draped in yellow silk, interlaced with mauve (to signify the Mauve Zone, no doubt). Li, robed in black, is sitting on a throne facing a large tank of water. She is in a state of semi-trance during the rite, reciting a singsong chant softly, assisted by acolytes. The Ku is successfully evoked, manifesting suddenly in the tank, and Li, disrobed now and swimming, is snatched by its slimy tentacles and brought to orgasm, while the acolytes appear to be possessed by the Deep Ones.

At the climax of the rite Li shed her robe and, like a white shadowy, incredibly reptilian, slithered over the rim of the tank. As her form clove the waters eight phallic feelers reached up and seized her. They engaged her in a multiple maithuna in which each tentacle participated in term. Li's hair, black as night, formed a slowly waving arabesque, each vivid tendril etched against the mauve-zone with Dalinian precision. The eightfold orgasm that finally convulsed her was registered by the votaries around the throne. Violent paroxysms displaced the black hoods, revealing bald shining heads and the protuberant eyes of the batrachian minions of Cthulhu.[231]

Elsewhere in *Hecate's Fountain*, Grant describes an invocation of Yog-Sothoth that was held during the summer solstice. The priestess was a woman named Yogadasi, a dancer who often incorporated dance moves into her rituals. She dances on the artificial turf covering the well-top while the acolytes recite the invocation. Eventually, Yogadasi is caught up by a dark form and swung down unconscious to the lid of the well, while alien entities in the well manifest again and coil their tentacles around one of the acolytes.

Some say that at this moment, precisely, a meteor flamed across the night sky. Others who were watching spellbound, declared that saurian forms oozed from the depths, and that slime-dripping tentacles coiled around Bemmel, who had indeed risen. He was offering upon the lid the living form of the priestess of Yog-Sothoth, as the head of John the Baptist may have been proffered to Salome. This remarkable feat of physical strength was achieved in a split second. Yogadasi awoke, leapt from the upraised disc—which plunged with a splash into the well—and with an agile bound embraced the shadow as it melted into the dark water with a hollow-sounding sigh.[232]

Grant refers to the outcomes of both rites as "tangential tantrums" and I have to agree— in fact, neither rite appears to yield much in terms of genuine power or knowledge. But the results are certainly Lovecraftian, at least in a superficial sense.

9

LOVECRAFT AND THE
CHURCH OF SATAN

When Anton LaVey founded the Church of Satan in the late 1960s in San Francisco, he did the same thing for Satanism that Gerald Gardner had done for witchcraft just over a decade earlier; LaVey essentially transformed a rather narrow, reactive, and loosely organized series of disparate cults into a viable black magickal system. LaVey, with the assistance of Michael Aquino, who was one of LaVey's highest ranked priests, constructed a series of ceremonies and rites which, if performed conscientiously by the black magickian, were instrumental in establishing a link between the black magickian and extraterrestrial forces. LaVey also set up five initiation degrees, which served the same purpose as the degree structures in other black magickal systems. Even more importantly, LaVey, through his published writings and various interviews and articles, formulated a philosophical and metaphysical framework for the practice of Satanic magick. Although there are many critics of the Church of Satan, particularly among the black magickal community, who dismiss LaVey as a mere showman and the Church of Satan as nothing more than a social club for individuals who are not interested in the practice of "real" magick, it must be remembered that the Church of Satan has managed to survive into the twenty-first century, and, moreover, continues to disseminate the tenets of its remarkable founder, unlike many of the other so-called "serious" black magickal organizations that are now defunct.

Lovecraft had a working knowledge of the early witch-cults, as I have shown in chapter 2, and he studied accounts of the medieval Witches' Sabbat in Murray's book on the early witch-cults and in the works of Cotton Mather. Lovecraft had undoubtedly read accounts of the activities of early Satanist groups such as the Knights Templar and the Hellfire clubs. Yet, there is no indication that Lovecraft understood the distinction between Satanism and traditional witchcraft, or that he even felt that there was such a distinction. Indeed, in early tales such as "The Horror at Red Hook," Lovecraft seems sympathetic to the view that the practice of Satanism and witchcraft are, in effect, synonymous. Of course, this has been the official view of the Catholic Church since 1484, when Pope Innocent VIII declared formally in a papal bull that the witch-cults were worshipping Satan, and that this amounted to heresy against the Church and society. This view was shared by the older sources that Lovecraft was familiar with.[233] But Lovecraft moved very quickly away from such concerns in his fictional works, and, in the Mythos stories, he developed a black magickal system that transcends Judeo-Christian concepts like God and Satan.

Nevertheless, Lovecraft's system does share some affinities with LaVey's Church of Satan, principally, in terms of LaVey's concept of the universe. Indeed, LaVey's Law of the Trapezoid, and his concept of the Powers of Darkness, are similar to Lovecraft's quantum view of the universe. The two men, however, held different views about the afterlife, and Lovecraft would have been shocked and appalled by

LaVey's rather frank and earthly opinions about human nature and behavior. LaVey, like Grant, utilized Lovecraft's Great Old Ones in magickal rites of his own composition. But LaVey is mistaken in asserting, in *The Satanic Rituals,* that "Lovecraft was an advocate of Satanic amorality."[234] A careful study of Lovecraft's tales, letters, and articles reveals that Lovecraft himself had strict opinions about morality, and he felt that the individual should always maintain a level of decorum and taste in all personal dealings that reflected, more or less, the conventional standards of behavior stipulated by society at large.

THE RISE OF SATANISM IN THE WESTERN WORLD

Satanism, unlike Vodou and Wicca, is not a natural outgrowth of the ancient Dionysian black magickal systems. In fact, at its inception, Satanism existed primarily as a small subset of the larger, loosely organized European celebration known as the Witches' Sabbat. Several factors led to the inclusion of the Satanic elements in medieval Sabbat rites, and these can rightly be perceived as the driving force behind the early beginnings of Satanism in Western culture. First, the populace of Europe had been accustomed to nature-based worship since the early Dionysian rites in ancient Greece, and the god that presided over the latter-day rites was invariably a Horned God. The Horned God, in turn, represented the natural attributes of the worshippers themselves, the basic (but not necessarily base) instincts of self-indulgence, pleasure, and pride; the Natural Man, writ on a cosmic scale. As the Christians demonized the pagan deities and started to associate the Horned God with Satan, the populace followed suit and associated Satan with the original, nature deity, and with the image of the Natural Man. Thus, the populace was predisposed to be comfortable with the Devil, since he was like them. Arthur Lyons, despite his generally negative view of Satanism in *The Second Coming: Satanism in America* (1970), describes this attitude correctly as follows:

> The people were told that the Devil was evil . . . The people nodded in agreement, for they knew that this was correct, but at a deeper level of consciousness something squirmed uncomfortably. It all struck a chord that was just a bit too familiar, for the Devil reminded them of somebody they knew very well—themselves . . . He painted a colorful picture, to be sure, much more attractive than the one of an overpowering, intolerant, faultless God whom none could ever hope to approach in perfection.[235]

A second reason why Satanic elements were an important part of medieval Dionysian rites stems from public perception of the nature and practices of the early Catholic priesthood. The principles of asceticism and denial were part of the teaching of St. Paul; they were fundamental to the establishment of monastic orders and the requirement of celibacy within the priesthood. The basic principles then filtered down to the people, who were taught by the Church to devalue the delights of material existence and focus instead on the afterlife. But the people could not ignore one undeniable fact: the clergy, monks, and spiritual leaders of Christianity did not themselves turn their backs on the material world, and the people were angered by this hypocrisy.

The widespread disaffection with Christian hypocrisy found expression in the devilish, rebellious elements of the Witches' Sabbat. After the Inquisition, which represented the most extreme manifestation of the Church's Apollonian zeal for crushing the remnants of the black magick cults, Satanism became more than simply a minor expression of disaffection. The ritualistic parodies that were part and parcel of the Sabbat were now formalized into Satanic rituals that were performed for their own sake, the most notorious of these being the Black Mass (I will be examining this rite in fuller detail later in this chapter). Concurrent with the development of a ritualistic infrastructure, the emerging Satanic congregations began to forsake the loose, informal structure of the covens.

As for the practitioners themselves, they were no longer drawn solely from the lower ranks of society. Among them were aristocrats, men of wealth and substance, and even individuals high in the Church. The Knights Templar, an essentially monastic order composed of laymen and mostly wealthy landowners, was established in the fourteenth century. This order frequently performed Satanic rites and presumably worshipped the Horned God Baphomet. In the fifteenth century, Gilles de Rais, Marshal of France and friend of Joan of Arc, operated a chapel where the Black Mass was performed; the chapel contained such lurid features as an inverted cross, black candles, and images of Satan. There was another case in France that attracted widespread interest in the seventeenth century. A priest, Abbe Guibourg; a woman named Catherine Deshays; and one of Louis XIV's mistresses, Marquise de Montespan, performed Black Masses for the purposes of maintaining their high positions in the court. The rituals were dedicated to the medieval demons, Astaroth and Asmodeus, and children were sacrificed, their blood used to consecrate a wafer that was to be used later as part of a potion secretly administered to the king. In the following century, a number of Satanic groups known as the Hellfire clubs were established in London and Ireland, the most famous being the West Wycombe lodge, under the leadership of Sir Francis Dashwood; these clubs were the inspiration for similar groups in the nineteenth and early twentieth centuries.

The subsequent consolidation of modern Satanism into a black magickal system is largely the work of Anton LaVey, who founded the Church of Satan on Walpurgis Night, April 30, 1966, in San Francisco. LaVey was as remarkable and colorful as any of the magickal practitioners described in this book. At the age of eighteen, he started his career in the carnival, where he served as the assistant to a sideshow magickian and also taught himself to play the organ. These early experiences not only gave him a firm grounding in life and human psychology at the rawest level, but also fostered a realization of the importance of showmanship in achieving worldly distinction. LaVey had been interested in magick, witchcraft, and occultism since childhood and his carnival experience, particularly the magick apprenticeship, allowed him to further develop his knowledge of these subjects. After LaVey married his first wife, Carole Lansing, he gave up his association with the carnival and became a photographer for the San Francisco Police Department. This job deepened his awareness of the grimy side of human nature and did as much as his carnival experience to lead him toward Satanism. After three years, he quit the police department and began playing the organ in nightclubs to earn a living while pursuing his studies in the occult. LaVey acquired a perfect house to reflect his interests: a large, Victorian mansion near the Golden Gate Bridge, which he promptly painted black. At this house, LaVey held weekly classes on ritual magick and lectured on a wide variety of subjects, including non-occult topics.

Initially, LaVey practiced ritual magick with a small coven of like-minded followers. This coven was informally known as the Order of the Trapezoid, and its members wore a special trapezoid symbol flanked by a bat-winged demon. This group of individuals ultimately became the first members of the Church of Satan. On Walpurgis Night, one of the most important festivals in the black magickal tradition, LaVey shaved his head, put on a clerical collar, and announced the formation of the Church of Satan. LaVey's teachings and rituals are embodied in two books: *The Satanic Bible* (1969) and *The Satanic Rituals* (1972). In *The Satanic Bible*, LaVey elaborates on the purposes of the Church of Satan. He argues that modern Satanism, unlike the Satanism in the Middle Ages, represents a viable worldview— that it is not meant to function in an adversarial manner against the Christian worldview, and is certainly not an attempt to blaspheme Christianity. The worldview of Satanism is basically that man should live life based on his natural instincts and reject the dogmas of religions that do not address man's true instincts and personality. This means a full acceptance of the truths yielded by modern psychology and science. But man still needs dogma, ceremony, and ritual. Thus, Satanism offers this without denying the truths of modern science and psychology. As LaVey phrases it:

> Satanism, realizing the current needs of man, fills the large gray void between religion and psychiatry. The Satanic philosophy combines the fundamentals of psychology and good, honest emotionalizing, or dogma. It provides man with his much needed fantasy. There is nothing wrong with dogma, providing it is not based on ideas and actions which go completely against human nature.[236]

The seriousness of LaVey's intent was, for the most part, reflected in the theory and practice of Satanic magick that he presented in *The Satanic Bible* and *The Satanic Rituals*. LaVey knew that in order to spread his theories and to attract a congregation, he would have to generate a little shock and outrage on the part of the public. Consequently, the "carny" side of LaVey's personality took over as he quickly developed his own brand of sensational Satanism. Despite his previous stipulations against the blasphemous and retaliatory nature of the Black Mass, LaVey performed highly publicized Black Masses, consistent with the lurid literary portrayals of these rites, and these rites did offer blasphemies against Christianity and other establishment dogmas. Similarly, he performed internationally publicized Satanic weddings and funerals and also held topless Witches'

Reviews in nightclubs. At his ceremonies, LaVey wore black, Dracula-like garments with a long, red-lined cape and a black skull-cap, complete with devil's horns.

LaVey's personal life reflected this flashy demonic image as well. He kept a large lion as a personal pet and divorced his first wife to marry a beautiful, seventeen-year-old blonde named Diane, who replaced Carole as hostess at the big, black house. Ultimately LaVey's personal and public campaign worked, and membership in the Church of Satan grew steadily in the 1970s. The Church claimed that their rosters had swelled to well over 10,000 members worldwide by 1975, but more realistic calculations put the actual number in the hundreds rather than thousands. Nevertheless, there were dozens of Satanic grottos, or covens, around the country and LaVey spent most of his time traveling, giving television, radio, and newspaper interviews. He got major coverage in magazines such as *Cosmopolitan* and *Time,* and was even on the August 24, 1971 cover of *Look.*

As Satanism grew, LaVey instituted a series of degrees, moving the Church of Satan closer in structure to the great magickal orders of Western magick like the O.T.O. and the Golden Dawn. However, after 1972, LaVey began to grow tired of his public persona and all public ceremonies under his personal direction ceased. He cut back on the administrative demands on his time and started focusing on his own magickal projects. At the same time, he became more selective about granting interviews, and the Church of Satan was no longer open to anyone who happened to casually drop by. In early 1975, LaVey increased the annual fees levied for membership in the Church of Satan and, in the *Church of Satan Newsletter,* stated that higher degrees of initiation would only be available in exchange for cash or other assets such as real estate. This irritated some of the longstanding members, and many key members of the priesthood left the Church. In the years before his death, LaVey separated from Diane. He preferred practicing his magick with only a close circle of friends and acquaintances. At the end, he lived a private life, letting the various grottos of the Church of Satan take care of themselves. LaVey died on October 29, 1997. His most recent mistress and High Priestess, Blanche Barton, took over the leadership of the Church of Satan in Southern California. In 2001, Barton retired, appointing Peter H. Gilmore, a Magus and one of the nine members of the administrative body of the Church, as High Priest—his wife Peggy Nadramia was High Priestess. Subsequently, the administration of the Church was relocated to New York City, where Gilmore and his wife reside. Currently, the Church of Satan is thriving, despite Nevill Drury's claim that the Church is now "defunct."[237] The original "grotto" in San Francisco still has a solid, growing membership base, and there are grottos in most major cities in the United States, including Louisville, Santa Cruz, Los Angeles, Denver, Dayton, Detroit, and Washington.

THE FOUR CROWN PRINCES OF HELL

In *The Satanic Bible*, LaVey lists seventy-seven infernal names which, he argues, can be used effectively in the performance of Satanic rituals. The list is very broad and includes entities from a wide variety of different cultures, both ancient and modern. There are deities from ancient Egypt, specifically Bast, the cat-headed goddesses of evil sendings, and Amon, the ram-headed god of life. There are deities from Greece and Rome, including Pan, the Dionysian archetype, and Hecate, the goddess of witchcraft. There are the standard Hebrew devils, including Asmodeus, demon of sensuality, who manifests usually as a four-headed, winged creature, and Beelzebub, the Lord of the Flies. There are even deities from American Indian culture, Aztec, Mayan, and Incan civilizations, and from Asian demonologies. However, the principal entities of the Church of Satan are the four Judeo-Christian demons, which LaVey calls the Crown Princes of Hell. These are Satan, Lucifer, Belial, and Leviathan, and significantly, LaVey names each of the separate books of *The Satanic Bible* after one of these entities.

The first of the Crown Princes, Satan, is associated with the southern quarter, which is attributed to fire. In the New Testament, Satan is an actual personage—an adversary to God who is the supreme tempter. Christ is tempted to renounce God on the mountaintop and, in Matthew 4:10, Christ resists the temptation and states: "Get thee hence, Satan." Later, Christ uses the term "Satan" to rebuke St. Peter (Luke 4:8). From the earliest period of the Christian Church, Satan absorbed into himself all biblical references to enemies of God. Thus, he is logically associated with anger, one of the seven deadly sins. A number of prominent medieval writers and demonologists also associated Satan with the serpent in Genesis, and this association stuck. However, most authorities agree that Satan did not actually take the form of a serpent; rather, he operated through the agency of this creature. Demonologists in Jewish literature gave Satan a grand heavenly pedigree as a great angel, chief of the Seraphim and head of the angelic order of the Virtues, but in his fallen state, Satan is usually visualized in zoomorphic, Dionysian terms, his upper body human and his lower extremities goat-like.

The second of the Crown Princes, Lucifer, is associated with the eastern quarter, which is attributed to air. The name "Lucifer" is Latin for "light-bearer." Originally, the name was used as a reference to the planet Venus when it appears as the morning star. In the Old Testament, the Hebrew prophet Isaiah used this term in a satiric allusion to Nebuchadnezzar, the king of Babylon, likening the frustrated ambition of the king to the morning star trying to rise higher than all the other stars in the sky. The identification of Isaiah's Lucifer with Satan began with St. Jerome and the other early fathers of the Church who argued that in describing Satan as a bolt of lightning falling from the sky, Jesus was making a reference to Lucifer. Thus, in early Christian literature, Lucifer became a synonym for Satan. In fourth-century Europe, the demonologists interpreted Lucifer as a separate aspect of Satan—one of the most influential members of the first hierarchy of angels. According to demonologists, Lucifer led the revolt in heaven against the Apollonian God and was promptly cast out by God, along with the other rebels. Thus, Lucifer became Satan. Given the fact that Lucifer is a pre-fallen Satan and that Lucifer remained a separate entity after the fall, the image of Satan can be equated closely if not exactly with the image of Lucifer. Lucifer is zoomorphic, like Satan—a horned, winged Dionysian entity, half human, half goat. He holds a burning torch between his horns or in his hand, signifying the light-bearing aspect to the legend.

The third of the Crown Princes, Belial, is associated with the northern quarter, attributed to earth. Belial was one of the principal demons in biblical times. Apostle Paul himself, in 2 Corinthians 6:15, makes a reference to Belial, and it is clear from his language that Paul regards Belial as more or less equivalent to Satan. According to the *Lemegeton of Solomon*, a famous grimoire of the seventeenth and eighteenth centuries, Belial was created by God immediately after Lucifer was created, and demonologists speak of Belial as the prince of the third hierarchy of devils. Belial can be translated as "without a master," suggesting that he is likely self-sufficient, perhaps even arrogant. But opinions regarding the appearance of Belial are divided. By some accounts, he adopts a thoroughly anthropomorphic form, manifesting as a beautiful angel riding in a fiery chariot, much like the Greek Phoebus Apollo. However, in Jacobus de Teramo's woodcut "Das Buch Belial," Belial's real appearance reflects his Dionysian status: he is depicted as a thin, sinewy devil, complete with horns, tail, and hoofed feet.[238]

The last of the Crown Princes, Leviathan, is associated with the western quarter, attributed to water. This attribution is entirely appropriate, for Leviathan, in the Old Testament, is one of the names of the primeval dragon subdued by the Apollonian God at the outset of creation: "You crushed Leviathan's heads, gave him as food to the wild animals," as it is written in Psalms 74:14. There are similar passages in Isaiah, Job, and Amos that reinforce the draconian symbolism. In Hebrew, "Leviathan" can be translated as "that which gathers itself together in folds"—reinforcing the serpentine associations. In the Enoch parables, Leviathan is spoken of as a primitive, female sea-dragon. In biblical lore, Leviathan is identified with the whale, the hippopotamus, and the Behemoth, a water monster supposedly created by God on the fifth day of creation. The biblical writers also refer to Leviathan as Rahab, the angel of the primordial deep (Job 9:13; Psalms 89:10), and as the Abyss (Habakkuk 3:10). The references to the battle between God and Leviathan in the Bible serve as prototypes for the later contests between the Olympian sky-gods and the titans in Greek mythology, and for subsequent contests in myth and literature between the so-called forces of "good" and the forces of "evil" in Western history. In this myth system, Leviathan invariably appears as a great dragon and the creation of the world is usually represented as the victory of the creator-god over the dragon of chaos, signifying the triumph of the Apollonian over the Dionysian.

It is interesting and perhaps instructive to note that all four of the Crown Princes of Hell are, in a sense, Lovecraftian. LaVey's fascination with Lovecraft's work and philosophy has been mentioned in previous chapters, but here, in LaVey's choice of suitable candidates for the Crown Princes, that fascination is clearly evident. Satan, Lucifer, and Belial manifest as typical Dionysian Horned Gods, the upper body human, the lower extremities goat-like. They are all equivalent archetypes to Cernunnos, the Oak King and Holly King of the Wiccan covens, and to Baphomet, as pictured by Eliphas Levi. LaVey's Crown Princes are also similar to Shub-Niggurath (see chapter 5). Although Shub-Niggurath is a female entity, unlike the Crown Princes, gender is not really an issue here. In fact, in the *Cthaat Aquadingen*, a fictitious book of magick created by Brian Lumley but purportedly written by a medieval scholar around 400 BC as the first in a series of occult works, Shub-Niggurath is spoken of as being both male and female. As such, Shub-Niggurath may represent a cosmic level of fertility and fecundity, the spawning of planets and nebula rather than children localized in space and time. This point is supported by Tyson, who, in *Grimoire of the Necronomicon*, argues that Shub-Niggurath has both male and female sexual organs, and thus can function as a goddess and a god.[239] As for Leviathan, this entity bears a remarkable resemblance to Lovecraft's two Great Old Ones associated with the sea and the element of water: Dagon and Great Cthulhu himself.

THE LAW OF THE TRAPEZOID

The Church of Satan makes no distinction between their Dionysian entities and the alternate, parallel realms inhabited by these beings. In fact, Anton LaVey sees both the beings and their habitats as a general manifestation of an all-inclusive force he labels the "Powers of Darkness," and which is clearly equivalent to the pan-psychic force field of the Vodouns and the quantum superstring theories of a universe consisting of pure energy. As LaVey describes it:

> Most Satanists do not accept Satan as an anthropomorphic being with cloven hooves, a barbed tail, and horns. He represents a force of nature—the powers of darkness which have been named just that because no religion has taken these forces out of the darkness. Nor has science been able to apply technical terminology to this force. It is an untapped reservoir that few can make use of because they lack the ability to use a tool

without having to first break down and label all the parts which make it run. It is this incessant need to analyze which prohibits most people from taking advantage of this many faceted key to the unknown—which the Satanist chooses to call "Satan."[240]

The intra-dimensional nature of the pan-psychic field is described by LaVey in an essay titled "The Law of the Trapezoid," which was published in a 1976 issue of *The Cloven Hoof.* According to LaVey, certain shapes, such as the trapezoid, can serve as windows to alternate dimensions, which LaVey referred to as the fourth dimension. LaVey based his speculations on the magickal system of Dr. John Dee and Sir Edward Kelley, who used a many-faceted crystal trapezohedron to "skry," or travel the astral realms. LaVey supplemented his studies by seeking out on the physical plane areas that functioned as windows to alternate dimensions. Examples of these types of areas include Devil's Slide, a coastside vortex south of San Francisco, and the White's Hill area in Marin County, north of San Francisco. LaVey discussed his findings in a series of lectures on Time Warps and Peculiar Areas, which he delivered in classroom settings at the Church of Satan. In the following passage, LaVey explains how the mere shape of a place can "change" a person's psychological state (in this particular example, the change is for the worse).

I had ample evidence that spatial concepts were not only able to affect those who were involved in visual confrontations, but far more insidiously, other parties with whom a viewer came into contact. As in any other form of contagion, family, friends and co-workers are affected by the signals of anxiety projected by another. The most tranquil and stoical person can be drawn into a chaotic situation if his surroundings are sufficiently disturbing ... Angles and space-planes that provoke anxiety—that is, those not harmonious with the visual orientation—will engender aberrant behavior, translate: change.[241]

The black magickian, of course, must use these types of "gates" or "windows" to effect positive change, as opposed to anxiety or insanity. The goal is to achieve altered perception, and the primary way that the magickian accesses the pan-psychic field is through the use of ritual workings, rituals that, in turn, utilize angles as passageways to alternate dimensions. In performing this type of magick, the black magickian achieves a high-energy or vibratory state reminiscent of the trance state achieved by the Vodou houn'gan or mam'bo who has been possessed by the loa. Once this state is achieved, then the black magickian can, in effect, simply "step" into another dimension.

The parallels between LaVey's and Lovecraft's systems are striking. The dark, otherworldly entity in Lovecraft's story "The Haunter of the Dark" materializes via a black, red-striated polyhedron crystal known as the "Shining Trapezohedron" (this, no doubt, inspired LaVey and Aquino when they composed their Satanic rite "Die Elektrischen Vorspiele," which appears in *The Satanic Rituals*). The use of angles and spatial shapes is most apparent in Lovecraft's tale "The Dreams in the Witch House," which I have already discussed at length in chapter 2. The main character of this story, Walter Gilman, lives in a crazily angled room, which makes it possible for the witch Keziah and her familiar, Brown Jenkin, to travel in alternate dimensions.

> Gilman's room was of good size but queerly irregular in shape; the north wall slanting perceptibly inward from the outer to the inner end, while the low ceiling slanted gently downward in the same direction . . . As time wore along, his absorption in the irregular wall and ceiling of his room increased; for he began to read into the odd angles a mathematical which seemed to offer vague clues regarding their purpose. Old Keziah, he reflected, might have had excellent reasons for living in a room with peculiar angles, for was it not through certain angles that she

claimed to have gone outside the boundaries of the world of space we know?[242]

There is, however, one fundamental difference between Satanism and the other systems that we have examined: Satanism offers no clear provision for the possibility of an afterlife for most individuals. Addressing the existential nature of mankind in *The Satanic Bible*, LaVey's viewpoint is characteristic, as befits a self-proclaimed proponent of earthly indulgence and delight. He does not believe that death is a great spiritual awakening, or that the Satanic magickian survives in any lasting or noumenal sense. Instead, LaVey argues that the Satanist, if he is a particularly vital person who has spent his existence developing his ego by the use of Satanic magickal practices, will not cease to exist after death. Rather, the Satanic magickian's ego will survive in some vague, earthly manner.

> Death, in most religions, is touted as a great spiritual awakening—one which is prepared for throughout life. This concept is very appealing to one who has not had a satisfactory life; but to those who have experienced all the joys life has to offer, there is a great dread attached to dying. This is as it should be. It is this lust for life which will allow the vital person to live on after the inevitable death of his fleshly shell . . . If a person has been vital throughout life and has fought to the end for his earthly existence, it is this ego which will refuse to die, even after the expiration of the flesh which housed it . . . It is this child-like vitality that will allow the Satanist to peek through the curtain of darkness and death and remain earthbound.[243]

This is considerably different than Vodou's dual concept of the Gros Bon Ange and the Ti Bon Ange; in both cases, these individual portions of the individual being are, in effect, immortal. LaVey's version of an "earthbound" immortality also differs greatly from the Wiccan concepts of reincarnation and immortality. However, Lovecraft, as we have seen, articulated a thoroughly rational, scientific concept of the individual as a disparate energy stream that ceases upon death; in Lovecraft's system, there is no immortality of any kind. LaVey would likely agree with this, at least with regard to the death of most individuals. But Lovecraft would not have accepted LaVey's vague notion of the possibility of "earthbound" immortality for strong-willed Satanists; to Lovecraft, the human will was no different than the human intellect, or any other aspect of the human mind—all facets of the human being were impermanent and thus could not withstand the death of the physical body.

THE SATANIC RITES

According to LaVey, there are three categories of Satanic magick. The first category is non-ritual, or manipulative magick. Non-ritual magick is the use of psychological manipulation, or "wile and guile," as LaVey refers to it, to effect changes in the world.[244] The second category is ritual magick proper, which is usually performed by the individual magickian. The goals of Satanic magick are the same as the goals of other black magickal rites: knowledge, power, and, of course, the basic "low" magick objectives, such as procuring lovers, finding better jobs, neutralizing enemies, and so on. In defining the sources of the magickian's power, LaVey emphasizes the psycho-physical nature of this power. LaVey also makes it clear that, in his estimation, the "outer" aspect to magickal power is minimal; power is drawn from latent resources inherent in the mind and body of the practitioner.

> Ritual magic['s] ... main function is to isolate the otherwise
> dissipated adrenal and other emotionally induced energy, and
> convert it into a dynamically transmittable force. It is purely an

emotional, rather than intellectual, act. Any and all intellectual activity must take place before the ceremony, not during it.[245]

The third category of Satanic magick is largely ceremonial. LaVey, along with his uncredited co-writer, Michael Aquino, provides a wealth of ceremonies, "psychodramas," as he calls them, in *The Satanic Rituals.* The most infamous and well-known Satanic psychodrama is the Black Mass, or "Le Messe Noir," as it was referred to by the Luciferian Society in the late nineteenth and twentieth centuries.[246] The rite is conducted by the priest, or celebrant, who is assisted by a deacon, a subdeacon, a nun, a naked woman, who serves as the altar, and various minor participants. They all wear hooded black robes, except for the nun and the woman. The celebrant starts out by reciting the Proclamation, renouncing God and acknowledging Satan and Lucifer as the true rulers of the earth. The first part of the Mass, the Offertory, then commences. In the Roman Catholic Mass, the Offertory section follows the saying of the Apostles' Creed, during which the bread and wine are exalted; in the Black Mass, the celebrant parodies these activities. The next part of the ritual is the Canon, which, in the Roman Catholic Mass, falls between the Sanctus and the recitation of the Lord's Prayer. But now, the celebrant asks Satan to accept the impending sacrifice, and offers praise and honor to the Four Crown Princes of Hell. The subdeacon then brings forth a chamber pot and the nun urinates into it, as the deacon recites a parody of the Christian blessing. The deacon takes up a representation of the phallus, bathes it in the fluid in the chamber pot, then holds it against his genitals and shakes it twice at each of the cardinal points, reciting the following phrase: "In the name of Satan, we bless thee with this, the symbol of the rod of life."[247] The Consecration follows, in which the celebrant identifies the wafer as the body of Christ, and the wine as the blood of Christ—he touches the wafer to the breasts and the vagina of the woman on the altar. He declares his trust in Satan, the Lord of the Flesh, and then recites a parody of the Lord's Prayer. Following this, the celebrant and the participants partake in the unholy communion and formally reject Christianity. When the chalice is drained, the candles are snuffed out and the rite is concluded.

Among the ceremonies published in *The Satanic Rituals*, LaVey includes two psychodramas directly inspired by the Lovecraftian Mythos. The first of these, "The Ceremony of the Nine Angles," purports to be an evocation of Shub-Niggurath. The participants, robed in black, stand before the image of a great Trapezoid and pay homage to Azathoth, Yog-Sothoth, and Nyarlathotep. Then, they evoke Shub-Niggurath, and Shub-Niggurath dutifully appears. However, since this Great Old One is subsequently given a speaking part in the rite, it is clear that Shub-Niggurath hasn't actually been evoked; rather, another member of the group is playing the role of Shub-Niggurath. Once the "evocation" has been successful, all of the participants, Shub-Niggurath included, recite the Bond of the Nine Angles. This consists of nine separate stanzas, the purpose of which is unclear. Presumably, each stanza is to be associated with one of the angles of the Trapezoid, but none of them make any sense. There are general, obscure references to entities such as the "hornless ones," the "Master of the Realms," and so on; there are also references to general concepts, such as "infinity," the "sleep of the Daemons" and "the flame of the beginning and end."[248] At the end of the recitation of the Bond stanzas, the actor playing Shub-Niggurath departs and the rite abruptly ends.

The second Lovecraftian psychodrama, "The Call to Cthulhu," is much more satisfactory, for there is an actual evocation. At night, the celebrant, assisted by participants, stands before a bonfire in some natural setting like a lake, river, or even the sea. Using words of power that actually do make sense, the celebrant and the participants evoke Cthulhu. Although this isn't the actual Cthulhu, since Cthulhu is imprisoned in the City of R'lyeh beneath the Pacific Ocean, it is, nevertheless, some type of otherworldly entity; a simulacrum of Cthulhu, perhaps, or an astral Cthulhu. In the presence of this entity, the celebrant and the participants pledge themselves to the Great Old Ones and the celebrant casts his or her torch into the bonfire, dissolving the simulacrum and effectively ending the rite.

10

LOVECRAFT AND THE CHAOS MAGICK PACTS

The chaos magick covens, or "pacts," represent one of the most recent permutations of the black magickal tradition. Most of the chaos magick groups started up in the late 1980s and early 1990s, and can best be described as disparate, autonomous organizations characterized by a desire on the part of their founders to align themselves with the most current, cutting edge theories of quantum physics, mathematics, and cosmogenesis. As for their actual magickal practices, the individual founders tend to favor an ad hoc, assemble-as-you-go approach, picking and choosing rites, god-forms and degree structures according to their diverse preferences. Despite the diversity in magickal practices, however, most chaos magickians share similar views of the universe, recognizing that all forms of energy and all types of matter behave in terms of probability waves rather than as particles in a patterned space-time continuum. In the estimation of the typical chaos magickian, there is, therefore, nothing that can be considered absolutely "real" in the universe, and this applies to magickal phenomena as well. A corollary of this view is that there is no one-and-only method to generate magickal power, thus rendering obsolete all the traditional tools, trappings, symbolic objects, and elements of other black magickal systems.

It is important to observe, however, there isn't really anything new about the chaos magick approach—because, as I have demonstrated in previous chapters, all the black magickal systems share a more or less quantum view of the cosmos, either overtly or otherwise. Indeed, Crowley himself, the supreme Apollonian magickian, appeared to be moving in the direction of the chaos magick pacts after his stint in the Golden Dawn. His teachings, and his reworking of the classical Golden Dawn rituals, demonstrate an honest attempt to break free from the hierarchical, symbolic, and cumbersome biases of traditional Western occultism. Crowley's motto, "the method of science," which he used as a subtitle for his *Equinox* publications, also reinforced his intent to align magick with modern science—this intent, however, was basically flawed from the start, due to Crowley's strong attachment to the very tradition that he was attempting to transcend. The fact that chaos magick isn't too different from other black magickal systems is further evident when one examines the actual chaos magick rites. For all their talk about the obsolescence of traditional tools and trappings, chaos magickians use the same materials as other black magickians; they also use the same languages, gestures, symbolic objects, and stylized settings. Even more importantly, the god-forms that serve as the basis for their rituals are equivalent in nature and scope to the god-forms of the older black magickal systems.

From the beginning, Lovecraft and his Mythos were wholeheartedly "adopted" by the chaos magick pacts; indeed, Lovecraft has become more of a darling to these groups than he has been for occultists like Kenneth Grant and Anton LaVey. On a practical level, the chaos magick pacts invariably use Lovecraft's pantheon of entities in their ritual work. On a more theoretical level, they identify with Lovecraft's amoral, inhuman view of extraterrestrial entities, and see Lovecraft as a prototypical chaos magickian, at least in theory. Richard Metzger describes the connection between "chaos culture" and Lovecraft's cosmogenesis.

> Lovecraft's fiction expresses a "future primitivism" that finds its most intense esoteric expression in Chaos Magic, an eclectic contemporary style of darkside occultism . . . For today's Chaos mage . . . [recognizes] the distinct possibility that we may be adrift in a meaningless, iterative cosmos within which human will and imagination are vaguely comic flukes (the "cosmic indifferentism" Lovecraft himself professed), the mage accepts his groundlessness, embracing the chaotic self-creating void that is himself.[249]

Lovecraft would have endorsed many of the philosophical underpinnings of the chaos magick pacts, and he would likely have approved of the postmodernistic view that extraterrestrial entities like the Great Old Ones are much more than merely static archetypes; rather, they are archetypes that change and adapt as cultural and historical conditions change, in contrast to the rather minor, brief, and ultimately inconsequential changes that occur in the human realm.

AUSTIN OSMAN SPARE AND THE ZOS KIA CULTUS

The basic tenets of chaos magick are derived from the works of Austin Osman Spare, whose use of dream control magick was explored briefly in chapter 1. Spare was born in Snow Hill, London, on December 30, 1886. His father was a policeman and his background was decidedly middle class. At an early age, Spare demonstrated a talent for drawing, and at the age of twelve, he was sent to Lambeth Evening Art School in South Kensington. He later attended the Royal College of Art and, in the early 1900s, his work gained the attention of the art world. Despite this success, Spare pursued a parallel career that had little to do with twentieth-century art. A few years earlier, Spare had been initiated into magick and witchcraft by a friend of his parents, a Mrs. Paterson who claimed descent from a line of Salem witches. First, she taught young Spare how to tell fortunes; as he grew older, she began to teach a very personal blend of paganism and witchcraft to her young disciple. As a result of these teachings, Spare had a life-long fascination with occultism, and his drawings reflected this fascination. For a brief period, Spare flirted with the traditional, Apollonian systems of magick; he became a member of Crowley's A∴A∴ in 1910, taking the motto "Yirohaum," a combination of IHVH and AUM. However, like Paterson herself, Spare was not content with the received doctrines and he quickly evolved his own brand of magick, which, according to Kenneth Grant, was an attempt to continue the tradition of the Petro rites of Vodou (see chapter 6) and Eastern Tantric sex magick, as embodied in the Vama Marg.[250]

The foundation of Spare's system was derived, in part, from his work with the Cult of the Ku, a Chinese occult order that flourished in London in the early nineteenth century. In fact, Spare adopted the name of this order when he articulated his concept of the Kia. In 1913, Spare published *The Book of Pleasure*, in which he formalized the tenets of his magickal system. This system was based on sex magick, like Crowley's system, and Spare followed Crowley's example in favoring unattractive or older women (mostly prostitutes) who, undoubtedly, reminded Spare of Ms. Paterson. Spare published his second book, *The Focus of Life*, in 1919, and spent the next thirty years perfecting his magickal system. He was in the process of completing his third major work, a bona fide magickal grimoire, *The Book of the Living Word of Zos and the Zoetic Grimoire of Zos,* when he died in 1956.

Spare postulated the existence of two primal principles, both of which were later adopted wholeheartedly by the chaos magick pacts. The first of these is known as the Kia, or the "Atmospheric I." The Kia is usually interpreted by occult scholars as an objective, rather vague force-field, or vortex of energy. This interpretation is due, in part, to Spare's own descriptions of the Kia, which seem to equate the Kia with the principle of creation in the cosmos. Indeed, Spare's descriptions of the Kia are strikingly similar to the portrayal of the First Cause in Qabalistic metaphysics (i.e. Kether, the first sephira on the Tree of Life). This is evident in the following passage from *The Book of Pleasure.*

> The Law of Evolution is retrogression of function governing progression of attainment, i.e. the more wonderful our attainments are, the lower in the scale of life the function that governs them. Man is complex, and to progress, must become simplified. This means that because more and more manifestations of Kia are appearing in the world all the time throughout reincarnation, as the source of creation expands "outwards," the true magical direction is "inwards" or more specifically "backwards" to the First Cause.[251]

Neville Drury, noting such phrases as "source of creation" and "First Cause," has concluded that the Kia is, indeed, Spare's counterpart to the Qabalistic concept of the Ain Soph Aur, the Limitless Light, the last phase of unmanifestation out of which Kether is concentrated.[252] Thus, Drury places Spare's first principle squarely in the center of the white magickal tradition. A close examination of Spare's concept of the Kia, however, contradicts Drury's assessment; the Kia is clearly allied with the Dionysian or black magickal tradition. The Kia is not merely another name for Kether, or for the

Ain Soph Aur—instead, it is equivalent to the Typhonian, Diony-sian goddess archetypes that we have been examining in this book. In his unpublished *Grimoire,* Spare makes it clear that the Kia is a full-fledged matriarchal deity: "Our Deity [is] The All-Prevailing Woman ('And I strayed with her, into the path direct')."[253] In fact, Spare's association with the Cult of the Ku provides full justification for seeing the Kia as the Dionysian goddess. This cult was basically matriarchal in structure; the initiates worshipped a serpent goddess, the Ku, and the High Priestess of the cult personified this goddess. The High Priestess would customarily become possessed during the course of the rites, just as the mam'bo or houn'gan were possessed by the goddess Mawu during the performance of the major Vodou rites. The High Priestess, intoxicated by the presence of the Goddess, then passed the current to other members of the cult. For the male members of the cult, this current took the form of "shadow-women," i.e. succubi, and the male devotees then had sexual intercourse with these beings, becoming possessed with the energies of the Goddess. For the female members of the cult, the current took the form of incubi, with the same result. Kenneth Grant, in his *Cults of the Shad-ow,* aligns the cult of the Ku with the Typhonian tradition, and by implication, with the Zos Kia Cultus of Spare.

> The Ku would seem to be a form of the Fire Snake exteriorized astrally as a shadow-woman or succubus, congress with which enabled the devotee to reify his "inherent dream." She was known as the "whore of hell" and her function was analogous to that of the Scarlet women of Crowley's cult, the Suvasini of the Tantric Kaula of the Cult of the Black Snake. The Chinese Ku, or harlot of hell, is a shadowy embodiment of subconscious desires concentrated in the alluringly sensuous form of the Serpent of Shadow Goddess.[254]

It is important to note, also, the similarity between Spare's term "Kia" and the "Ku." Although Grant does not address this similarity, it is clear that Spare adapted the term "Ku" in the formulation of his own primary personae.

The second persona of Spare's system is known as the Zos. There is little confusion on the part of occult scholars about the meaning of this term. The Zos represents the body, the physical and mental nature of the magickian, "the body considered as a whole."[255] By interpreting the actual, embodied magickian as the lesser persona in his system, Spare is following the classic black magickal tradition, as manifested in the Wiccan and Vodou religions. As we have seen, the Vodou High Priest, or houn'gan, awakens the magickal power by coupling with the Goddess, either physically or metaphysically. The High Priest is, technically speaking, a human body, as is the Zos, and in both cases these bodies are utilized by the loa during the crisis of possession. Similarly, the Wiccan High Priest, the earthly representative of the Horned God, is always incarnate in a human body; he is chosen by the High Priestess of the coven, and is usually her husband or lover. Indeed, Spare's view of the Zos is nearly equivalent to Crowley's view of the magickian. Crowley saw the whole physical and mental being of the magickian as the "god" or male polarity in the grand equation of the universe. When the magickian realizes his godhead—when he discovers his true will—then he can be understood as a "star," as Crowley refers to this state in *Liber Legis*. At this point, the man is magickally potent, and can utilize the powers of the universe. Crowley's view is expressed clearly in theorem 14 in his *Introduction* to *Magick*.

> Man is capable of being, and using, anything which he perceives, for everything that he perceives is in a certain sense a part of his being. He may thus subjugate the whole Universe of which he is conscious to his individual Will . . . Man has used

the idea of God to dictate his personal conduct, to obtain power over his fellows, to excuse his crimes, and for innumerable other purposes, including that of realizing himself as God.[256]

There is, however, an important difference between Crowley's concept of the will and Spare's Zos. Crowley elevated the will, making it the primary component of his white magickal system. But Spare, approaching the Zos from the black magickal standpoint, realized that the ego has a tendency to isolate the magickian from the true sources of magickal power. The exaltation of the ego brings with it the debris of the subconsciousness, and the magickian can end up being unable to distinguish between reality and illusion in the course of his magickal explorations. Thus, Spare took on a magickal name to indicate the proper use of the magickal mechanism known as the Zos. He called himself Zos vel Thanatos—the body qualified, or purified, by the death of the ego. According to Spare, when the individual magickian is in a state of simulated death or mental vacuity, then he is fully open to the Kia, the supreme principle of the universe. And this ultimate openness, in turn, allows the magickian to utilize his magickal powers in the fullest sense. The actual technique for accomplishing this end is labeled the Death Posture by Spare, and was based on a method of dream control that Spare developed himself. Kenneth Grant perceives an affinity between Spare's view of the body and Egyptian and Tantric mysticism.

> The Death Posture [was] a formula evolved by Spare for the purpose of reifying the negative potential in terms of positive power. In ancient Egypt the mummy was the type of this formula, and the simulation by the Adept of the state of death—in Tantric practice—involves also the total stilling of the psychosomatic functions. The formula has been used by Adepts not necessarily working with specifically Tantric or magickal formulae, notably by the celebrated Advaitan Rishi, Bhagavan Shri

Ramana Maharshi of Tiruvannamalai, who attained Supreme Enlightenment by simulating the processes of death; and also by the Bengal Vaishnavite, Thakur Haranath, who was taken for dead and actually prepared for burial after a "death trance" which lasted several hours and from which he emerged with a totally new consciousness that transformed even his bodily constitution and appearance.[257]

Interestingly, the theoretical basis of Spare's Death Posture can be found in Western philosophy, not Eastern metaphysics. Plato uses the life of Socrates as the prototype of the ideal philosophical life. The actual practice of the philosophical life, however, is much closer to Spare's mystical conception of the magickal life. According to Socrates, the philosopher must live purely, avoiding association with material and physical pleasures, in order to gain a clearer perception of reality and understand the difference between reality and appearances. In particular, the true philosopher must not fear death, but must look forward to it; his life should in fact be a training for death.[258] The parallels between this argument and Spare's own approach to the magickal path are clear. The magickian makes use of the Death Posture to circumvent the ego, essentially "training" himself for a more enduring escape from the cycle of birth and rebirth after the death of the physical body.

Spare's magickal system culminates in a state, or more appropriately, a conceptualization, that he referred to as the Neither-Neither. The Neither-Neither is equivalent to the Vodou concept of the pan-psychic field; it is immaterial, yet ubiquitous; it can be experienced only by a "disaggregated" being, i.e. a being that is no longer localized in space and time. The Neither-Neither is also equivalent to the highest level of disincarnation posited by the Wiccan religion, the level that the Wiccan themselves are unwilling to define because they recognize that such a level is beyond conception. As indicated in *A Witches' Bible*:

The immortal individual, freed by its own efforts from the need for further incarnations on this plane, can then move on to the next stage. The nature of that stage we can only envision dimly, at our present level of development; if we could grasp its essence and its detail, we should not still be here.[259]

The parallels between Spare's Neither-Neither and the quantum physicists' views of the universe are obvious. When a sentient being is incarnate, or localized, then he or she is not part of the Neither-Neither. But when this same being is disaggregated, or energized, then he or she is partaking in the Neither-Neither and the peculiar, alternate levels of reality envisioned by modern science. In *Outer Gateways,* Grant argues that Spare's Neither-Neither is comparable to the Buddhist Madhyamaka proposition of Absolute Zero, or Emptiness, as articulated by Nagarjuna, who was among the first Buddhist monks and scholars to perceive that Emptiness was at the core of Buddhist doctrine.

> At about the time Crowley embarked upon his "Equinox" period, Austin Osman Spare was elaborating his doctrine of the Kia which he described as the philosophy of Neither-Neither ... [he introduced] into his system the Asiatic metaphysic of the Madhyamaka, or "Middle Position," which eschewed the two extremes—Existence (Is) and Non-Existence (Not Is) ... Spare assumed a standpoint which represents precisely the Madhyamaka position, although it is, rather, the abolition of all positions, for Kia implies not only "neither is, nor is not," but also, neither of these.[260]

Spare developed his concept of the Neither-Neither intellectually, not magickally. Yet, his intellectual intuition arose from his own level of illumination. This explains why many of the chaos magickians are so quick to embrace Spare as one of their own. Basically, the idea of the Neither-Neither was derived from Spare's understanding of the ancient Chinese formula 0=2. Crowley's research into the meaning of this formula is fairly well known among occultists, and illustrates his Apollonian approach to the practice of magick. Crowley's first analysis of this formula appears in *An Essay in Ontology* (1902) and later, in a passage from *The Book of Thoth* (1973). Crowley starts out viewing zero as an Absolute Zero, as a symbol for nothingness. But later, Crowley moved away from this view of zero and interpreted it in terms of the Hegelian dialectic; this interpretation reflected Crowley's own white magickal approach to occultism and metaphysics. He saw zero as the union of +1 and -1, both of which are something rather than nothing, and the result of this union as a third "something." Thus, 0=2 signifies the creation of the universe out of a nothingness that is still seen as a somethingness. The reason why this interpretation is Apollonian is because it eschews chaos—there is a positive and negative element, and thus, nothingness is qualified. Also, the need for synthesis as opposed to genuine negation is preserved. Spare circumvents this problem by interpreting +1 as non-negative rather than positive, and -1 as non-positive. The union of the two is therefore non-two, or non-duality. Thus, in Spare's estimation, 0=2 yields a genuine nothingness, a genuine Neither-Neither. Grant expresses Spare's view succinctly in another passage from *Outer Gateways*.

> Spare did not fall into the error of 0=2; his nought is Absolute Zero ... Spare understood profoundly the inbetweenness concepts, the Middle Position (Madhyamaka) which is no position at all for it is the negation of two positive concepts, "Is" and "Not-Is" ... The non-negative (+1) plus the non-positive (-1)= non-two, which is advaita, or non-duality. The difference in physical terms is unnoticeable because both formulae yield Nothing, but metaphysically, the difference is total, because the residual Nothing is absolute nothing, or Nothingness, the Two having been utterly abolished.[261]

Spare never articulated a definite position on the afterlife, but his views are clear enough. As mentioned previously, the methodology of Spare's magickal practice is centered around the Death Posture, a form of dream control modeled on the death of the body, or phenomenal existence. The physical magickian, the Zos, experiences the Kia, and the magickian temporarily attains the Neither-Neither. Over the course of his life, the magickian becomes more and more accustomed to the Neither-Neither, and learns to function in the "inbetweenness" as easily and effortlessly as he functions in the phenomenal world. After death, the magickian becomes pure energy, or pure "quanta," and his transcendence of duality is complete.

CHAOS MAGICK THEORY AND
THE ETHERIC SELF

All three of Austin Osman Spare's magickal concepts, or paradigms—the Neither-Neither, the Kia, and the Zos—have been adopted and only slightly modified by the contemporary chaos magick pacts (and by many postmodern black magickians, who are drawn to chaos magick but who prefer to maintain their independence from all magickal organizations). Peter J. Carroll, in *Liber Null & Psychonaut*, identifies the three "realities" of the universe, as envisioned by the chaos magick pacts.

> Primary Reality: The Void, Chaos, Ain Soph Aor, God, the Empyrean, Universe B, the Meon, The Pleroma or Plenum, Mummu, the Nagual, the Archetypal or Formative World, the 5th Dimension, Cosmic Mind, the Hologram, the Night of Pan, Hyperspace, Acausality, Quantum Realm.
>
> Second Reality: The Aethers or Astral, Probability, the Gods, Morphic Fields, the Shadow World, the Side, the Wind, the Astral Light, Potentia, Aura, Middle Nature.

Tertiary Reality: The Physical or Material World, Malkuth, Universe A, the Tonal, the 4th Dimension, the Body of God, the Holograph, Causality.[262]

Here, Carroll provides a full set of comparison terms for each paradigm, leaving no confusion as to how these realities should be compared to their prototypes in Spare's system and, also, to some of the other black magickal systems we have examined. The primary reality in Spare's system, as we have seen, is the Neither-Neither, and this is equivalent to Carroll's primary reality. This equivalence is evident from a close reading of Spare's interpretation of the Neither-Neither as 0=2, or as genuine nothingness, since nothingness is clearly synonymous with chaos, or the void, or the quantum realm, as defined by Carroll. In describing exactly what chaos is (or more appropriately, isn't), Carroll dismisses the alternate terms for this primary reality (or God, or the Ain Soph Aur) because he argues that such terms distort the pristine simplicity and incomprehensible nature of the primary reality.

> Consider the world of apparent dualisms we inhabit. The mind views a picture of this world in which everything is double. A thing is said to exist and exert certain properties. Being and Doing. This calls for the concepts of cause and effect or causality. Every phenomenon is seen to be caused by some previous thing. However, this description cannot explain how everything exists in the first place or even how one thing finally causes another. Obviously things have originated and do continue to make each other happen. The "thing" responsible for the origin and continued action of events is called Chaos by magicians. It could well be called God or Tao, but the name Chaos is virtually meaningless, and free from the childish, anthropomorphic ideas of religion.[263]

Spare's concept of the Kia, according to Carroll, is also part of the Neither-Neither, or the chaos, but the Kia is actually a fragment of chaos that is specifically connected with the planet earth, and with the chaos magickian. When the Kia, or life force of the planet, is viewed from a macrocosmic standpoint, then this is not the "Atmospheric I" that Spare describes, but when the Kia is viewed from the microcosmic standpoint, (the standpoint of the individual black magickian), then this Kia is, indeed, the "I." Carroll, in his description of the Kia, associates this paradigm with Baphomet, the Horned God of the Witches, and then, generally, with the goddess image of the black magickal systems.

> There is a part of Chaos which is of more direct relevance to the magician. This is the spirit of the life energy of our planet. All living beings have some extra quality in them which separates them from inorganic matter. The ancient shamans mainly sought to represent this force by the Horned God. In more modern times this force has reasserted itself in our awareness under the symbol of Baphomet. Baphomet is the psychic field generated by the totality of living beings on this planet . . . it has been variously represented as Pan, Pangenitor . . . as Ishtar or Astaroth—goddess of love and war—as the Anima Mundi or World soul, or simply as "Goddess."[264]

It will be remembered from the previous section that Spare, likewise, associated the Kia with the image of the Goddess. Therefore, the chaos magick pacts, at the very basic, metaphysical level, represent a magickal system that is closed allied with the previous Dionysian, matriarchal black magickal systems that have been the subject of this book. The two other paradigms of reality identified by Carroll as central to chaos magickal theory (or CMT, as Carroll refers to it in *Liber Kaos*), the second and tertiary realities, are similarly based on Spare's magickal system, though only the third paradigm can be identified specifically with one of Spare's principal concepts, the Zos. The Zos, being the actual body and mind of the magickian, is obviously equivalent to Carroll's view of the physical, material world, particularly in terms of the subjective aspect of this world.

The second reality refers to the Aether, or Astral realm. Spare did not actually identify the Aether with a separate principle, but much of his magickal work was conducted via the Aether, and he would have agreed with Carroll's view of the Aether as "a realm of half-formed substance . . . Between Chaos and ordinary matter."[265] Carroll utilizes the concept of the Aether as a synonym for the alternate levels of existence postulated by modern quantum physics. In ancient Greek and Roman philosophy, the Aether represented the root of the four elements, fire, air, water and earth. Aether was seen as a semi-solid substance, elastic and invisible, pervading space and time, and responsible for the transmission of energy—particularly heat, light, and electricity. Most Western occultists, white and black alike, associated the Aether with the astral realm and with the invisible substance known as "ectoplasm," which can be modeled by lesser, incorporeal entities into temporary bodies. Western science was known to accept the concept of the Aether between the seventeenth and nineteenth centuries, but in the twentieth century, it was relegated to the realm of the miraculous.

However, with the advent of quantum theory, the concept of the Aether was given a new lease on life. Because Aether is envisioned as both solid and semi-solid, it does seem to correspond at least superficially to the concept of the quanta. The minimum particle of matter, the quanta, exists as a discrete point in space, a solid point, like one aspect of the Aether. Yet, the quanta also exist as a probability wave, and this corresponds to the semi-solid nature of the Aether. Given the fact that one part of matter is, in a sense, all matter, then the Aether could be understood as an etheric pattern or "shadow" that defines the probability of all material events. The chaos magickians extend the Aether into precisely this type of pattern, and associate the Aetheric pattern with the alternate realities that comprise the shadow-matter dimensions. As Carroll describes it:

> The CMT paradigm states that the wave functions are actually a mathematical description of etheric patterns . . . which can be considered as a kind of shadow substance . . . I now identify the contents of the etheric time dimension with the parallel universes which are an optimal consequence of the wave equations of quantum physics.[266]

There are a number of important principles of the Aether, as envisioned by CMT. First of all, the Aether is emitted by all matter and all mental activity, past and present. Second, the Aether provides information about the entities that produce it. Finally, Aether, as noted previously, combines with all other Aether, creating a vast, ubiquitous Aetheric pattern. The god-forms that the chaos magickian utilizes take their forms from the Aether; this view of the god-forms is akin to Spare's interpretation of god-forms as impressions of mythic impulses in the Kia. Most of these impressions are derived from earlier human incarnations, but they are reawakened in the mind of currently incarnate humans via the use of magick, particularly the technique of dream control. Indeed, contemporary chaos magickians would not dispute the following description of gods and goddesses that appears in Spare's *Book of Pleasure*: "All gods have lived (being ourselves) on earth, and when dead, their experience of Karma governs our actions in degree."[267] The human self, of course, is necessarily part of the Aetheric pattern, differing from the gods and goddesses in degree rather than in kind. According to CMT, the self is merely a concept, not a reality, since in the quantum universe, there is no reality; there is only an arbitrary, random coupling of particles and events.

The chaos magical view of self is that it is based on the same random capricious chaos which makes the universe exist and do what it does. The magical self has no center; it is not a unity but an assemblage of parts, any number of which may temporarily club together and call themselves "I." This accords with the observation that our subjective experience is not constant. Our subjective experience consists of our various selves experiencing each other ... In the magical view of self there is no spirit/matter or mind/body split and the paradoxes of free will and determinism disappear.[268]

The self may appear to be a stable thing, but this isn't really so; there is no certainty that the self will remain as it appears to be—stability is only probability. Similarly, the experiences based on the illusion of self, and the mental activities based on this same illusion—emotions, intellect, free will, and so on—are equally unstable and probabilistic. Given these facts, there can be no afterlife for the self, or survival of any sort after the death of the physical body and the mind. The only possibility of immortality is inherent in the Aetheric pattern, but this is hardly a personal immortality.

As we have seen, Lovecraft accepted the views of the early quantum physicists, and he would have also sanctioned the scientific speculations of those later quantum physicists who envisioned the existence of shadow-matter dimensions. Indeed, how could he have done otherwise—Lovecraft, arguably, helped inspire those same theorists with his own views of alternate dimensions, as articulated in his Mythos. Consequently, Lovecraft's view of the universe is more or less equivalent to the views of the chaos magick pacts. In chapter 2, I speculate that Lovecraft's materialistic view of the universe may have been inspired by Edgar Allan Poe's cosmological treatise, *Eureka*. Poe pictures the universe like a gigantic "Heart Divine," originating in a radiation outward from the center, swelling into existence, and then, ultimately, collapsing into nothingness. This Heart, in Poe's estimation, is not a unity or a god, but rather non-matter, or Emptiness. Thus, the primary reality of the cosmos is Emptiness, or chaos. In developing the cosmology of the chaos magick pacts, Carroll describes the universe in terms that are remarkably similar to Poe's description.

> For out of Chaos arise the two prime forces of existence, the solve et coagula of existence. The Light power and the Dark. The light power is the expanding, outgoing, dualizing, increasing expression of Chaos, responsible for the new birth, creation, incarnation, and variety. The dark power is the contracting, returning, transcending, withdrawing expression of Chaos, responsible for death, dissolution, reabsorption, simplicity and return to the source.[269]

Likewise, Lovecraft had no belief in the afterlife, and this is shared by the chaos magick pacts; both Carroll and Lovecraft would agree that no human being can survive the death of the body. When the individual human being experiences "death, dissolution and reabsorption," then this individual no longer exists. There is no return to the godhead; there is no rebirth into an ideal level of existence, since the "source" referred to above is pure nothingness.

CHAOS MAGICK RITES

The practice of chaos magick is founded on an independent, "in-your-face" approach to black magick; thus, this system is designed particularly for the solitary magickal practitioner. A number of chaos magickians, like Peter Carroll and Phil Hine, author of *Condensed Chaos* (1995) and *The Pseudonomicon* (1998), have formed groups, or "pacts," all of which bear a close resemblance to the covens of other black magickal practitioners, and, in fact, to the organizational structure of many of the existing white magickal systems. Each of the male members of the pact are denoted by the term "Fra" (i.e. Frater or brother) and the female members are called "Sor" (Soror, or sister). The chaos magick pacts offer their adepts the opportunity to perform invocation and evocation rites, which are not very different from the invocation and evocation rites taught by the other black magickal systems. Both types are based on a technique known as "sleight of mind," which derives from Spare's notion that the conscious mind of the magickian is a "distraction" that interferes with the magickian's ability to access the subconsciousness (LaVey makes this same argument in *The Satanic Bible*). The chaos magickian solves this problem by providing words of power that are, in effect, nonsense syllables; by so doing, the conscious mind is "tricked" into losing track of the intent of the ritual, and magickal power is activated at the level below (or above) conscious awareness. There are three components to a successful evocation: first, the entity must be "implanted" in the magickian's subconsciousness; second, the entity must be charged with magickal energy; and, finally, the entity must be sent on the task for which the rite has been designed. Likewise, there are three components to a successful invocation: the magickian must first identify himself with the god-form; next, the magickian attains some type of union with this entity; and lastly, the magickian must manifest the powers of the god-form.

A good example of a chaos magick evocation is provided by Carroll in *Liber Kaos*. The god-form in this particular ritual is Azathoth, one of the Great Old Ones (see chapter 5). Carroll's interpretation of Azathoth differs significantly from Lovecraft's, and from all of the other interpretations I have examined previously. Carroll tends to see Azathoth as part of the broader context of Western black magick.

> Azathoth is an egregore associated with the emergence of
> sentience from the primeval slime and the quest of sentience to

reach for the stars . . . Azathoth has no shape or name for itself that is meaningful to humans, yet, it will respond to the names Azathoth, Atazoth, and occasionally Astaroth; although this last name, which is a confused derivate from the Babylonian goddess Ishtar, should be avoided to prevent confusion. Historically, this egregore was known to certain alchemists whose name for it, Azathoth, means an increase of azoth, or increasing etheric (morphic) fields in contemporary terms.[270]

The word "egregore" literally refers to an entity that has been intentionally created by the black magickian for some specific purpose; in my estimation, this term is not really appropriate for an extraterrestrial entity such as Azathoth, whose existence likely predates the existence of most of the god-forms used by the Western magickal systems. Nevertheless, this rite is similar to evocation rites in the other black magickal systems. The magickian uses Uranian, Solar, or Jupiterean incense to perfume the temple. The magickian also uses fresh blood to anoint the material basis; in this case, the basis is a triangular pentacle with a chaos-like swirl in the center. As for the evocation, the magickian vibrates the name AZATHOTH nine times, and then the barbarous names: AZAK GRIFE DAGARSH AZATHOTH. [271] The "sleight of mind" identified previously is accomplished by a random shouting out of the letters of the alphabet, and the entity will then make its appearance.

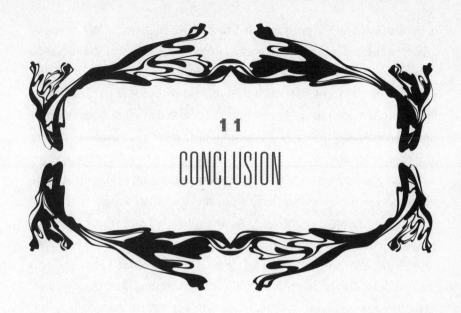

11

CONCLUSION

As the new millennium progresses, H. P. Lovecraft's influence and reputation continue to expand, becoming, in a sense, a microcosm of that great expansion among the finest minds of this century toward the cold, black vastness of space and time, the realm where Lovecraft's fascination finds its epicenter and purpose. The high culture, which still exists as a symptom of human imperfection and earth-consciousness, strives to keep the cosmic at bay. Man is only earthly with earthly concerns, the Harold Blooms of this world often argue, but thankfully the Blooms are dying out, passing away in the presence of a great, inexorable, embryonic universe in which God has no place, but the Great Old Ones reign as perfect expressions of the cosmos as it truly is. S. T. Joshi, in his Introduction to *Black Wings of Cthulhu 2: Eighteen New Tales of Lovecraftian Horror* (2014), identifies horror fiction as a perfect medium to grapple with the great philosophical issues, and, in so doing, designates H. P.

Lovecraft as the patron saint of this cosmic questing: "What is our place in the cosmos? Does a god or gods exist? What is the ultimate fate of the human species? These and other 'big' questions are perennially addressed in Lovecraft's fiction, and in a manner that conveys his 'cosmic' sensibility—a sensibility that keenly etches humankind's transience and fragility in a boundless universe that lacks a guiding purpose or direction."[272]

These are fine words. Clearly, they represent an aesthetic of sorts directed primarily at the high culture—a call to arms, as it were. But at the basic, and arguably most profound levels—the realm of popular culture, where readers feel as well as think and act instead of talking about action—the witchcraft of Lovecraft's thought and images has always exerted a perennial fascination. In turn, this fascination has garnered not merely fans or even converts but fledgling initiates as well, who are willing to follow him into the darkness and entangle themselves in compelling alternate universes. Indeed, Lovecraft's work has it all: horror, science fiction, fantasy, cosmicism, supernaturalism, non-supernaturalism, mythology, metaphysics, quantum physics, antiquarianism, escapism, paganism, neopaganism, white magick, black magick, religion, occultism, psychology, parapsychology, sociology, socialism, philosophy, sentimentalism, cheap sensationalism, and sheer fun. There is something for nearly everyone in Lovecraft's work.

The occultists in particular have found much to admire and emulate in Lovecraft, as I have demonstrated in this book. At the very least, I have shown that Lovecraft has had an indirect, though clearly definable, influence on current Vodou and Wiccan practices. With regard to more modern permutations such as the Typhonian tradition, the Satanic cults, and the chaos magick pacts, the connection has been immediate and vital. In recent years, we have seen Lovecraft's influence broaden to include a diverse variety of magickal practitioners and groups. On average, these groups tend to favor the organizational format of the typical chaos magick pact, being generally small, independent, and loosely structured. Their links to similar groups are often tenuous at best and, in many cases, predicated only on the fact that each group makes use of Lovecraft's pantheon of extraterrestrial entities, either magickally or as a metaphysical underpinning. A good example of such a group is the thirty-year-old Esoteric Order of Dagon, headquartered in Eugene, Oregon and headed by Grand Master Frater Obed Marsh (a name taken from Lovecraft's "The Shadow Over Innsmouth"). Another example is the K'rla cell in London, described by Kenneth Grant in the eighth book of his nine-volume *Typhonian Trilogies, Beyond the Mauve Zone*. Members of this cell make use of Tantric sex magickal methods to forge a link between the earth and the Great Old Ones.

To the uninitiated and to interested parties who have no connection with occultism, this interest in Lovecraft among occultists and magickal practitioners might seem, at first glance, rather difficult to understand. After all, as I have made clear in this study, Lovecraft identified himself as a "mechanistic materialist," by which he meant that he was a believer in the doctrine that nothing exists apart from matter and that all the facts of existence and experience can be explained in reference to the laws of material substances. Since spiritual beings such as gods or goddesses are immaterial, Lovecraft denied their existence. Thus, the question arises: why would any occultist be interested in the work of a self-professed atheist? In attempting to offer a viable answer, it must be remembered that Lovecraft, for all his veneration of pure intellect and reason, also acknowledged that humans have an incomplete and limited knowledge of reality. Thus, he tended to keep an open mind on the issue of spirituality, accepting the premise that there might be alternate levels of being that "supplement" rather than contradict the laws of material substances. And in his dreams, Lovecraft drew even closer to a frank acceptance of certain basic truths that occultists have known for centuries.

Thus, the reader must look to Lovecraft's fictional composition, which naturally arose from his avid dream world and nighttime speculations, to find a more balanced, accurate view of such problematic issues as the existence of gods, goddesses, and the soul, or the likelihood of paranormal phenomena and psychic sensibility. In one of Lovecraft's earliest tales, aptly titled "Beyond the Wall of Sleep," the narrator ends up being able to experience an alternate dimension via an apparatus that links him to the disembodied alter-ego of the story's protagonist, Slater. The insight that this alien, extraterrestrial entity ends up sharing with his rescuer is, as Paul Rolland rightly observes, one that the initiates of any esoteric order would recognize and understand.[273]

> I am an entity like that which you yourself become in the freedom of dreamless sleep. I am your brother of light, and have floated with you in the effulgent valleys. It is not permitted me to tell your waking earth-self of your real self, but we are all roamers of vast spaces and travelers of many ages ... How little does the earth-self know life and its extent! How little, indeed, ought it to know for its own tranquility![274]

NOTES

INTRODUCTION

1. H. P. Lovecraft, "Supernatural Horror in Literature," in *Dagon and Other Macabre Tales*, ed. August Derleth (Sauk City, WI: Arkham House, 1965), 347.
2. Peter Straub, ed., *H. P. Lovecraft: Tales* (New York: Library of America, 2005).
3. Kenneth Grant, *The Magical Revival* (York Beach, ME: Weiser Books, 1972), 99.
4. Peter Levenda, *The Dark Lord: H. P. Lovecraft, Kenneth Grant and the Typhonian Tradition in Magic* (Lake Worth, Florida: Ibis Press, 2013), 189.
5. Anton Szandor LaVey, *The Satanic Rituals* (New York: Avon Books, 1972), 177.

CHAPTER 1

6. Aleister Crowley, *Magick* (York Beach, ME: Weiser Books, 1974), 131.
7. Ibid., 151.
8. Camille Paglia, *Sexual Personae* (New York: Vintage Books, 1991), 12, 96, 98.

9. Janet and Stewart Farrar, *A Witches' Bible* (Blaine, WA: Phoenix Publishing, 1996), 17–8.
10. Anton Szandor LaVey, *The Satanic Bible* (New York: Avon Books, 1970), 81–3.
11. Kenneth Grant, *Nightside of Eden* (London: Skoob Books, 1994), xiii.
12. Kenneth Grant, *Outer Gateways* (London: Skoob Books, 1994), 154–57.
13. Isaac Bonewits, *Real Magic: An Introductory Treatise on the Basic Principles of Yellow Magic* (York Beach, ME: Weiser Books, 1993), 116–17.
14. Grant, *The Magical Revival*, 111.
15. Crowley, *Magick*, 448–59.
16. Grant, *The Magical Revival*, 112.
17. Crowley, *Magick*, 224–26.
18. Ibid., 228.
19. Konstantinos, *Nocturnicon: Calling Dark Forces and Powers* (St. Paul, MN: Llewellyn, 2006), 15–16.
20. Ibid., 23.
21. S. L. MacGregor Mathers, *The Grimoire of Armadel*, ed. Francis King (York Beach, ME: Samuel Weiser Books, 1980), 8.
22. Konstantinos, *Nocturnicon*, 25–27.
23. Crowley, *Magick*, 49-50.
24. William G. Gray, *Magical Ritual Methods* (Great Britain: Helios, 1969), 255.
25. Farrar, *A Witches' Bible*, 83.
26. Kenneth Grant, *Cults of the Shadow* (York Beach, ME: Weiser Books, 1976), 204.
27. Gray, *Magical Ritual Methods*, 179.
28. Crowley, *Magick*, 251.
29. Ibid., 251.

CHAPTER 2

30. Erik Davis, *Calling Cthulhu: HP Lovecraft's Magick Realism, Book of Lies*, ed. Richard Metzger (New York: The Disinformation Company, 2003), 138–148.
31. L. Sprague de Camp, *Lovecraft: A Biography* (New York: Doubleday & Company, 1975), 427.
32. H. P. Lovecraft, *Selected Letters: 1925–1929*, ed. August Derleth and Donald Wandrei (Sauk City, WI: Arkham House, 1968), 160
33. Ibid., 266–67.

34. Ibid., 267.

35. Arthur Hobson Quinn, *Edgar Allan Poe: A Critical Biography* (Baltimore, MD: Johns Hopkins, 1941), 543.

36. Lovecraft, *Selected Letters: 1925–1929*, 197.

37. Ibid., 293–96.

38. S. T. Joshi, *The Rise and Fall of the Cthulhu Mythos* (Poplar Bluff, MO: Mythos Books, 2008), 90.

39. S. T. Joshi, "H. P. Lovecraft: The Decline of the West," *The Weird Tale* (Austin, TX: University of Texas Press, 1990), 168–229.

40. Grant, *The Magical Revival*, 115–16.

41. Ibid., 114.

42. Donald Tyson, *Grimoire of the Necronomicon* (St. Paul, MN: Llewellyn, 2008), xvi.

43. H. P. Lovecraft, *Tales* (New York: Library of America, 2005), 385.

44. Lovecraft, *Selected Letters: 1925–1929*, 267.

45. de Camp, *Lovecraft: A Biography*, 108.

46. Cotton Mather, *Cotton Mather on Witchcraft: The Wonders of the Invisible World* (New York: Dorset Press, 1991), 16.

47. H. P. Lovecraft, *The Transition of H. P. Lovecraft: The Road to Madness* (New York: Del Rey Books, 1996), 148.

48. Lovecraft, *Selected Letters: 1925–1929*, 28.

49. Margaret Alice Murray, *The Witch-Cult in Western Europe* (Great Britain: Oxford University Press, 1921), 12–13.

50. Lovecraft, *Tales*, 374.

51. Ibid., 380.

52. Ibid., 615.

53. Montague Summers, *The Vampire: His Kith and Kin* (New York: University Books, 1960), xvi.

54. Montague Summers, *A Popular History of Witchcraft* (New York: Causeway Books, 1973), 258–60.

55. Daniel Harms and John Wisdom Gonce, III., *The Necronomicon Files* (York Beach, ME: Weiser Books, 2003, 96.

56. H. P. Lovecraft, *Selected Letters: 1934–1937*, ed. August Derleth and Donald Wandrei (Sauk City, WI: Arkham House, 1976), 286.

57. Lovecraft, *Tales*, 137.

58. Ibid., 137.

59. Arthur Edward Waite, *The Book of Ceremonial Magic* (New York: Citadel Press, 1971), 258.

60. Gustav Davidson, *A Dictionary of Angels* (New York: The Free Press, 1967), 8, 106, 191, 251, 277–8.

61. Waite, *The Book of Ceremonial Magic*, 277.

62. Ibid., 295.

63. Davidson, *A Dictionary of Angels*, 11, 60, 216.

64. Ibid., 105.

65. Lovecraft, *Tales*, 271.

66. Ibid., 319–20.

67. Ibid., 275.

68. Ibid., 275.

69. Eliphas Levi, *Transcendental Magic*, ed. A.E. Waite (York Beach, ME: Weiser Books, 1970), 320.

70. Ibid., 320.

71. Lovecraft, *Tales*, 399.

72. Ibid., 701.

73. H. P. Lovecraft, *The Best of H. P. Lovecraft* (New York: Ballantine Publishing Group, 1982), 327.

74. Ibid., 327–8.

75. Lovecraft, *Dagon and Other Macabre Tales*, 193.

76. Lovecraft, *Tales*, 146.

77. Ibid., 309.

CHAPTER 3

78. de Camp, *Lovecraft: A Biography*, 409.

79. Ibid., 409–10.

80. Ibid., 410.

81. Al-Hazred, Abdul. *Al Azif (The Necronomicon)* (Philadelphia, PA: Owlswick Press, 1973), ix.

82. Daniel Harms and John Wisdom Gonce III, *The Necronomicon Files: The Truth Behind Lovecraft's Legend* (York Beach, ME: Weiser Books, 2003), 35.

83. Ibid., 35.

84. Robert Turner, *The Necronomicon: The Book of Dead Names* (Great Britain: Neville Spearman, 1978), 50.

85. Ibid., 138.

86. Ibid., 101.

87. Harms and Gonce, *The Necronomicon Files*, 50.

88. Ibid., 50.

89. Fred Pelton, *A Guide to the Cthulhu Cult* (Seattle: Armitage House, 1998), 87.
90. Ibid., 128.
91. Ibid., vi–vii.
92. Ibid., 30.
93. Kostantinos, *Nocturnicon*, 159.
94. Donald Tyson, *Necronomicon: The Wanderings of Alhazred* (St. Paul, MN: Llewellyn, 2004), 49.
95. Ibid., 82.
96. Ibid., 89.
97. Ibid., 103.
98. Ibid., 78.

CHAPTER 4

99. Harms and Gonce, *The Necronomicon Files*, 146–7.
100. Ibid., 174–8. Gonce's contention here is supported by Jason Colavito, who, in *The Cult of Alien Gods: H.Lovecraft and Extraterrestrial Pop Culture* (2005), argues that "Simon Peter" is actually Peter Levenda (hence the suffix "Peter"). Colavito supports this argument by referring to a statement made by Alan Cabal in 2004, in "The Doom That Came to Chelsea" published by New York Press. As Colavito writes: "In 2004, Alan Cabal finally told the true story behind the Simon tome, identifying Peter Levenda as the elusive Simon and explaining that the whole book was cooked up by devotees of Satanist Aleister Crowley's Ordo Templi Orientis by inserting Lovecraftian names into Sumerian and Babylonian myths." (New York: Prometheus Books, 2006). I'm not so sure that Cabal is a valid source here. First, he is clearly not a competent authority when it comes to occult literature; his statement that Aleister Crowley was a Satanist demonstrates a superficial understanding of Crowley, and furthermore, Cabal's point that the Simon Necronomicon was derived by simply inserting "Lovecraftian names" into Sumerian mythology is just plain wrong: there are no specific Lovecraftian names in the Mad Arab's text at all. Nevertheless, when one compares Levenda's work in terms of style, tone, and substance to Simon's work, there are similarities. For example, in Levenda's *The Dark Lord*, there is the same sort of "ranting" against the establishment and status quo that one finds in Simon's *Gates of the Necronomicon* (2006) and in his *Papal Magick: Occult Practices Within the Catholic Church* (New York: Harper Col-

lins, 2007). Of course, this doesn't amount to actual proof that Simon and Levenda are one and the same, but it does encourage further speculation.

101. Simon, *Dead Names: The Dark History of the Necronomicon* (New York: Avon Books, 2006), 174; 175–85.

102. Ibid., 171.

103. Harms and Gonce, *The Necronomicon Files*, 132.

104. Konstantinos, *Nocturnicon*, 156–158.

105. Konstantinos, *Summoning Spirits* (St. Paul, MN: Llewellyn, 2005), 121.

106. Simon, *Necronomicon* (New York: Schlangekraft/Barnes Graphics, 1980), 14.

107. Ibid., 15.

108. Ibid., xxxiv.

109. Ibid., 22.

110. Harms and Gonce, *The Necronomicon Files*, 159.

111. Simon, *Necronomicon*, 46.

112. Harms and Gonce, *The Necronomicon Files*, 150.

113. Simon, *Necronomicon*, liii.

114. Harms and Gonce, *The Necronomicon Files*, 161.

115. Simon, *Necronomicon*, 70.

116. Ibid., 73.

117. Ibid., 73.

118. Harms and Gonce, *The Necronomicon Files*, 162.

119. Ibid., 155.

120. Ibid., 161–4.

121. Simon, *Necronomicon*, 183.

122. Ibid., p207–8

123. Ibid., 216.

124. Simon, *The Gates of the Necronomicon* (New York: Avon Books, 2006), 67–70.

125. Simon, *Necronomicon*, 19.

126. Simon, *The Gates of the Necronomicon*, 162–3.

127. Ibid., 135–7.

CHAPTER 5

128. Grant, *The Magical Revival*, 117.

129. de Camp, *Lovecraft: A Biography*, 333.

130. Ibid., 139.

131. H. P. Lovecraft, *Selected Letters: 1911–1924*, ed. August Derleth and Donald Wandrei (Sauk City, WI: Arkham House, 1968), 160–62.
132. de Camp, *Lovecraft: A Biography*, 138–9.
133. S. T. Joshi, ed., *The Ancient Track: The Complete Poetical Works of H. P. Lovecraft* (San Francisco: Night Shade Books, 2001), 72–3.
134. In *The Cthulhu Mythos Encyclopedia* (2008), forty-four of these avatars are listed; the author informs his reader that these are only a few of the recorded forms that Nyarlathotep has used to manifest on earth. In this chapter, I have focused on only a fraction of these avatars; the interested reader should consult the aforementioned *Encyclopedia* for the complete listing.
135. Grant, *Nightside of Eden*, 182.
136. Simon, *Necronomicon*, xix–xx.
137. H. P. Lovecraft, *At the Mountains of Madness and Other Novels* (Sauk City, WI: Arkham House Publishers, 1964), 291–92.
138. Daniel Harms, *The Cthulhu Mythos Encyclopedia* (Lake Orion, MI: Elder Sign Press, 2008), 15.
139. Joshi, *The Ancient Track*, 73.
140. George T. Wetzel, "The Cthulhu Mythos: A Study," in *H. P. Lovecraft: Four Decades of Criticism*, ed. S. T. Joshi (Athens, OH: Ohio University Press, 1980), 83.
141. Harms, *The Cthulhu Mythos Encyclopedia*, 327–28.
142. Aleister Crowley, *777 and Other Qabalistic Writings of Aleister Crowley*, ed. Israel Regardie (York Beach, ME: Weiser Books, 1979), 89.
143 Grant, *The Magical Revival*, 116–17.
144. Lovecraft, *The Best of H. P. Lovecraft*, 134.
145. Grant, *Outer Gateways*, 13.
146. Simon, *Necronomicon*, xix.
147. Harms, *The Cthulhu Mythos Encyclopedia*, 58.
148. Lovecraft, *The Best of H. P. Lovecraft*, 79–80.
149. Tyson, *Grimoire of the Necronomicon*, 31.
150. Aleister Crowley, *The Holy Books* (Dallas, TX: Sangreal Foundation, Inc., 1972), 83.
151. Levenda, *The Dark Lord*, 103.
152. Ibid., 133.
153. Tyson, *Grimoire of the Necronomicon*, 47.
154. Simon, *Necronomicon*, xx.

155. H. P. Lovecraft, *Selected Letters: 1934–1937,* ed. August Derleth and Donald Wandrei (Sauk City, WI: Arkham House, 1968), 303.

156. Harms, *The Cthulhu Mythos Encyclopedia,* 259.

157. Lin Carter, *Lovecraft: A Look Behind the Cthulhu Mythos* (New York: Ballantine Books, 1972), 100.

158. Pelton, *A Guide to the Cthulhu Cult,* 23.

159. Harms, *The Cthulhu Mythos Encyclopedia,* 286.

160. Clark Ashton Smith, *A Rendezvous in Averoigne* (Sauk City, WI: Arkham House, 2003), 156.

161. Ibid., 140–1.

162. Lovecraft, *Tales,* 462.

163. Ibid., 745.

164. H. P. Lovecraft, *The Horror in the Museum and Other Revisions* (Sauk City, WI: Arkham House, 1970), 262.

165. Lovecraft, *Tales,* 464.

166. Lovecraft, *Selected Letters: 1925–1929,* 232.

167. It is beyond the scope of this book to elaborate fully on all the entities, gods, and demons added by other writers to the Lovecraftian pantheon since Lovecraft's death. The interested reader can consult Daniel Harms' *The Cthulhu Mythos Encyclopedia* (2008) for an updated list. There are four other sources which might be useful to the student and scholar of the Mythos: Chris Jarocha-Ernist's *A Cthulhu Mythos Bibliography and Concordance* (Armitage House, 1999); Francis T. Laney's *The Cthulhu Mythology: A Glossary,* which appears in *Beyond the Wall of Sleep* (Arkham House, 1943); Fred L. Pelton's *A Guide to the Cthulhu Cult* (Armitage House, 1998); and Donald Tyson's *The 13 Gates of the Necronomicon: A Workbook of Magic* (2010).

CHAPTER 6

168. Farrar, *A Witches' Bible,* 17.

169. Robert Tallant, *Voodoo in New Orleans* (Toronto, ON: Collier Books, 1969), 89.

170. Reginald Crosley, *The Vodou Quantum Leap* (St. Paul, MN: Llewellyn, 2000), xxv.

171. Ibid., 97.

172. Ibid , 97.

173. Milo Rigaud, *Secrets of Voodoo* (San Francisco: City Lights Books, 1969), 58.

174. Crosley, *The Vodou Quantum Leap*, 101.
175. Rigaud, *Secrets of Voodoo*, 75.
176. Crosley, *The Vodou Quantum Leap*, 99.
177. Rigaud, *Secrets of Voodoo*, 74.
178. Ibid, 73.
179. Crosley, *The Vodou Quantum Leap*, 86.
180. Ibid., 118–20.
181. Ibid., 264.
182. Lovecraft, *Selected Letters: 1925–1929*, 265–6.

CHAPTER 7

183. Montague Summers, *Witchcraft and Black Magic* (New York: Causeway Books, 1974), p.14.
184. Farrar, *A Witches' Bible*, 22.
185. Bonewits, *Real Magic*, 104–5.
186. Lovecraft, *Selected Letters: 1911–1924*, 223.
187. Lovecraft, *Selected Letters: 1929–1931*, 181.
188. Gerald Gardner, *The Meaning of Witchcraft* (New York: Magickal Childe, 1988), 25.
189. Ibid., 49.
190. Murray, *The Witch-Cult in Western Europe*, 11–12.
191. Ibid., 12.
192. Gardner, *The Meaning of Witchcraft*, 78.
193. Rossell Hope Robbins, *The Encyclopedia of Witchcraft and Demonology* (New York: Crown Publishers, 1959), 215.
194. Gardner, *The Meaning of Witchcraft*, 273.
195. Ibid., 6.
196. Francis King, *The Rites of Modern Occult Magic* (New York: The MacMillan Company, 1970), 179.
197. Gardner, *The Meaning of Witchcraft*, 6.
198. Neville Drury, *The History of Magic in the Modern Age*, (New York: Carroll & Graf Publishers, 2000), 153.
199. Farrar, *A Witches' Bible*, 28–9.
200. Ibid., 107.
201. Margaret Murray, *The God of the Witches* (New York: Oxford University Press, 1977), 29.
202. Ibid., 33–4.
203. Farrar, *A Witches' Bible*, 23–4.

204. Ibid., 17–8.
205. Anne Baring and Jules Cashford, *The Myth of the Goddess: Evolution of an Image* (New York: Penguin Books, 1993), 305.
206. Farrar, *A Witches' Bible*, 71–2.
207. Ibid., 365.
208. Baring, *The Myth of the Goddess*, 328.
209. Grant, *Cults of the Shadow*, 207.
210. H. P. Lovecraft and August Derleth, *The Lurker at the Threshold* (New York: Ballantine Books, 1945), 158.
211. Levi, *Transcendental Magic*, 307.
212. Farrar, *A Witches' Bible*, 107.
213. Ibid., 117.
214. Gardner, *The Meaning of Witchcraft*, 25.
215. H. P. Lovecraft, "The Materialist Today," in *Miscellaneous Writings: H. P. Lovecraft*, ed. S. T. Joshi (Sauk City, WI: Arkham House, 1995), 178.

CHAPTER 8

216. Kenneth Grant, *Aleister Crowley and the Hidden God* (London: Skoob Books, 1992), 73.
217. Grant, *Nightside of Eden*, 115, 135, 137.
218. Ibid., xiv.
219. Ibid., xii–xiii.
220. Ibid., 139–255.
221. Ibid., 52–3, 87.
222. Grant, *Outer Gateways*, 76–92.
223. Lovecraft, *Selected Letters: 1925–1929*, 267.
224. The concept of the aeons is derived from an astrological phenomenon generally known as the Precession of the Equinoxes. When the earth wobbles slightly on its axis, the sun seems to rise in a different place along the Zodiac each year. Most ancient cultures measured the year from the start of the spring equinox, March 21. Due to the precession referred to above, the sun appears to rise one degree off from where it started each 71.6 years, and thus, after 25,776 years, the sun makes a complete circuit of the Zodiac. If we break this down into twelve more or less equal periods, every 2,148 years there is a new constellation behind the sun at the spring equinox. These are the "ages" or "aeons." According to the Thelemites, of course, Aleister Crowley instituted the Aeon of Horus in 1904; this is the Age of Aquarius

that replaced the previous Age of Pisces, the aeon of the "Crowned and Conquering Child," as Crowley and his Thelemic O.T.O. refer to it.

225. Kenneth Grant, *The Ninth Arch* (London: Starfire Books, 2002), xx.

226. In his stimulating book *The Cult of Alien Gods: H. P. Lovecraft and Extraterrestrial Pop Culture* (2005), Jason Colavito makes the claim that Lovecraft was the guiding force and inspiration behind the UFO craze that attained its first flowering in the late 1950s and 60s. As Colavito describes it: "H. Lovecraft was the seminal figure in the world of alternative archaeology and it was from his imagination that nearly all the strange theories and alternative explanations were channeled. Lovecraft towered above all the other figures of fact and fiction as the First Cause of the ancient astronaut hypothesis, and it was from him that all subsequent tales of extraterrestrial gods and lost civilizations came" (New York, Prometheus Books, 2005, p.22). If this is true (and certainly, Colavito, an able philosopher, offers some solid reasoning to support his views), then an argument could be made that Lovecraft himself was the first cause of Grant's own metaphysical views, since Grant bases his theories on the some of the same specious sources as the ancient astronaunt theorists, such as Erich von Daniken, author of *Chariots of the Gods?* (1968) and Robert Temple, author of *The Orion Mystery* (1998).

227. Tyson, *Grimoire of the Necronomicon*, 48–9.

228. Kenneth Grant, *Beyond the Mauve Zone* (London: Starfire Books, 1999), 133–34.

229. Kenneth Grant, *Outside the Circles of Time* (London: Muller, 1980), 28.

230. Kenneth Grant, *Hecate's Fountain* (London: Skoob Books, 1992). This argument is rather disingenuous, however. Throughout the corpus of the *Typhonian Trilogies*, there are reams of overly technical and repetitive material. I suspect that Grant's omission of the magickal texts in his work is due to other, unrelated issues.

231. Ibid., 18–9.

232. Ibid., 134.

CHAPTER 9

233. This view still persists to this day, particularly among devout, non-scholarly persons of all the major Christian denominations. In fact, among scholars, this view can still be encountered; Peter Haining, in *The Anatomy of Witchcraft* (1972), mistakenly equates Satanism with witchcraft, and views these separate practices as virtually the same thing.

234. LaVey, *The Satanic Rituals*, 177.

235. Arthur Lyons, *The Second Coming: Satanism in America* (New York: Award Books, 1970), 34.

236. LaVey, *The Satanic Bible*, 53.

237. Neville Drury, *The History of Magic in the Modern Age* (New York: Carroll & Graf Publishers, 2000), 190.

238. Davidson, *A Dictionary of Angels*, 73.

239. Tyson, *Grimoire of the Necronomicon*, 27.

240. LaVey, *The Satanic Bible*, 62.

241. Blanche Barton, *The Secret Life of a Satanist: The Authorized Biography of Anton LaVey* (Los Angeles: Feral House, 1990), 161–62.

242. H. P. Lovecraft, *The Best of H. P. Lovecraft* (New York: The Ballantine Publishing Group, 1982), 320–21.

243. LaVey, *The Satanic Bible*, 91–4.

244. Ibid., 111.

245. Ibid.

246. LaVey, *The Satanic Rituals*, 129–53.

247. Ibid., 44.

248. Ibid., 189–191.

CHAPTER 10

249. Richard Metzger, *Book of Lies: The Disinformation Guide to Magick and the Occult* (New York: The Disinformation Company, 2003), 142.

250. Grant, *Cults of the Shadow*, 100.

251. Drury, *The History of Magic in the Modern Age*, 123.

252. In *The Ladder of Lights* (1968), William G. Gray observes: "If Kether is a dot, the Ain Soph Aur is the circle around it" (223).

253. Grant, *Cults of the Shadow*, 197.

254. Ibid., 203.

255. Ibid., 234.

256. Crowley, *Magick*, 134.

257. Grant, *Cults of the Shadow*, 199.

258. Plato's argument here is extrapolated from the *Phaedo*: C.M.A. Grube, trans., *Plato: Five Dialogues* (Indianapolis: Hackett, 2002), 101–4.

259. Farrar, *A Witches' Bible*, 121.

260. Grant, *Outer Gateways*, 67.

261. Ibid., 68–71.

262. Peter J. Carroll, *Liber Null & Psychonaut* (York Beach, ME: Weiser Books, 1987), 199-200.

263. Ibid., 28.

264. Ibid., 158.

265. Ibid., 29.

266. Peter J. Carroll, *Liber Kaos* (York Beach, ME: Weiser Books, 1992), 34.

267. Drury, *The History of Magic in the Modern Age*, 123.

268. Carroll, *Liber Kaos*, 59–60.

269. Carroll, *Liber Null & Psychonaut*, 96.

270. Ibid., 148.

271. Ibid., 150.

CHAPTER 11

272. S. T. Joshi, ed., *Black Wings of Cthulhu 2: Eighteen New Tales of Lovecraftian Horror* (London: Titan Books, 2014), 8.

273. Paul Rolland, *The Curious Case of H. P. Lovecraft* (London: Plexis Publishing Ltd., 2014), 54.

274. H. P. Lovecraft, *Beyond the Wall of Sleep*, eds. August Derleth and Donald Wandrei (Sauk City, WI: Arkham House, 1943), 38.

INDEX

Materialist Today, The, 195
Mather, Cotton, 43–45, 179, 224
Mauve Zone, 120, 212, 220
Mawu, 6, 20, 153, 186, 188, 196, 202, 209, 218
Meaning of Witchcraft, The, 173–74, 175–76, 180, 182, 195
mechanistic materialism, 32, 34
Melville, Herman, xiv
Messe Noir, Le. See Black Mass
Metzger, Richard, 245
Modern Science and Materialism, 34
moon goddess. See Mawu
Murray, Margaret, 46–48, 171, 174, 224
Mysteries of Magic, The, 58
Myth of the Goddess, The, 188, 189–90

Necronomicon, xvii, 39, 42, 61
Necronomicon (The Book of Dead Names), 76–80
Necronomicon (Al Azif: Owlswick Press), 73–76
Necronomicon (Simon/Schlangekraft Recension), xvii, 93–112
Necronomicon (The Wanderings of Al-hazred), 86–92
Necronomicon Files, The, 95, 102–05, 107–09
Neither-Neither, 251–52, 254
New Isis Lodge, 7, 201–02, 205–06, 220
Nightside of Eden, 7, 207, 219
Ninth Arch, The, 214
Nocturnicon, The, 13–14, 16, 98
nkisi—see veve
Nu Isis Lodge. See New Isis Lodge
Nyarlathotep, 78, 83, 89, 91, 119–23, 216, 218, 241
Nyarlathotep (sonnet), 120–21
Nyarlathotep (story), 120

Oak King, 186–87, 192, 197–98, 234
Order of the Old Ones, 40–41
out-of-body-experience (OBE), 26, 66, 160, 194
Outer Gateways, 7, 98, 252–53

Paglia, Camille, 4–5, 14
pan-psychic field, 159–164, 159–60, 235–36, 251
Pelton, Fred, 81, 84–86; 137
Petro Vodou pantheon, 156–57
Phillips, Whipple, 28–29
Plato, 251

Poe, Edgar Allan, xiv, 29, 34–36
Popular History of Witchcraft, A, 49
possession, 20–22, 63–65, 146, 160, 165–67
Pseudonomicon, The, 260

Qabalah of Nine Chambers, 16–17, 86, 89–90
Qliphoth (Qliphotic), 3, 7, 114, 126, 142, 202, 207–210, 211–12, 219
quantum physics, 32, 41–43, 146, 159, 159–60, 164, 195, 235, 243, 252, 257–59

Rada Vodou pantheon, 152–56
Real Magic, 8
Reed, Zealia Brown, 32
Riddle of the Universe, The, 34
Rigaud, Milo, 152–55; 159
Rites of Eleusis, 21
ritual magick, 24–26
Ritual of Transcendental Magic, The, 58–59, 191–02
R'lyeh, city of, 82–83, 128, 130, 241
Roba el Khaliyeh, 87, 122
Robbins, Rossell Hope, 178

Sabbats, 21–22, 48, 171, 197–99, 225–26
Sadducismus Triumphatus, 71
Salem Witchcraft Trials, 43–44, 179
Sanders, Alex, 182–83
Satan, 47, 186, 225–26, 232, 235–36
Satanic Bible, The, 6–7, 228–29, 231, 238, 261
Satanic Rituals, The, 228–29, 237, 240–41
satanic rituals, 239–42
Satanism (history), 225–27
Satanism's gods and goddesses, 231–35
Satanism's law of the trapezoid, 235–38
Satanism's view of the afterlife, 238–39
Second Coming, The, 226
Secrets of Voodoo, 152–55, 159
Set-Typhon, 130–31
Sexual Personae, 4, 14
shadow-matter dimensions, 7, 41–42, 160, 164–65, 194, 202, 258
Shadow Out of Time, The, 64–64, 87, 140, 143, 167, 214
Shadow Over Innsmouth, The, 46, 48–49, 84–85, 220
Shadow-Woman, 24, 248
Shub-Niggurath, 79–80, 94, 132–34, 143, 173, 191–92, 234–35, 241
sigils (magickal weapons), 16–17